Paullina Simons is the author of *Tully* and *The Bronze Horseman*, as well as ten other beloved novels, a memoir, a cookbook and two children's books. Born in Leningrad, Paullina immigrated to the United States when she was ten, and now lives in New York with her husband and an alarming number of her once-independent children.

Praise for Paullina Simons

Tully

"You'll never look at life in the same way again. Pick up this book and prepare to have your emotions wrung so completely you'll be sobbing your heart out one minute and laughing through your tears the next. Read it and weep—literally."

Company

Red Leaves

"Simons handles her characters and setting with skill, slowly peeling away deceptions to reveal denial, cowardice and chilling indifference … an engrossing story."

Publishers Weekly

Eleven Hours

"*Eleven Hours* is a harrowing, hair-raising story that will keep you turning the pages late into the night."

Janet Evanovich

The Bronze Horseman

"A love story both tender and fierce" (*Publishers Weekly*) that "recalls *Dr. Zhivago*." (*People Magazine*)

The Bridge to Holy Cross

"This has everything a romance glutton could wish for: a bold, talented and dashing hero [and] a heart-stopping love affair that nourishes its two protagonists even when they are separated and lost."

Daily Mail

The Girl in Times Square
"Part mystery, part romance, part family drama … in other words,
the perfect book."
Daily Mail

The Summer Garden
"If you're looking for a historical epic to immerse yourself in,
then this is the book for you."
Closer

Road to Paradise
"One of our most exciting writers … Paullina Simons presents the
perfect mix of page-turning plot and characters."
Woman and Home

A Song in the Daylight
"Simons shows the frailties of families and of human nature,
and demonstrates that there's so much more to life, such as
honesty and loyalty."
Good Reading

Bellagrand
"Another epic saga from Simons, full of the emotion and heartache of
the original trilogy. Summer reading at its finest."
Canberra Times

Lone Star
"Love is never grander than that in Paullina Simons novel …
I just can't get enough of her writing."
Good Reading

By the same author

FICTION
Tully
Red Leaves
Eleven Hours
The Girl in Times Square
Road to Paradise
A Song in the Daylight
Lone Star

The Bronze Horseman Series
The Bronze Horseman
Tatiana and Alexander
The Summer Garden
Children of Liberty
Bellagrand

NON FICTION
Tatiana's Table

CHILDREN'S BOOKS
I Love My Baby Because
Poppet Gets Two Big Brothers

Paullina Simons

Six Days
in Leningrad

HarperCollins*Publishers*

Photo Credits

All the pictures (internal and back cover) taken of young Paullina alone or with parents are by Anatoly Studenkov. Every single one.
The picture of my mother from 1958, I don't know. It's lost to posterity.
The photo of me dressed up holding my son's hand, by Kevin Ryan.
The photo of me with my grandparents, by Elizabeth Handler.
The photo of me in August 1998 with my parents, by Elizabeth Handler.
The photos from Leningrad of me with my dad, are by Viktor Smirnoff.
The rest of the photos are by Paullina Simons.

HarperCollins*Publishers*

First published in Australia in 2015
by HarperCollins*Publishers* Australia Pty Limited
ABN 36 009 913 517
harpercollins.com.au

HarperCollins*Publishers*
Level 13, 201 Elizabeth Street, Sydney NSW 2000, Australia
Unit D1, 63 Apollo Drive, Rosedale, Auckland 0632, New Zealand
A 53, Sector 57, Noida, UP, India
1 London Bridge Street, London SE1 9GF, United Kingdom
2 Bloor Street East, 20th floor, Toronto, Ontario M4W 1A8, Canada
195 Broadway, New York NY 10007, USA

National Library of Australia Cataloguing-in-Publication data:

Simons, Paullina, 1963– author.
  Six Days in Leningrad / Paullina Simons.
  ISBN: 978 0 7322 9880 7 (paperback)
  Subjects: Simons, Paullina, 1963 – Travel – Russia (Federation) – Saint Petersburg.
  Saint Petersburg (Russia) – Social conditions.
  Saint Petersburg (Russia) – Economic conditions.
  Saint Petersburg (Russia) – Description and travel.
813.546

Cover design by HarperCollins Design Studio
Front cover image by shutterstock.com
Author photograph by Renaissance Studio
Typeset in Minion Pro by Kirby Jones
Printed and bound in Australia by Griffin Press
The papers used by HarperCollins in the manufacture of this book are a natural, recyclable product made from wood grown in sustainable plantation forests. The fibre source and manufacturing processes meet recognised international environmental standards, and carry certification.

For Yuri Handler, my darling Papa, who took me to the new world and gave me a new life, and then took me back to the old world and gave me a new heart.

GLOSSARY OF STRANGE AND UNFAMILIAR
RUSSIAN WORDS

blini: yeast dough

crèpe: like pancakes

Comsomols: Young Communists,

dacha: summer house

elektrichka: short-distance train

khrushchyobi: residential tenement-style buildings built during the
Khrushchev era

koshmar: nightmare

matryoshkas: nesting dolls

metro: subway

pelmeni: Russian meat dumplings

perestroika: rebuilding

Pioneers: pre-Communists

pozhalusta: please

Prospekt: Avenue

Shepelevo: sheh-peh-LYO-voh

shosse: highway

solyanka: a thick meat soup

Ulitsa: street

zakuski: hot and cold appetizers

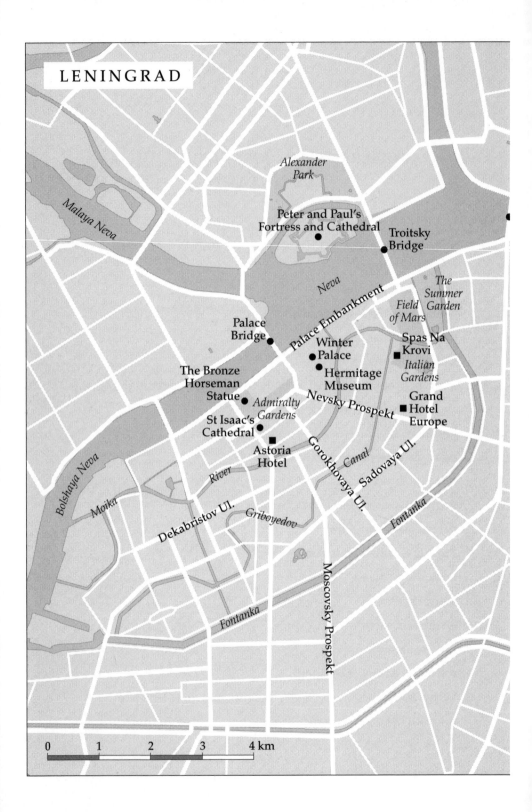

LENINGRAD

Malaya Neva

Alexander Park

Peter and Paul's
Fortress and Cathedral

Troitsky
Bridge

Neva

The Summer Garden

Field of Mars

Palace
Bridge

Palace Embankment

Winter
Palace

Spas Na
Krovi

Italian Gardens

Hermitage
Museum

The Bronze
Horseman
Statue

Admiralty Gardens

Nevsky Prospekt

Grand
Hotel
Europe

St Isaac's
Cathedral

Astoria
Hotel

Gorokhovaya Ul.

Canal

Sadovaya Ul.

Bolshaya Neva

Moika

River

Dekabristov Ul.

Griboyedov

Fontanka

Moscovsky Prospekt

Fontanka

0   1   2   3   4 km

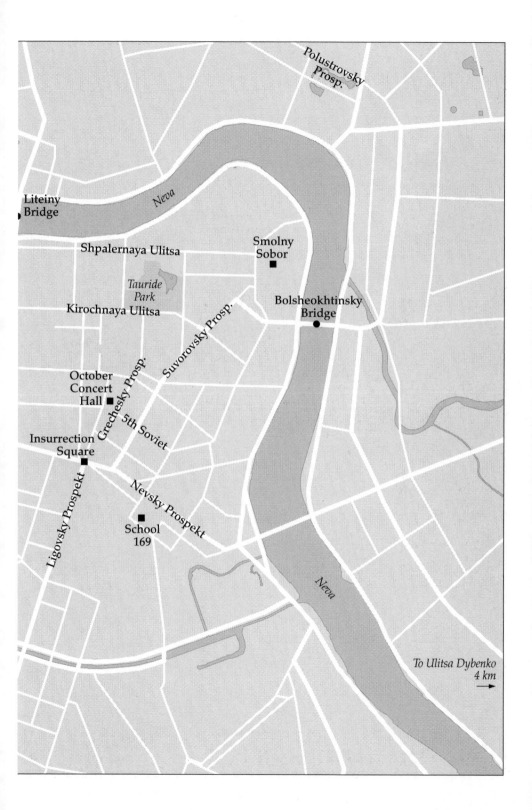

Polustrovsky Prosp.

Neva

Liteiny
Bridge

Shpalernaya Ulitsa

Smolny
Sobor

*Tauride
Park*

Bolsheokhtinsky
Bridge

Kirochnaya Ulitsa

Suvorovsky Prosp.

October
Concert
Hall

Grechesky Prosp.

5th Soviet

Insurrection
Square

Nevsky Prospekt

Ligovsky Prospekt

School
169

Neva

To Ulitsa Dybenko
4 km

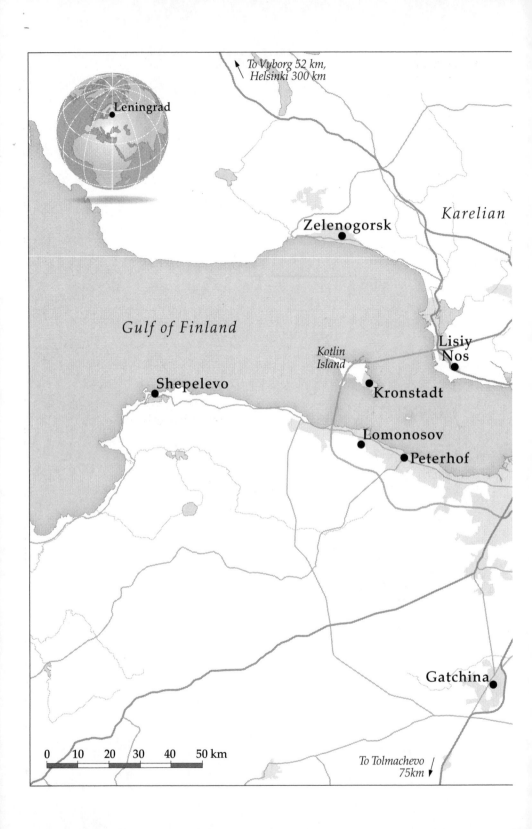

To Vyborg 52 km,
Helsinki 300 km

Leningrad

Karelian

Zelenogorsk

Gulf of Finland

Kotlin
Island

Lisiy
Nos

Shepelevo

Kronstadt

Lomonosov

Peterhof

Gatchina

0   10   20   30   40   50 km

To Tolmachevo
75km

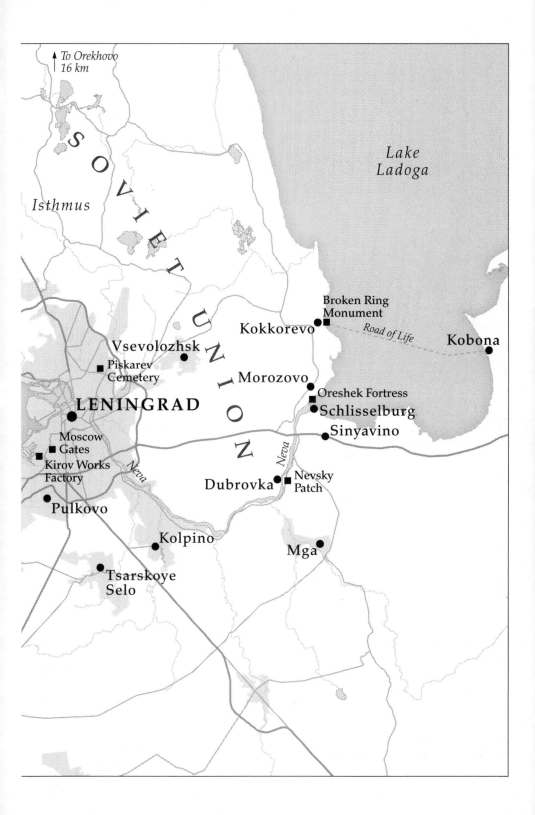

To Orekhovo
16 km

S O V I E T

Isthmus

U N I O N

Lake
Ladoga

Broken Ring
Monument

Kokkorevo

Road of Life

Kobona

Vsevolozhsk

Piskarev
Cemetery

Morozovo

Oreshek Fortress

LENINGRAD

Schlisselburg

Sinyavino

Moscow
Gates

Neva

Kirov Works
Factory

Neva

Nevsky
Patch

Dubrovka

Pulkovo

Kolpino

Mga

Tsarskoye
Selo

We live, not as we wish to, but as we can.

— Menander

PART I

BEFORE: THE TEXAS LIFE

MOVING DAY

Kevin and I got to our brand new house at 8:20 in the morning and not a moment too soon: the moving truck was already parked in front of the driveway. We had to drive on the grass to go around it. We had barely opened the garage doors when the guys started laying down their blankets and getting out their trolleys. The next thing we knew, they were bringing stuff into the house.

Into a house, I might add, that wasn't quite ready yet. The builder's cleaning crew had just arrived and were in the kitchen, scrubbing. The movers started piling boxes onto the carpet, which had not been vacuumed since the day it was installed.

I asked the cleaning women to please vacuum the rooms before they continued with their other tasks so that the movers could pile the boxes onto clean carpets. You would have thought I'd asked them to carry heavy objects on their backs upstairs in 100-degree heat. First the diminutive ladies huffed and puffed, and then they said they spoke no Inglés. Phil, my building manager, explained to me that the women worked at their own pace and according to their own schedule. I looked at him as if *he* were not speaking Inglés and finally responded, "Phil, I don't know if you've noticed, but we're moving in. Please ask them to vacuum the floor in the bedroom and living room."

"Problem is," Phil said, "they don't speak any English."

My two young sons, Misha, three, and Kevie, one, zigzagged in front of the movers. I think they were trying to trip them. Misha was crying. "I don't want to go to Burger King for breakfast, I don't want to go to Burger King for breakfast." Natasha, eleven, was reading, perched on top of a box of books, wisely ignoring everyone and everything.

The babysitter cajoled Misha, but in the meantime, Kevie had toddled off to the pool. The dogs were barking non-stop. They wanted either to be let in, let out or shot.

My husband ran in and said, "Please go out to the garage and talk to the movers. They need one of us there at all times to tell them where things are going."

"But I labeled all the boxes!"

"Well, they don't know where boy bedroom is or where guest bedroom is," Kevin replied. "Every bedroom looks the same."

The pool guy knocked on the back porch door. "Hey, guys? Is this a bad time to show you how to use the pool equipment?"

The one-year-old ran in from the pool, draped himself around his father's leg and wouldn't let go until Kevin picked him up. The babysitter pried him off eventually. The dogs continued to bark. Misha continued to scream about Burger King. Apparently he didn't want to go, he really wanted to stay right here at the new house.

Our builder walked in. "Well, good morning! We needed just a couple more days with this house, but that's okay, we'll make it work. Hey, do you have a few minutes to go over the change orders? I have your closing contract. I need both you and Kevin to sign."

One of the moving guys stuck his head in and said pointedly, "*Mrs.* Simons, could we see you in the garage right now, please?"

The phone rang.

How could that be? I didn't think we'd unpacked a phone yet.

Open boxes stood on the kitchen counter.

The front door bell rang. It was the delivery guy from Home Depot. He'd brought the barbecue. Where would I like it?

Another delivery truck stopped in front of the house. This one was unloading a dryer and a television.

Another truck pulled up, with my new office desk. The two desk guys steadfastly refused to take the desk upstairs, "because we're not insured for damage." They asked if the moving guys could do it.

The moving guys said they *certainly* weren't insured to move a desk that wasn't on their truck upstairs. So I told the desk guys that either they took the desk upstairs or else they could take it right back to the warehouse.

They took the desk upstairs.

"*Mrs. Simons!*"

In the garage, the four large moving guys stood with their arms folded and impatiently told me they were having a problem with the cleaning ladies, who really needed to stay out of their way. "We cannot do our job, *Mrs. Simons.*"

The dogs were still barking. My young sons were now running around in the street as the babysitter chased after them, trying to corral them into the minivan.

Pressing my fingers into my temples, I glanced at my watch. 8:45 a.m.

The phone rang again. It was my father calling from Prague.

"Hey, Papa," I said weakly.

"Well?" he asked. "Are you excited?"

"What?"

"About our trip. It's no small thing, you know, you going back to Russia for the first time in twenty-five years. Are you thinking about it?"

"Absolutely, Papa," I said. "I'm thinking about it right now."

My newly-built house in Texas, June 1998.

July 1998.

THE BRONZE HORSEMAN

We had been planning our trip to Russia for a year. Ever since the summer of 1997, when I told my family that my fourth novel, *The Bronze Horseman*, was going to be a love story set in World War II during the siege of Leningrad. I said I couldn't write a story so detailed and sprawling without seeing Russia with my own eyes.

My family had listened to me carefully, and then my grandfather said, "Plina, I hope I'm not going to be turning over in my grave reading the lies you're going to write in your book about Russia."

"I also hope not, Dedushka," I said. "Though you're not dead." He was only ninety, a "spring chicken" in his own words.

Going to St. Petersburg was not an option before the summer of 1998. The logistics of the trip had been too overwhelming. How would I get a non-Russian-speaking husband and three non-Russian-speaking kids, one of them barely walking, to Russia? And what would they do there? Either my husband would be watching the kids full-time in a foreign country — and not just any foreign country, but Russia! — or we would be watching them together, and I wouldn't be doing any research.

I didn't need to go all the way to Russia to take care of my kids. I could stay home in Texas and do it. Kevin and I considered leaving them and just the two of us going, but in the end decided that was a bad idea. Leave the kids with a babysitter for ten days? Too much: for them, for us.

Still, thoughts of Russia would not go away. Also, there was no book. Eighteen months earlier there had been a nebulous vision of two young lovers walking in deserted Leningrad on the eve of a brutal war, but a vision did not an epic story make. How could I not go to Russia?

I finally said to Kevin that it looked like I would have to go on my own. He didn't love the idea, my going to "a place like Russia" by myself. He said I should take my sister.

I ran the idea by my father. "Kevin thinks I should take Liza to Russia with me," I said.

My father was quiet on the phone for what seemed like an hour, smoking and thinking. Then he said, "*I* could come with you."

I hadn't thought of that.

*

A girlfriend of mine said, "Oh, that's neat! When was the last time you and your dad took a trip together?"

"Never."

During the course of a year, the trip gradually took shape. My father told me he was planning to retire from Radio Liberty at the end of May, 1998. "We have to go before I retire." My father was the

Director of Russian Services for Radio Free Europe/Radio Liberty, a government-run radio station where my father worked his entire American life since we left Russia and came to New York in 1973. Working had defined and consumed him. Working was his life. And with good reason. For the last quarter-century, he and his team of writers translated Western news, both political and cultural, into Russian and then broadcast it over shortwave to Eastern Europe and the Soviet Union. They broadcast to Russia 24/7, with twelve hours of original programming every day. He had been stationed at the New York bureau until 1991 when Communism fell. In 1992 he was made Director of Russian Services, the largest of Radio Liberty's bureaus and transferred to Munich, and then Prague, where he was at the moment. In my opinion four people were responsible for bringing down the Berlin Wall and Communism: Ronald Reagan, Margaret Thatcher, Pope John Paul II, and my father.

But May was not a good month for me. After much discussion, my father agreed to postpone his retirement and we settled on July, 1998. It was the perfect time to go, my dad told me, because we stood a chance of having some nice weather. Also the nights would be white. "That's a sight to see. You do remember white nights, Plina?"

"Pfft, of course, Papa." I didn't want to tell him how little I remembered them. I was just a kid then. In the city, at ten in the evening, I was already asleep.

How long could I be away and not traumatize my kids? I figured a day to travel there, a day to travel back, and then six days in St. Petersburg. But even then, when it was almost finalized, I vacillated, procrastinated, delayed.

Truth was, I didn't want to go back.

*In Vienna, September 1973, in a coat my mother
hand-knitted for me.*

IN 1973 THERE WERE SHARKS

I was born in St. Petersburg when it was still called Leningrad and came to America when I was ten. We left Leningrad one fall day and lived in Rome while waiting for our entry visa to the United States.

Those were blissful months we spent in Rome. Every Thursday my mother gave me a few lire, enough to go to the movies by myself *and* buy a bag of potato chips. I'd never eaten anything so delicious in Russia as potato chips. The movies were all in Italian of course, of which I spoke exactly three phrases: *bella bambina, bruta bambina* and *mangiare per favore.* Cute baby, ugly baby, and food please. It was two more phrases than I spoke in English.

We spent my tenth birthday in Rome. My parents asked me what I wanted, and I said gum. So I got gum. Also some strawberry gelato, and then we went to the American theater across town to see the 1966 Oscar winner *A Man for All Seasons.* I liked the gum better than the movie. I didn't understand a word of it, but at the end, the man for all seasons had his head cut off.

We came to America two days before Thanksgiving 1973. Our first big American meal was turkey and mashed potatoes and something called cranberry jelly. We celebrated in Connecticut, at the home of a young man we had met briefly in Vienna and who'd invited us to his house for the holidays. We gave thanks for our amazing luck, for getting out of Russia, for coming to America. America seemed like heaven. True, first you had to die, to leave behind the only life you knew how to live, but *then* you had — America! The death was leaving Russia. Because once you left, you could never go back. My father had told me that when we were leaving.

America was life after death.

That Thanksgiving, when everyone else was done with their meal, my father walked around the table and finished the food the Americans had left behind on their plates. My mother was so embarrassed. "What are you doing?!" But my father calmly explained what we all knew to be true: Russian people of a certain age born in Leningrad do not leave food on their plates.

Our second American meal was the lasagna our landlady brought up to our apartment in Woodside, Queens. Don't ask me how this is, but during our stay in Rome, *Italy,* I had not tasted tomato sauce once. I had not had lasagna. I had not had pizza. I did not know tomato sauce until our Italian landlady knocked on our door.

In America there was Juicy Fruit gum, and chocolate ice cream, which I had never had, and corn, which I also had never had, and something called Coca-Cola. And television. I found a children's cartoon: *Looney Tunes.* I'd never seen anything like it. In Russia, we had black-and-white war movies, black-and-white news. There was some animated programming, but it looked like war movies, just less interesting.

War movies and news. And the Olympics, which was the single most exciting thing on Soviet television — unfortunately the Olympics came only once every four years.

Suddenly there was *Looney Tunes*! Bugs Bunny! Elmer Fudd! Porky Pig! Our first TV set was black and white, but the cartoons were straight out of someone else's Technicolor dream. The war movies in Russia were set in gray tents and invariably starred two gray men who talked non-stop until there was a battle, followed by more dialogue, all concluding in a blaze and eventual victory for Mother Russia. The movies lasted, it seemed to me, as long as the war itself.

In Queens, the *Looney Tunes* bunny blew up a pig, blew up a hunter, ran away, blew up a cave and fell off a cliff, all in eight minutes. Then he disappeared and was instantly replaced by a lady selling towels made of paper. Towels made of *paper*? The cartoon was over, so I turned off the TV, utterly disappointed.

It took me many weeks to discover that the cartoon did not end but was merely interrupted by the lady selling towels made of paper. Imagine my happiness!

I used to read in Russia, and who could blame me? What else was there to do? Now that I had Bugs Bunny, all reading stopped for four or five years.

In school I would occasionally be asked to talk to the other students about my experience of life in the Soviet Union. That's how it was put: "Your *experience* of life in the Soviet Union." I wanted to say even then that it wasn't my *experience* of life, it actually *was* my life, but I didn't. Instead, I gave my little talk in broken English: about the communal apartment, the small rooms, the cockroaches falling on my bed while I slept, the bed bugs and the smell like a decomposing skunk they made when I accidentally squished them, about the lack of food, the lack of stores, the lack of my father.

When I was asked, "How did it feel living with that kind of deprivation?" I would shrug and say, "I didn't know it was deprivation. We all lived the same way. I thought it was just life."

My American friends grew up with Coca-Cola and Jesus Christ.

I grew up with hot black tea and the astronaut Yuri Gagarin — the first man in space.

My husband grew up watching *I Dream of Jeannie* and *Star Trek*.

I watched Gagarin's funeral, and a 120-part series called *Liberation* — full of burning tents and dark winter nights — which they rebroadcast every December because Decembers near the Arctic Circle weren't bleak enough.

I'd never seen a palm tree, I'd never seen an ocean, I'd never heard a church service, I'd never read *Charlotte's Web*. I read *The Three Musketeers*, *Les Misérables* and a Russian writer named Mikhail Zoshchenko. By the time I was ten I had read all of Anton Chekhov and Jules Verne, but what I wanted, though I did not know it, was Nancy Drew and Laura Ingalls Wilder.

What was baseball? What was peanut butter? I didn't know. I knew what soccer was, what mushroom barley soup was, what perch was.

And who was this Jesus Christ?

I, who had not grown up with Christmas carols, cookies, decorations and a divine baby in a cave, had only a dim understanding of what Jesus had to do with Christmas. My first Christmas Eve in New York my parents went out, leaving me alone to joyfully watch *Bonanza* — or so I thought. But to my great dismay, Michael Landon (on whom I had quite the crush) was replaced on Channel 11 by a log burning on a fire and instrumental muzak. As you might imagine, my Pavlovian reaction to the discovery that this Christmas was responsible for ousting my Michael Landon was less than spiritually appropriate.

While my husband was vacationing near Lake George, I was learning how to swim in the icy Black Sea.

Kevin knew Atlantic Ocean beaches. I knew the dirty sand on the Gulf of Finland. It had been enough for me when I was a child. I spent ten summers of my life in a tiny Russian fishing village called Shepelevo near the Gulf of Finland. Three months of every year, I slept, read, fished, swam, and played with other kids, from dawn to dusk, free and in bliss.

I didn't want to go back there.

I lived ten years of my life in a communal apartment, nine families sharing thirteen rooms, two kitchens, two bathrooms.

I didn't want to go back there.

When I was four, my father was arrested and spent the next five years of his life — and mine — in a Soviet prison, in a Soviet labor camp, in exile.

I lived alone with my silent mother. I was not interested in reliving any part of that.

There was no romanticizing our life in Russia. If it weren't for my unwritten book, why on earth would I go back?

Papa and his (then) only child. February 1965.

MOLOTOV'S GRANDSON

My father got me a travel visa through Radio Liberty. The already painful Soviet visa process was further complicated by the fact that we were going to stay with my father's best friend Anatoly, instead of in a hotel like normal, non-suspicious tourists.

"Papa, why don't we stay in a hotel?"

"What hotel?"

"I looked in my St. Petersburg guide, and it lists two great hotels in Leningrad —"

"Don't call it Leningrad."

"Fine. St. Petersburg. Two great hotels: Grand Hotel Europe, and Astoria."

"Astoria *is* a very nice hotel."

"So it says. It says it's located conveniently close to the statue of the Bronze Horseman. That's good for me. As you know, that's what I'm calling my book *The Bronze Horseman*."

"I want to speak to you about that. I think it's a terrible title."

I sighed. "Papa, it's a very good title, and everybody likes it."

"Who is everybody?"

"My agent, my editor. My former editor. My husband."

"They don't understand."

"Fine. Can we go back to hotels? Astoria is nice?"

"Yes, but Paullina, I can't stay in Astoria. I'm retiring in August. And my company won't pay for such a hotel."

"Grand Hotel Europe?"

"Very nice hotel, in the center of town, close to Nevsky Prospekt. So convenient." He sounded like a travel agent.

"So which one is better?"

"Paullina, we can't stay in either. We have a perfectly decent apartment to stay in with Anatoly and his wife, Ellie. They loved you very much when you were a child. They can't wait to see you. Their daughter Alla can't wait to see you either. You remember her, don't you?"

Of course I remembered her. She had been my best friend.

"Anatoly and Ellie have room. You'll be comfortable. It'll be fine."

I thought about it. "How close are they to the center of town?"

"Okay fine, their apartment is not the Grand Hotel Europe. It's not going to be fifty paces from Nevsky Prospekt. They live on the outskirts of town, the last stop on the metro. You do what you like, but I have to stay with them. They'll never forgive me if I don't."

I continued to quiz him about the two hotels. My father finally admitted to me that my parents' wedding reception was held on the top floor of Grand Hotel Europe.

"I have to stay there then. There is no question."

He told me that when I was a baby, I had helped him to smuggle strictly forbidden books out of Grand Hotel Europe. He received them from an American friend who was visiting Russia and staying at the hotel. KGB agents checked every bag that left the hotel as a matter of course. They were watching my father particularly carefully because of a provocative letter he had sent to *Pravda*; he had to be cautious. So when he received the books from his American acquaintance, he put them underneath me in my baby carriage, wrapped the blanket around me and the books, and wheeled us out into the street.

He smuggled out *Thirteen Days That Shook the Kremlin: Imre Nagy and the Hungarian Revolution* by Tibor Meray, *Bitter Harvest: The Intellectual Revolt Behind the Iron Curtain*, a collection of essays and stories edited by Edmund Stillman, *The New Class* by Milovan Djilas, and *The Communist Party of the Soviet Union* by Leonard Schapiro.

Years later, in 1994, a former KGB agent who used to watch my father met him at a gathering in Munich and asked him, "Yuri Lvovich, tell me, that winter night, how did you get those books out of the hotel? We were watching you so carefully."

After my father told him how, the KGB agent shook his head and said, "We underestimated you, Yuri Lvovich."

*

During our next conversation, I said to him, "Papa, how about if we stay with Anatoly and Ellie for a few days, but then I will get us a suite at Grand Hotel Europe and we'll stay there the rest of the time."

"How much is a room there? Four hundred dollars a night?"

"Five hundred."

"Oh my goodness."

"Don't worry about it. It will only be for a few nights."

But because I was going to be staying part of the time with friends, I couldn't get a simple tourist visa. I needed to get a letter of invitation from a business. My father said he would take care of it. Radio Free Europe/Radio Liberty, which had bureaus in Prague, Munich, Washington, Moscow and St. Petersburg, would provide me with an invitation.

My father's colleague in Washington personally walked my visa application over to the Russian embassy to be processed.

"The man who is walking with your application, doing you a favor, processing your visa, treat him with respect," my father told me. "He is Molotov's grandson."

Vyacheslav Molotov had been Stalin's foreign minister, responsible for the war with Germany and the war with Finland, and for unwittingly giving his name to the incendiary cocktails the Finns invented in his honor.

"Not Molotov's grandson!"

"Yes," my father said, lowering his voice, "but don't say anything to him."

"Why?" I asked. "Doesn't he know whose grandson he is?"

My father said it was a very complicated subject and spoke no more about it. I did think there was something Homeric about Molotov's grandchild traipsing to the Russian embassy to get me my Russian visa so that I could go to Russia and write about the period when his grandfather had been making history. I sent Molotov's grandson my three published books, all signed to his wife, and thanked him for helping me. I really wanted to ask him about his grandfather, but didn't.

GRAND CENTRAL STATION

Grand Central Station wasn't in New York. It was in my house in Texas.

With barely two weeks between our move and my trip, and having not yet unpacked, I was trying to get some work done before we left. But not only was my mother-in-law visiting from New York for ten days, my builder must have had every contractor in Dallas stopping by my house at least twice a day.

I had made a firm commitment to myself that I would finish reading one of my Russian research books before we left, but that was before Eric, the screen-door guy, came to replace the screen door — twice. The painters hadn't finished painting before we moved in, and a quarter of the power outlets weren't working, including the one my computer was supposed to be plugged into. The faucet in the kitchen was leaking. The icemaker upstairs wasn't making ice, while the frost-free refrigerator was making frost.

The days were too full for me to do my regular work — research, beginning my new novel, plus being a mom to three small kids, all home for the summer — much less prepare to travel to Russia. But every once in a while, my dad would call and say, "Are you ready for our trip?"

"I am," I'd say. "But I have to go because the Rotor Rooter guys are at the door. We have an overflow problem in one of our shower drains."

Somehow, a week before I left for Russia, I managed to squeeze in an event at a local bookstore in Dallas for the publication of *Eleven Hours*, and a live TV interview in Austin, Texas, eight round-trip hours away.

Meanwhile the door latches in the house were nearly all broken, the garage door keypad was not opening the garage, and the concrete driveway was getting dents in it as if it were made of dough not cement.

The front fence was not fully installed, and our dogs kept running out onto the road.

The grass was dying, which could have had something to do with the fact that it had been over a hundred degrees in Dallas every day for the past six weeks and no rain.

In Russia I had read a book about a place Americans called the west, and in this west there were endless prairies and on these prairies rode cowboys with lassos. I didn't know what a lasso was, but it sure sounded exciting when I was a little girl growing up in Russia. One day, I wanted to see this prairie.

And here I was. We had built our house on the edge of the prairie. Ours was the last lot in the development that ended a few hundred yards past our house. There the prairie began — a savannah that disappeared into the sky. A lone tree. Some bales of hay. The sun rose in the backyard and set in the front yard. Nothing marred our view of the relentless sun or the prairie. Nothing. Dead grass, burnt corn, coyotes, lightning storms. And rats in the pool. Not dead rats either.

Time inched its way toward July 12.

Where the magic happens. Note the drawn blinds to keep out that glorious daylight.

May 1964, at six months. Must have just realised how far I am off the ground.

FLY AEROFLOT!

A few days before our trip, my father instructed me to get a single room at a hotel and forget about a suite for him and me. "I will stay with Anatoly," he said. "He will never forgive me if I don't stay with him. You stay by yourself. Getting a single room will be cheaper for you. I will meet you at your hotel every morning and we will go about our business."

I booked the hotel for six days. My father was surprised. He thought I would stay at least a few nights with him at Anatoly's apartment. But I was thinking of myself. How inconvenient, to pack and unpack twice.

Besides, it was only for six days.

*

The airfare I booked was one of the cheapest. The travel agent was thrilled when after an hour of looking — while I stayed on the line — she finally found something inexpensive for my exact dates.

"What airline is it?" I asked.

"Aeroflot."

I wasn't too sure about Aeroflot. When every other airline was quoting me a return fare of twelve hundred to nineteen hundred dollars, what was Aeroflot doing selling me a ticket for five hundred and thirty dollars? They were practically gifting me a seat. I fretted.

"Is it standing room only or something?"

"No, no. It's their regular fare. They don't have a lot of these special seats left. And it's a non-stop flight."

Now I got excited. Other airlines were refueling in Paris or London. Aeroflot did not need to refuel!

"Non-stop all the way from Dallas? Wow."

"No, no," the woman said hurriedly. "Not Dallas. JFK. New York."

I pointed out to her that I did not live in New York. I lived in Texas, and needed a ticket from Dallas.

"I don't have a ticket from Dallas. Well, I do — on Air France, with a three-hour layover in Paris, for $1900."

I remained silent.

"Don't worry," said the travel agent. "You can fly Aeroflot. The rest is easy. We just have to find you a connecting flight."

I knew it couldn't be that simple, and it wasn't. My Aeroflot flight was leaving New York at 1:15 p.m. on Sunday. My flight from Dallas would not arrive in New York until 11:30 a.m.

Into LaGuardia, twelve miles away from JFK.

Which would give me an hour and forty-five minutes — assuming my first flight was on time — to get my luggage, find a cab, drive across town, and check into an international flight — check-in time for which was strictly three hours before departure.

"I'll take it," I said.

I told Kevin I would pack only a garment bag, as carry-on luggage. How was I going to fit a week's worth of clothes and shoes into one garment bag?

*

My father had given me weirdly specific instructions about what time to meet up in St. Petersburg. I was flying from Dallas, while he would be arriving from Prague.

Of course I got it all wrong. Apparently I was arriving too early.

"I told you," he said when I gave him my flight details, "don't come before Monday, July 13."

"But Papa, I *am* coming Monday, July 13."

"Yes, but you're coming in at 5:30 in the morning. I can't be there that early."

"So come when you can and meet me at the hotel."

I could tell he was frustrated, but I couldn't understand why. Did he want to meet me at the airport?

"I can't be there at five in the morning," he repeated.

"I understand," I said. "Come when you can. You don't have to meet me at the airport. I can take a taxi."

Two days later he called again. "You won't take a taxi. I will have a man meet you. Viktor. He will meet you, holding up a sign with your name on it. In Russian. You know how to read your name in Russian, don't you?"

"Yes, Papa."

"Pay him. Pay him like thirty rubles. Look, and if something happens and he's not there, then take a taxi. There are plenty of taxis.

But make sure you negotiate the fare in advance. Because if you get in and say you're going to Grand Hotel Europe, they'll take all your money. Negotiate in advance. If they quote you a hundred rubles, don't go. If they quote you fifty rubles, talk them down to thirty."

"Okay," I said, but I must have sounded hesitant, because my father quickly added, "Viktor will be there. He will be there most assuredly."

My father is nothing if not a planner. It's a control thing, having been a manager of people for twenty-five years. "I will meet you at the hotel, probably around 3:45," he continued. "Be ready at 3:30, though, just in case I'm early. Don't go anywhere. Maybe go for a short walk, but better yet, sleep, have a nap for a few hours, but whatever you do, be at your room and ready at 3:30. Understood? We'll go for dinner at Anatoly's. They're very excited you're coming. Then on Tuesday we'll go to *Shepelevo*." He paused for effect. He knew how I felt about Shepelevo.

"Great," I said. "How will we get there?"

"Viktor will drive us. We will have him and his car at our disposal for the whole week."

"Great," I said, not enthusiastically. I didn't know this Viktor; why would I want a total stranger coming with us to Shepelevo of all places? It made no sense. I wanted to take public transportation. Just me and my papa, like we used to. I said nothing.

"On Wednesday we will go to Piskarev Cemetery," my father went on. "Friday is the funeral of the Romanovs. It's a historic day, and I got you and me a press accreditation. It's impossible to get in, but I got it for you. You will see history being made."

"Wow."

"I don't know what else you want to do."

"I want to go to the Siege of Leningrad Museum."

"Yes, that's at Piskarev Cemetery."

Not according to my map, but who was I to argue? My father had lived in Leningrad for thirty-five years, not including the years he spent in labor camp. He knew better than my stupid map.

With my grandparents, Lev and Maria, for Deda's 93rd birthday, July 2000.

MY GREAT-GRANDMOTHER'S GRAVE

I called my grandparents, my father's parents, on July 2, my grandfather's ninety-first birthday. He said he was happy I hadn't forgotten with all the things I had to do.

"How could I forget your birthday, Deda?" It was with them I had spent every summer in Shepelevo. Every year of my life in Russia we were together on his birthday.

I had been less close to my mother's parents. My mother's mother died when my mother was sixteen, before I was born. I am named after her. My mother's father was a Red Army man — not prone to easy attachments. My last memory of him was his coming to our communal apartment to talk my mother out of leaving for America. I was told to go into the kitchen, so the adults could talk privately in our rooms. I hung around the hallway, hoping to hear a word or two — with no luck. Suddenly the door opened, and he walked out, not even glancing my way. His hat was in his hands, his mouth tightly closed. He marched past me down the hall and out the front door. That was the last I saw of him.

But my father's father was a different story. Lev Handler, born 1907, had lived through World War I, the Russian Revolution, the Russian Civil War, the Stalin years, the Leningrad blockade, World War II, the Khrushchev years, the Brezhnev years, and through fishing on the Gulf of Finland with me. When he turned ninety-one, I remembered.

"Happy birthday," I said to him.

My grandmother picked up the second telephone. "Happy birthday, nothing. Are you and your father planning to go to Shepelevo? He told us you were."

"Yes, Babushka, we are."

"Plinka," she said. "You are going to go and visit your great-grandmother's grave, aren't you?"

"Of course."

She started to cry. "Because probably no one has been at her grave since we left Russia — nineteen years ago!"

"What about Yulia?" Yulia was my only cousin, my father's only brother's only child. She still lived in St. Petersburg. The Shepelevo summer *dacha* was left to her when my grandparents left Russia in 1979.

"Yulia, Yulia. I don't know if she's even been back to Shepelevo."

"We'll find it. It's marked, right?"

"I don't know. I don't think so."

"It's not marked?"

"I can't remember. It was a long time ago."

"Do you remember what the gravestone looked like?"

"No."

"Do you remember where in the cemetery you buried her?"

"Not really. Somewhere on the right-hand side, toward the back. I'm not sure."

"I see," I said. "We'll find it. How hard can it be?"

She cried.

My grandfather interrupted, asking if I would be coming to New York before July 12. I told him I didn't think I would be coming to New York in the next ten days with a trip to Russia looming. What was he thinking? "Because there are some people in Russia I want you to go and visit," he said. "The Ivanchenkos. Do you remember them?"

"Are they dead or living?"

"Don't joke. Living, living. They want to see you very much."

Interrupting him right back, my grandmother said, "I'm sure her grave has not been taken care of. I don't know if Yulia takes care of it. Probably not. Who knows? I hope you and your father spend some time with her. But do you remember the Likhobabins? They still live in Shepelevo — "

"If they're not dead," Deda interjected.

"Leva, stop it," said Babushka. "Plinka, I want you to give the Likhobabins money. Give them a hundred dollars. That's a lot of money for them but not so much for you. You have a hundred dollars, don't you? Give it to them and ask them to take care of my mother's grave."

"So you're not coming to New York?" my grandfather said. He sounded disappointed. "That's a pity. I really wanted to talk to you about the Ivanchenkos. I have to go. Now is really not a good time to talk, Paullina. I'm having a birthday party."

With 22-month-old son the night before I fly to Russia. July 11, 1998.

TO LENINGRAD

At 4:30 in the morning on the day of my flight, I slithered out of bed, having gone to sleep just two and a half hours earlier. We had gone to my husband's boss's fiftieth birthday bash, and because I thought ahead, I had partaken in seven vodka-cranberries. Or it could have been six, or eight; being a lightweight as a drinker, very un-Russian of me, after the first two I had lost my ability to perform simple math.

I couldn't remember the last time I'd had that much to drink. In college, maybe. But back then, I'd go to sleep for fourteen hours and wake up nearly sober. Today, less than three hours after going to bed, I had to get up and travel 5000 miles. And I had woken up *not* sober.

My flight to New York was leaving at 7:10 a.m. We were in the car at 5:45 for the fifty-minute ride to the airport.

I sat stiffly, staring straight ahead. As Kevin drove, I asked him to please not make any right or left turns and at all costs to avoid coming to a complete stop. By the time we got to the airport, I felt a bit better. The vodka behind my eyes wasn't sloshing inside my brain anymore.

I had squeezed everything I was bringing into a single garment bag, as planned. My publisher had arranged for a car to pick me up at LaGuardia and take me across town to JFK, so that I wouldn't be delayed flagging a yellow cab. Even with these precautions, however, it was clear I would not have enough time to make my flight. When I had called Aeroflot to inquire about check-in times, the woman told me in her Russian-accented English that I had to be at the check-in counter three hours before departure. Since that was clearly not possible, I asked what she recommended as the *minimum* check-in time, explaining my situation. She said, "As long as you're there at least two hours before, you'll be all right."

I had one hour and forty-five minutes to get to JFK from LaGuardia. Anyone who has battled the Van Wyck Expressway and lost will understand what I was facing.

Bottom line: my garment bag simply *had* to come with me as carry-on.

Not according to the American Airlines woman at DFW in Dallas printing my boarding pass. The first thing she said was, "That can't come with you."

"It has to," I said. "I have a connecting flight at JFK at 1:15."

I'm not sure she knew what JFK was. If she knew, she didn't care.

Shaking her head, she said, "It has to be checked. See?" She flung her hand in the direction of the metal frame into which I was supposed to fit my carry-on bag. "It has to be *that* size."

"But this isn't a carry-on," I pointed out. "It's a garment bag."

"It has to be *that* size," she said, and turned away from us to fill out a gate check ticket.

"What are you talking about?" my husband said. "We've taken this bag with us three times and every time they've let us take it on the plane."

"Uh-uh," she said and pulled the bag out of my hands.

I was suddenly endowed with the ability to see the future. I saw my future at LaGuardia, trying to find my bag, waiting for the luggage carousel, missing my plane to Russia.

The woman was clearly a graduate of the Advanced Rudeness Training seminar given at an American Airlines Rudeness night school.

Just then, a muscular young man rushed up to Kevin and began to assure him that everything was going to be all right because there were forty more just like me also going to St. Petersburg on my flight. Their group leader had already called Aeroflot, who agreed to hold the plane until they made their way from LaGuardia to Kennedy.

This made Kevin and me feel better. Consequently we did not do what we usually do when confronted with graduates of the American Airlines Advanced Rudeness Training program, which is to prominently display our own higher learning degrees from the School of Angry and Defensive Travelers.

*

I sat in seat 7A — a bulkhead seat! The first time I'd ever had one.

As I was climbing over the girl in the aisle seat, I noticed she was unusually friendly. Her name was Carrie. She made lots of eye contact, said hello, was interested in the contents of my purse, in my magazines, in my Walkman, and in finding out if I was well.

She turned out to be a missionary, one of the forty traveling to St. Petersburg. She told me they were all from a mission near Dallas.

"Oh," I said. "A Catholic mission?" Catholics were the only kind of missionaries I knew. It made sense that the Catholics would be headed to Russia to preach Roman Catholicism to the Russian Orthodox. The Catholics have been trying to reunite with us ever since our one Holy Catholic and Apostolic Church split in the Great Schism in 1054. Boy can the Orthodox hold a grudge. We still haven't forgiven them for what they did to the Nicene Creed way back then.

But no, these missionaries weren't Catholic. Carrie said they were a non-denominational mission, going to preach the word of God to the Russians. As though the Russians were heathens.

I wanted to tell Carrie that although the Communists tried to stamp out Orthodoxy and create their own religion with Lenin and Stalin worship, they failed. But before I could speak, she looked out the window, at the clouds and the sun, and said, "Isn't this beautiful? How can anyone doubt there is a God when you see the beauty He made?"

I mumbled incoherently, glanced indifferently out the window and turned on my Walkman. Guns n' Roses screeched about paradise city while Carrie tried to engage me for a few more moments. Blessedly she gave up, put on her own headphones and took out her diary. I could tell she was not inspired, even by the lovely clouds. I read over her shoulder. She began, "I thank my Father for ..." and stopped.

She closed her notebook and went to sleep.

She snored. Loudly. I could hear her through the din of the 747 and Guns n' Roses' *Appetite for Destruction*.

My stomach, still queasy after my liquid dinner the night before, could take no more than half a banana. When Carrie woke up, she offered me hers and her yogurt, too. I politely accepted. I do not turn down offered food.

*

It had been such a mad dash for the door and so early in the morning that I'd had no time for long goodbyes with the kids. My youngest boy, Kevie, had watched me get ready the day before. He would bring me items from my purse, saying, "Here, Mommy," as he handed over each one. Later that afternoon, Misha got out of his crib when he woke from his nap, opened his bedroom door and came downstairs. He took my hand and said, "Come, Mama. Kevie wants you." You could say Kevie wanted me. He was crying hysterically.

I felt unsettled, overwhelmed.

I didn't want Misha to get out of his crib. It made it impossible for me to finish whatever I was doing. Packing for Russia, blow-drying my hair, getting ready for the birthday party.

"You know, Misha," my husband said. "You have to stay in your crib till we get you."

Misha replied, with a roll of the eyes, "But I had to get out, Dad. I didn't want to stay there anymore." Big, exasperated three-year-old sigh.

When it was time for us to leave, Kevie was too busy playing with his toys to look up. The kids barely stirred. Natasha grunted something like, "Have fun in Russia, Mom."

I couldn't believe how much had happened in such a short time. How could we be in our new house already? How could I be going to Russia already? I felt woefully unprepared. My oldest friend, Kathie, sent me an impromptu letter, pages long, full of her life and her kids, signed "I love you." But her birthday had come and gone in June, and I'd been too crazed by my life to send her so much as a card. I wasn't spending enough time with my own children. I had no time for anything but the house.

Kevin went to work *outside* the home. He published children's books about a dog who reads. I worked *inside* the home. Which meant my work stopped when the painters came. When the security men came, the pool guys, the lawnmower guys, the appliance guys, the plumbers, the electricians: it was me, each and every day, calling them, arranging times, answering questions. And carrying the baby. That's what I did — and when I was in my office for the briefest of minutes, I remained filled with the house and filled with the kids.

I was filled with my life. I was not filled enough (which is to say nearly at all) with World War II, with Leningrad under siege, with my ghosts as characters. The house was formed, the children were formed, but the new novel remained an elusive space in my heart. Half a million people froze to death or died of hunger in Leningrad during the winter of 1941. In Texas in 1998, I sat in my office, which was 80 degrees, and called the air-conditioning guy because it was not cool enough.

Somewhere I had read that during the siege of Leningrad, each child received only 125 grams of bread a day, about four ounces — bread cut with glue and cardboard. But that was all in another life, not my own. In my life, I said, "Misha, would you like a baked potato with butter and cheese and bacon bits?"

"No," he replied. "I don't want anything. Just Tootsie Rolls."

I had built my office upstairs so I could have a lovely view, but I had to close my ivory blinds so I wouldn't see the view, so it wouldn't distract me, so I wouldn't see my children frolicking and the dogs leaping into the pool. I might as well have been sitting in the rented house we'd been living in before, sitting in the small, hot attic room over the garage, looking out onto the driveway and the road and the neighbor's house. The blinding Texas sunshine, all well and good in theory, was disastrous for computer screens. I couldn't write if I couldn't see.

During the winter of 1941, my grandfather used to pour a bit of paraffin oil onto a plate, put a piece of wick in the middle, and light the wick. When the oil ran out, he would sit in darkness. He allowed himself only a tablespoon of paraffin oil every twenty-four hours. There was no electricity, and barely six hours of murky sunlight each day — the flipside of the sublime white nights my father and I were traveling to.

Still, my refrigerator was not making ice and the hot water dispenser was not dispensing hot water. When would the plumber come and fix them? Then I would be comfortable in my home office, where I could write about people starving to death.

My grandfather and great-grandmother had to burn furniture for firewood in their portable ceramic stove. They could have used it to cook some food, had there been any food to cook.

Thus their granddaughter did not say no to a proffered yogurt and banana.

*

We landed in LaGuardia at 11:30: right on time.

My bag wasn't at the gate where it was supposed to be, like children's double strollers that magically appear by the door as you leave the plane. I went to the baggage-claim area and met my soon-to-be driver, a polite, fiftyish West Indian man, who stood with me and watched the baggage carousel go round and round and round.

And round.

And round.

The missionaries' bags came, all three hundred of them. The other passengers' bags came. People were lifting off three, four bags at a time. But my one lousy garment bag was nowhere to be seen.

I was so tense, if someone had blown on me, I would have snapped in two. I imagined my bag on a different flight: to Las Vegas, Chicago, Seattle. The way the kids' car seats sometimes disappeared. Other times our suitcases would not make the plane and would arrive on a later flight.

It was now certain that I would miss my flight to St. Petersburg. Because I could not go to Russia without my clothes. Could I buy what I needed there? Shoes, underwear? Jeans, makeup? What about the ten T-shirts I brought for my father's friends? What about my coat?

No, I'd have to miss the flight. My six days in St. Petersburg were about to become five. And what if the bag was irretrievably lost? All this because of one unhelpful woman in Dallas. I never hated anybody more than her during those traumatic twenty-five minutes. My body shuddered with anxiety.

Meanwhile my driver, courtesy of the publicity department at St. Martin's Press, stood next to me, serenely humming a happy tune. Bobby McFerrin's "Don't Worry, Be Happy." I wanted to stuff a sock in his mouth.

I was so tightly wound that when the bag finally did appear — one of the last ones on the conveyor belt — I could not immediately feel relief.

Cheerfully the driver grabbed my single piece of luggage and began to wheel it. I hurried. He sauntered. We ambled across the road into the parking garage and guess what? He couldn't find his car.

It was 12:05 p.m. My plane was due to leave at 1:15, whether I was on it or not. And he couldn't find his car. But he was happy about it. He was whistling.

He approached a black Lincoln Town Car, laughed and said, "Wait: that's not mine."

Ha ha.

Aimlessly we searched. He looked at another Town Car license plate. "Nope, that's not mine, either."

And then he stood. He just stood in the middle of the parking garage, looking to the left, looking to the right, even looking up, as if he had absolutely no idea what to do next. Perhaps he was thinking of hailing a cab.

I said nothing for fear of offending him. If I had said what I was thinking, he might have refused to drive me even if he did eventually find his vehicle.

And he did eventually find it. He laughed again, leaning into my face, inviting me to laugh too, and said, "They all look the same!"

I smiled thinly. "Are you sure this is yours?"

He laughed harder.

We took off at 12:12 p.m. and made fantastic time, getting to Kennedy in fifteen minutes. The Van Wyck Expressway didn't defeat me. On July 12 1998, I came as close as Elaine on *Seinfeld* had ever come to beating the Van Wyck. I wheeled my bag to the Aeroflot counter, and joined the line of at least seventy people. After five minutes, someone yelled in Russian, "Anyone for the St. Petersburg flight?" About ten of us stepped forward.

"All of you?" the man yelled with exasperation, still in Russian. "But it's completely full!"

I looked around for the missionaries. Had they made it to Kennedy before me? They'd certainly retrieved their hundreds of bags before I got my lousy one.

In any case, I was shepherded "over there," and waited for the woman behind the counter to deal with me. She was Asian and spoke no Russian, which at first seemed a blessing — but a small one, for she seemed to speak no English either.

Her computer broke down in front of my eyes, and she looked as helpless as the driver searching for his black car. She spent five minutes threading paper into the computer's printer, and another five looking quizzically at the screen.

"Is there a problem?" I finally said.

"Yes," she said in heavily accented English. "The computer broke."

"I still don't have a seat assignment."

"Yes, yes. I will take care of it." She looked around. "I have to go use another computer. Wait here."

I waited, tapping my fingers on the counter, watching her fiddle with someone else's machine.

Thirty minutes passed. When she came back, I asked if I could have a window seat.

"A window seat?" she echoed, as if she were about to laugh. "Oh, no. There are no window seats left."

"Why would there be."

"This is a completely full flight. I can give you aisle."

I kept my mouth shut, took aisle, and ran to my gate. When I got there, the flight hadn't even started boarding. Bless Aeroflot. I called Kevin, who didn't answer: probably in the pool with the kids.

It was now 1:20. Aimlessly I shuffled around. A vague line had formed near the gate; I didn't know whether or not to join it. Behind the counter, an Aeroflot woman was busy on the phone, snapping at someone in Russian. I overheard a young woman and young man conversing in English. I asked them, in English, "Excuse me, do you know when they're going to start boarding?"

They looked at me vacantly.

The guy said, "*Mhy ne govorim po Angliyski.*" ("We don't speak English.") I stared at him. I nodded. "I see," I said, edging away.

Before I had a chance to ask anyone else, we started boarding. It was now 1:30 p.m.

While I waited for takeoff, I wondered what the chances were I'd be fed *pelmeni* on the plane. *Pelmeni* is my favorite Russian food — meat dumplings in chicken broth. I also like mushroom and barley soup, Russian potato salad, and caviar. Thinking of all this food, I realized I was *starving*.

What did a four-ounce ration of bread look like?

I was finally anxiously excited about returning to Leningrad.

*

My mother, who had recently moved to Maui, called me while I was packing and Kevie was bringing me offerings from my purse.

"You know it upsets me when you don't call me," she'd said. "I know you're busy. I know you have children. But Paullina, you can have many, many children. You only have *one* mother."

Who could argue with that?

"Your father doesn't like the title of your new book," she continued. "*The Bronze Horseman*. He says it's like calling a book *Romeo and Juliet*."

"No, it isn't. No one in America has heard of Pushkin's poem, 'The Bronze Horseman'."

"Well, I don't think you should call your book *Romeo and Juliet*."

I paused. "Okay, Mama. I won't call my book that."

My mother told me she was jealous of my father and me going to Leningrad together, without her. With a heavy sigh, she added, "Under different circumstances, I would have liked to come with you."

All I could say was, "Yeah. That would've been *great*."

Back in 1991, my father, my mother and my sister Liza drove down from New York to Sanibel Island in Florida. I wasn't invited.

My father said, "Paullina, I would love for you to come, but you and your mother — you know you just keep going at each other."

When they got back, I asked my sister how the vacation had gone.

She rolled her eyes and said, "You wouldn't believe it. They had the hugest fight about forgetting their sunglasses by the time we got to the bridge."

I laughed. The Verrazano–Narrows Bridge was about ninety minutes' drive from our house. The drive to Florida took two full days.

"They had a fight on the Verrazano over dumb sunglasses?"

"What Verrazano?" Liza said. "They had a fight at the bridge over the Long Island Expressway!"

It wasn't a bridge; it was an overpass — a mile from our house. They had to turn back to get the sunglasses. Liza said they didn't speak again until North Carolina.

So when my mother said she wished she could come with us to Russia, I kept my mouth shut.

*

Forty-five minutes after we boarded, we were still on the ground. It was now an hour past our scheduled departure time. I could have *walked* from LaGuardia to Kennedy.

The missionaries still had not materialized.

*

In 1996, with my father's retirement a few years away, my parents went to Maui on a fact-finding vacation. They'd never been, so they went to find out whether they liked it, and whether it really was paradise on earth like the internet said.

They came back two weeks later, tanned, converted, and the proud if slightly stunned owners of a plush new condo.

No one in the family could understand why they'd done it. My father's elderly parents were still alive and living in his house on Long Island. My sister, Liza, was nineteen and attending art school in New York. I had three children. Moving to Hawaii would take my parents 5000 miles away from us, a continent and half an ocean away.

Oh but the weather was apparently glorious on Maui. Everything worth having requires some sacrifices, my mother said. There was a price to be paid for fabulous weather, and complete separation from the family was the price she was willing to pay. My father wanted to make my mother happy so he said nothing.

A year later, in 1997, my mother suddenly left my father in Prague where they had been living and moved to the empty Maui condo by herself. Which is, by the way, why she couldn't come with my father and me to St. Petersburg — she had moved to Maui *by herself*. Had she remained in Prague with my father, she would have come with us to Russia.

My mother had adjusted dismally to Europe when my dad was transferred in 1992. She became blackly depressed. She was lonely, and my father spent all his days and nights working. The best years of his adult life were the worst years of hers. So she up and went to Maui, where she was now completely by herself and not much happier. Her one consolation was my dad's impending retirement, when they would finally be able to spend *all* their time together.

As I attempted to stuff eight changes of clothes into one garment bag, my mother said, "I don't like Hawaii anymore."

I stopped packing. "What are you talking about?"

"I've made a terrible mistake. It's all my fault."

"But Mama," I said. "It's Hawaii. Paradise on earth. That's what you told me. You know, if you can't be happy in paradise, you can't be happy anywhere." My mother had been looking for paradise every place she lived.

"That's the problem," she said. "It's sunny *all* the time. It's very depressing to have sun like that. You want a rainy day once in a while."

"I see." I didn't really. Texas was sunny. I didn't want rain.

"Hawaii is a nice place to visit for two weeks, but not to live. I've made a terrible mistake," she repeated. At noon every day, she explained, the winds began. They whipped up red dust from the earth and blew it all around the island: into all the open windows, onto the tables and the sofas and the shelves and the chairs. If she didn't dust daily, in less than a week she'd have an inch of red dust to deal with.

"Why don't you close the windows?" I asked.

"Close the windows? But it's so hot."

I was afraid to ask. "Don't you have central air?"

"Central air? What is central air? There is no central air. We have one air-conditioner in the bedroom, but it's small."

My father didn't know about the red dust. My mother was afraid to tell him.

"Didn't you both notice the red dust when you visited?"

"No. Who notices anything? We stayed in a hotel. The cleaning people dusted everything. You know, if it wasn't for you and this trip he's taking with you, he'd be here with me already. I can't wait until he retires. Then we can suffer the dust together."

*

The missionaries finally started filtering through. There had been six announcements, all in Russian, apologizing for the delay.

The muscular blond guy who had talked to my husband in Dallas walked by me, shouting something to one of his friends. When he saw me, he said, beaming, "See? I told you you'd make the plane no problem."

The plane taxied off at 2:30 p.m.

My head throbbed. My left eye throbbed, even six Advils later.

Aeroflot tried hard to emulate British Airways. But where was the back-of-the-chair TV screen? Where was the beautifully presented four-color menu? *Grilled salmon, exquisitely prepared with sautéed onions and Hollandaise sauce, served with new potatoes and string beans.*

On Aeroflot they took a more informal approach. The man in blue and gray wheeled his trolley to my seat and barked in Russian, "*Shto?*" which means, "What?"

I looked at him inquiringly, but before I could ask, he said, "Fish or turkey."

"What kind of fish?" I asked in Russian.

He shrugged.

"I'll take the fish," I said.

A woman came around with the drinks tray.

"*Shto?*" she demanded.

"Please could I have some tomato juice and some water?"

She nodded, and poured me a plastic cup of tomato juice and another of water. Both were filled only halfway, and both were room temperature. Ice was not offered. Later I was told that they'd give you ice if you asked — but they'd have to go to the back and chip it off the air-conditioning unit. Which, by the way, seemed to be running at full power. No matter how I wrapped the blanket around my shoulders, I could not get warm.

I downed both cups of liquid, but after eating my meal became thirsty again. The fish was cod. *I think.* It came with rice, peas and carrots, two kinds of salad, carrot cake for dessert, and plastic utensils. When I pressed too hard into a pea, one of the fork tines broke off. I ate the fish. I ate the Caesar salad with vinaigrette — no, *vinegar* — dressing. I ate the potato, ham and pepper salad in thick mayonnaise. I ate the small carrot cake, and then I started on the bread roll. I ate as if I fully expected to starve in Russia for the next six days. Further preparing me for the trials ahead, the roll was ice cold and decidedly unfresh. Oh, so the bread was ice cold! I smothered it with unsalted butter and ate it. Russians don't eat salted butter; they consider that a travesty.

I wondered if the roll of stale cold bread weighed more or less than 125 grams.

When a stewardess in a garish red uniform walked by, I asked in my politest Russian, "Could I get some more water, please?"

"No!" she barked. "Not now. Maybe later." She walked away.

Later, she did come back with half a cup of tepid water. I drank it gratefully.

After dinner, I had two cups of black tea with sugar. To Aeroflot's credit, the sugar was not doled out in tiny Western one-teaspoon allowances, but in thick Communist packets of heaped tablespoons. Much better.

Then I slept. It wasn't easy: the Russian married couple across the aisle were immensely entertaining. They made up for the lack of TV screens. In their sixties, they sat as far away from each other as possible without actually sitting in different rows. The wife could not stop commenting on her husband's every move.

"Vova, why are you putting your hands there? This isn't your magazine. Don't touch it. They're bringing our food soon."

Vova pulled out the in-flight magazine anyway.

"Why are you looking at that, Vova? What is so interesting about it?"

"Do you want to get a new suitcase?" Vova asked in his gruffly appeasing voice. His face was lined with resignation.

"Get a new suitcase? Vova, put the magazine down. I've had enough of your nonsense. And don't drag the blanket on the floor."

After dinner, Vova wanted to have a smoke. Being Russian, he pulled out a cigarette.

"You can't smoke in here, idiot," she said. "Didn't you hear the captain?"

So Vova got up from his seat and, standing in the aisle, lit up.

"Idiot! What are you doing? They told you not to smoke here!"

He shrugged, extinguished his cigarette and sat back down. She wanted him to pass her a blanket, but he wasn't moving fast enough. "Can you just give it to me? Can't you see I'm cold? I'm getting a headache from the cold. Just pass it already."

Kevin had suggested that on the long flight, perhaps I could write a few pages of *The Bronze Horseman* — the first chapter or two. Yeah, sure. When I woke up, I read *Good Housekeeping*, *Redbook*, *McCall's*, *InStyle*, *Reader's Digest*, *People*, and half of *Shape* before I got bored and finally picked up one of my research books, *The 900 Days*, an account of the siege of Leningrad. My goal was to finish it in 900 days, not at all a given.

Drifting off, I recalled what I could of Russia.

I was afraid to see it. Shouldn't some things remain a memory? Memory is so kind. I had left too young to have any regrets. I had not left love behind. We left family behind, but many of our relatives were now with us in America. My father had seen to that. My grandparents, my father's brother and his family, my father's oldest friend and his family — my father had given them all an American life.

I didn't want to go, but I knew I needed to see it with my own eyes. My grown-up eyes. I imagined it would be like gawking at an old boyfriend. You hope he is well, but not too well — not better than you. I wanted Russia to be well.

*

When we first came to America, I knew little about it, except that there were sharks and they ate people. That I had learned in school. The Americans killed their presidents, and the sharks ate the Americans.

When my father told me that we were going to America, the first question I asked him was, "In America, are there sharks? And will they eat us?"

"No," he said. "They won't."

The second question I asked was, "Do you think we will ever come back?"

He looked at me for a long time before he answered, "Never." He said it with sadness. We were walking down Nevsky Prospekt and as always he held my hand.

"Maybe when there are no more Communists?"

He shook his head. "Not in my lifetime," he replied. "Not in yours, either."

Yet here we both were, proving him wrong. My father isn't wrong often.

When we had left, in 1973, the Union of Soviet Socialist Republics was an all-powerful monolith, designed to perpetuate the power of the Communist Party, fourteen million members strong. We could choose to become Communists if we wanted to. We could become Pioneers in third grade; then we could become Komsomols or young Communists in tenth grade; eventually, we could get a party card, which meant we could get into all the best stores. Since the rest of us couldn't get anything in any store at all, party membership seemed pretty appealing. One of my dad's standard replies when people spoke to him about inequality in the Western world as opposed to Russia was, "Yes, in Russia everybody is equal. Everybody has nothing, so we're all equal."

From the day I spat on a statue of Lenin when I was eight, I knew I would not make a very good Communist.

In 1987, nearly fifteen years after we had left Russia, my mother made an unprecedented trip back to visit her dying father. Mikhail Gorbachev had come to power and travel restrictions were relaxed a little. She went by herself, shocking the whole family. My father was afraid to go with her. *Perestroika* or no, the Communists might throw him back into labor camp and not be as kind this time.

So she went by herself. Two years later, the Berlin Wall came down. After the wall fell, my father, despite all his protestations, made a trip to Russia. Then Communism fell. My father's friend Anatoly visited us on Long Island, and my Uncle Misha from Moscow came, and finally in 1994, my mother and father went to Russia together for the fifty-year celebration at my father's alma mater. My father was invited as an honored guest, a man who had left Russia and made a great success of himself.

I am not saying all these events transpired because of my father's persistent radio broadcasts to the Eastern bloc, but I can't rule it out.

*

If there's one question I'm always asked after I say that I was born in Russia, it's, "Have you been back?"

During Communist rule, my answer was always a puzzled, "Of course not."

But after 1991, the answer became more complicated. There were children involved, to be sure. There was a sense of danger, of unstable economic and political times. There were logistical issues — but most important of all, there was the question of me: why *would* I go back? What did I hope to gain by it? What would be the point?

I was happier thinking I would never go back.

There was a certain romance in being a kind of outcast. A refugee for life. Woman leaves Russia as a young child, forever carries Russia in her soul, but never again sees the place where she was born and raised. Such melodrama!

But now, I had a reason to go back. It was for my book.

I had to see the Leningrad streets where my hero and heroine walked, where they fell in love and said their goodbyes, and fought against a mortal enemy, embodiment of evil, and against the Nazis, too. I had to see the city where people starved to death by the thousands.

I had to see the city where I was born.

During my teenage years, what I would not have given to be less Russian, less foreign. I wanted a pair of new jeans, not flared hand-me-downs hopelessly out of style. I wanted American hair, which meant hair not bushy and not cut at home by my mother. I wanted a coat that was not knitted by my mother.

I wanted to speak the language of the hip kids at school. I wanted to say "Hi," in English without sounding like a dork.

I carried the feeling of wanting to be an American with me wherever I went.

When I was twenty, I went to England.

The British, smiling their sly, sardonic smiles at me, would ask, "So … where're you from?"

"New York," I'd say.

Those smiles again.

"Really? We never would have guessed."

They would tease me, thinking they were being *so* clever, mocking my adopted country. "What have Americans ever given us?" they'd say. "Except McDonald's and herpes?"

I couldn't believe my luck. To the British, I wasn't Russian; I was American. In England, I wasn't from Russia. I was from *Noo Yawk.*

It took five years of living in London for me to become an American. But despite my best efforts, I knew I was only an American on the surface. I knew that I could make a really good show of it, get a nice American haircut, buy nice American shoes, and a pair of Levi's. I could drive a Chrysler minivan, and even learn a word like *equivocate* and use it in a sentence.

Yet regardless of what the English believed, my soul was painfully Russian. It was Russian music that would bring tears to my eyes, and Russian food that made me fullest, and Russian language that would make me feel as if I were home.

Having turned myself inside out to become what I wanted to be but was not, deep down I still craved pumpernickel bread with sunflower oil and fried potatoes with onions. I was still a big mushroom-eating dork.

For twenty-five years, I tried to hide it, but now I was being called home.

*

We were landing soon. Breakfast was served. We were fed roast beef, which was not considered by Russians to be a perishable food, so it was kept at room temperature. It was served with a 125 gram cold bread roll and a slice of pale tomato.

The captain announced — in Russian first and then reluctantly in English — that the temperature in St. Petersburg was 18 degrees Celsius. I spent five minutes converting to Fahrenheit. We were landing. It was raining.

Mama chasing 15-month-old Plink, February 1965.

PART II

HERO CITY

DAY ONE
Monday

HERO CITY

When we landed at Pulkovo Airport, the missionaries clapped.

All I could see out the window at six in the morning was wet buildings and tarmac. And uncut grass.

Inside the terminal, I joined the line to have my American passport checked. Behind me, two women clucked away in Russian. I made a mental note to stop being surprised at hearing Russian all around me. The women were talking about the missionaries. One of them said, "Yeah, I wish them well, but I think they're going to have a hard time over here."

At the luggage carousel, my garment bag appeared almost instantly. On my customs form, I declared that I was bringing in six hundred American dollars and a camera.

While I was waiting in line, the customs officer at the head of the queue suddenly got up from his desk and wandered off. I stood dumbly for about five minutes, and then concluded he was not coming back any time soon, so I joined another line. Good call, for he had permanently disappeared.

The international arrivals area was jammed with people, none of whom would let me pass. I came to an impasse with one man: he glared at me, then at my bag, before finally stepping half a hostile foot back. I may have run over his foot with my bag as I wheeled by.

I saw a sign in Russian that said, Полина Саймонс. I went over to the sign. It was held by a skeletally thin man of indeterminate age with big lips and blue eyes. He was Viktor Smirnoff, our driver for the week.

When we reached his little white Volkswagen in the parking lot, we found it trapped between four other vehicles. There were no marked parking spaces; drivers parked wherever they felt like. We were stuck.

After we sat in the car for some minutes, staring at the terminal building as if for guidance, the car in front of us mercifully pulled out and we started to drive away. Before we could get anywhere, however, another car approached to take up the empty space in front of us. Viktor and the other driver glowered at each other. Viktor motioned in the direction of … I don't know. Possibly the exit, although it was hard to tell where the exit was.

The other man motioned back.

Viktor nodded.

The other driver rolled his eyes, but reversed his car a few feet, barely enough to let us pass. We pulled out of the parking lot and were soon on the Pulkovo *shossé*, or highway, on our way into St. Petersburg.

All I wanted to do was look at the countryside. Pulkovo is twenty kilometers south of St. Petersburg. The Germans bombed

the city from Pulkovo Heights for the duration of the war — before
the airport had been built. I expected to see the foliage of northern
Maine in the trees and the leaves and the fields. My father told me
that's why so many Russians settle in Maine — because it looks a lot
like Russia. I've been to Maine many times, but I didn't recognize
that state in the countryside near Pulkovo. Here was flat and slightly
swampy, more like Holland than Maine. With the overgrown
uncut grasses, it looked unkempt like a neglected village, not the
entranceway to Russia's second largest city. Certainly there were no
skyscraper pines of Maine, or the sugar maples of New England, or
any white cedar-shingled farmhouses with their silver grain silos.

It stopped raining. The sun was peeking out.

*

On a map, Leningrad looks like a glob of cotton candy surrounded on
two sides by water — Gulf of Finland to the west, Lake Ladoga to the
east. The city was built on the narrow neck of a wide isthmus, on the
banks of the Neva River.

To the north is Karelia and beyond that, Finland. The Finns and
Russians have fought bitterly over the Karelian Isthmus for three
hundred years, ever since Peter the Great built St. Petersburg in
the swampy mud and then decided he wanted to put some distance
between his spanking new capital and the Finns. The Karelian
Isthmus changed hands a number of times, the last time during
World War II. Today, nearly all of Karelia belongs to Russia. Unlucky
Finland had sided with Hitler, and to the victor went the spoils.

No one knows this except Russians, but Lake Ladoga is the
largest lake in Europe. The river Neva forms in this lake and flows

seventy-three kilometers or about forty-five miles to empty into the Gulf of Finland, just outside Leningrad city limits. In fact, the Gulf *is* the city limits. To the south is the rest of Russia.

In blockading Leningrad from 1941 until 1944, the Nazi Panzer tanks formed a semi-circle just south of the city. The German–Russian southern front looked like a smile on the face of death. The Germans knew they didn't have to encircle the entire city. Finland, a German ally, stood ready to fight the Red Army in Karelia, and to the east and west there was water. The Nazis had to worry only about the south. It looked so certain that Leningrad would starve and surrender, that Hitler had booked the Astoria Hotel in Leningrad for a victory celebration. The invitations had been printed, with the exact time of the party. Only the date had been left blank.

Hitler never set foot in the Astoria.

At first, in 1941, he was too busy keeping his men from frozen collapse during the invasion of Moscow. Moscow would not surrender. Stalingrad would not surrender. And Leningrad would not surrender. After Hitler lost the Battle of Moscow, the Battle of Stalingrad, and the Battle of Leningrad, it was just a matter of time.

Time and twenty million Soviet dead.

As we neared the city limits, the *shossé* turned into a *prospekt*, which is an avenue or a boulevard. Moscovsky Prospekt, also called Prospekt of Victory, runs in a straight line from the south of St. Petersburg, all the way into the heart of the city. Finally, I saw something familiar: a wide road flanked by four-story buildings.

The buildings were in pretty bad shape, though. Their faded pastel façades were finished in stucco: blues, greens, yellows, grays. The paint looked to be pre-war — not that I would know what pre-war paint looked like.

Everywhere I looked, I saw rotting window frames and unhinged doors. I wanted to look away, but there was nowhere to look.

In the movie *White Nights* with Mikhail Baryshnikov, Leningrad was so beautiful — and pristine. Had the film been made in a different city? I hear my father's voice from years ago: "Of course it wasn't filmed in Leningrad. Who would allow them to come inside Russia to make a movie about that defector Baryshnikov of all people? It was filmed in Helsinki. That's why it looks so beautiful."

There were very few trees. In the center of the wide boulevard stood a low concrete divider and barricaded behind it, tram tracks: a bus on rails.

The tram tracks were set in concrete that was in varying states of disrepair, from badly cracked to ravine-like. The rails were uniformly rusted. Oxidation had removed so much of the rails, it was a wonder electricity still surged through them.

There was something else, too. The streets were empty of people. Where was everyone? I looked at my watch.

10:45.

My mind was blank. 10:45 what? Was it morning or night? Had I already changed my watch to Russian time? My attention was temporarily diverted from the window as I tried to subtract nine hours from 10:45, then add nine hours to 10:45. After five minutes I gave up and asked Viktor. He told me it was 7:45 on Monday morning. Viktor was quiet. Telling me the time was the first phrase he spoke all car ride.

I know well Monday mornings in New York City — teeming with chaotic, purposeful life.

Here, nothing looked open and no one was out.

Well, why should they be out? Nothing was open.

But didn't they have work to go to?

There were a few stores. I was baffled by the large-scale billboards — SONY, and SANSUI, and NOKIA — some translated into Russian, some bilingual, some left solely in the Latin alphabet. Were there stores in Russia selling cellular phones and consumer electronics and small appliances?

"Viktor, these stores weren't here before, when I lived here, were they?" I asked.

"Of course not. There was nothing here then. It's much better now."

I nodded — and my head nearly went through the roof as the car dived into a pothole.

My father told me, after I had emailed him with a possible title for this book — *Thinking About Leningrad* — "Paullina, please, don't ever call it Leningrad. Call it St. Petersburg."

I tried.

In my defense, my book *The Bronze Horseman* is set during World War II, and in those days St. Petersburg *was* Leningrad.

My Aeroflot tickets stated that I would be landing at LED. When I asked the helpful airline attendant what LED stood for, she looked at me like I was the weirdo and brusquely said, "Leningrad." As if, *duh.*

After Communism fell, four million citizens voted by referendum and overwhelming majority to restore their city's original name. They had been waiting eighty years to call Leningrad St. Petersburg. The affectionate name all Leningraders use for the city is *Peter.*

We drove past Moscow Station — one of the five major railroad stations in St. Petersburg, and a very famous building in its own right. It is a large, imposing blue building with white window frames, apparently the twin, in every detail, of the Leningrad Railroad Station in Moscow. It also looked fifty years unpainted.

Directly opposite the station, across the big city square, is another large, imposing blue building. On its roof, in monumental Cyrillic letters that light up at night, stand the words ГОРОД-ГЕРОЙ ЛЕНИНГРАД (HERO-CITY LENINGRAD).

Viktor told me the sign was there to greet travelers arriving from the rest of Russia as they emerged from the train station. *Hero-City Leningrad.* Those three words scream in the night: *We starved and we fought and we died, but we did not surrender.*

Rename *that*, I thought. Change *that*.

I felt better about not adjusting easily to calling Leningrad St. Petersburg.

The letters on the sign were twenty feet tall and shakily faced every which way. They looked as if they were about to fall down on the street and kill somebody. Oh, sure, all glory to the hero-city, but the letters were not to be straightened out.

We are still on the outskirts, I assured myself. It had only been seven years since the fall of Soviet Union. They just hadn't gotten around to repairing it yet. Viktor, as if reading my mind, said, "Don't worry. Everything is better in the center of town."

Then we got to the center of town.

The road we needed to take to get to my hotel was cordoned off for repairs. It looked every bit as rough and full of holes as the road we'd just been driving on.

Viktor smiled. "They're fixing it, see? They do little by little. They're starting at the center and working their way out."

I nodded.

"It's much better than before," he said, as if on the defensive.

My father was right about my hotel, Grand Hotel Europe. It couldn't have been in a better location, on the corner of Nevsky Prospekt, the Rodeo Drive of St. Petersburg, and Mikhailovskaya Ulitsa. In 1991, the hotel had been extensively renovated and was now run by Kempinski, the oldest luxury hotelier in the world. The side of the hotel that faced Nevsky Prospekt was freshly painted yellow stucco with white window trim. The side that faced Mikhailovskaya was freshly painted brown stucco, with ornate window detail. Inside and out, the hotel looked as if it belonged on the streets of Paris.

Dutifully I offered Viktor money, just as my father had instructed, but he flatly refused, saying we would take care of it later. As per my father's directive, we agreed to meet at 3:30 that afternoon.

The desk clerk spoke to me in courteous, accented English as he took my passport and visa, promising to return them to me in a few hours. I asked him why he needed them. "You're going to be exchanging currency," he replied, as if that explained anything.

"Yes, that's true," I said.

Self-satisfied, he smiled.

"But I'm not exchanging currency *now*."

"Yes, but later."

Ah, yes, later. So he took my passport and visa, and I went to my room.

"Will there be more bags, madam?" said the bellman.

"No," I replied, all puffed up and proud of myself. "Just the one."

It was Monday morning, 13 July 1998, 8:30 a.m. Russian time, or 11:30 p.m. Sunday, Dallas time. Aside from less than three hours of drunken sleep and an hour's tense nap on the Aeroflot flight, I hadn't slept — in any time zone — since Saturday morning. How many hours was that? Thirty-six? Forty-four? Then and there, I made myself a promise to stop counting after thirty hours of sleeplessness.

My room had a large entranceway, and was taller than it was wide. It had twenty-foot ceilings, a crystal chandelier, and gilded ceiling trim. The two twin beds had down pillows, down mattress pads, and down quilts. I was reluctant to sit on either bed, for fear that I would fall asleep sitting up. I didn't come to St. Petersburg to sleep. I was going to call Kevin, unpack, and explore.

The window had a sill about eighteen inches deep. How thick the walls must be, I marveled, comparing them with the two-by-fours that I'd just watched frame our house in Texas. It had looked like a house of sticks before the sheetrock and the stucco went up.

I opened the window. It had a side view of the leafy Italian Gardens and beyond them the Russian Museum.

A road crew was repairing the street below. What they were repairing didn't look so much like a pothole as a crater. The repair crew was two men, both wearing white dress shirts. They were taking a cigarette break, and then they picked up their jackhammers and got back to work, making the crater even larger.

I perched on a stone ledge beneath a crystal chandelier, and gazed out onto the tall oaks of the Italian Gardens for about a minute. All was quiet in St. Petersburg — aside from the two deafening JACKHAMMERS going full bore right below my window. As a soundtrack, it didn't work. I was about to close the window when the noise suddenly stopped. The men were taking another cigarette break!

Just then, I noticed a sign on the window latch: "To keep insects out of the room, kindly keep the windows closed."

The room was the nicest I'd ever been in. The bathroom was the size of a bedroom, with a separate shower and tub. The toilet was a standard white toilet, a magnificent feat of ingeniously simple technology. It wasn't quite as nice as my all-time favorite hotel toilet, at the BoardWalk Villas at Walt Disney World — but then what was?

I unpacked slowly. I wasn't sure what to do with my bounty of alone-time. Should I go for a walk? Should I, without a map, just using childhood intuition, find Fifth Soviet, the street where I lived for the first ten years of my life?

I decided to have breakfast. I was hungry, and my eyes were getting that glassy, sandpapery feel from being up too long. But first I walked down a flight of stairs to the hotel health club, which advertised a number of different services: massage, acupuncture, sauna, weight room, small pool, pedicures, facials. I booked a massage for 10 a.m. and a blow-out for eleven. My hair is untamed at best; if my father's friend and his entire family were turning out to see me, I intended to have my wild hair conquered by a professional.

Bookings made, I rushed downstairs to breakfast. Stepping out of the stairwell, I thought I'd walked outside, yet I wasn't chilly. When I looked up, I saw a glass ceiling a hundred feet above me. It gave the illusion of being outside, without any of the disadvantages of, say, rain or wind. The patrons of the hotel could sit and sip their tea and eat their finger sandwiches and read their newspapers, as if they were on a warm *rue de Paris*, surrounded by fresh flowers, untouched by Arctic weather. It was the famous glass mezzanine of the Grand Hotel Europe, a partial floor between two stories.

On the mezzanine were two restaurants — the Caviar Bar, and the opulent European. Both were open, but the European offered a breakfast buffet that included red caviar and *blini* — yeast-raised pancakes. I opted for caviar. I love *blini*. I took two. They cost me twenty-four units per *blini*, fat and small, like silver-dollar pancakes, instead of thin and crèpe-like, as *blini* are supposed to be.

Everything in the Grand Hotel Europe was charged in units — not rubles, not dollars, but units. When I asked the hostess about it, she cheerfully told me that units were dollars.

"So nothing is in rubles?"

Smiling courteously, she shook her head. "Not in this hotel," she said. "Outside, yes. But the dollar is more stable at the moment."

After my *blini* with caviar and sautéed mushrooms and potatoes, I bolted to the health club. It was a few minutes past my appointment time, and I don't like to be late. Svetlana, the girl behind the counter, gave me a towel and robe and told me I could use the sauna while I waited.

"Waited?" I repeated. "Waited for what?"

"For the masseuse, of course."

"Oh. I won't be waiting long, right?"

"No, no. Not too long."

In an American health club, if you arrive for your appointment a few minutes late, the masseuse is already waiting for *you*, towel in hand, tapping her impatient foot on the floor.

I disrobed, sat for ten minutes in an empty locker room, caught myself falling asleep. I went back to the reception area.

"Will it be long?"

"No, no, not long," Svetlana assured me.

I ambled over to the pool. It was an oversized Jacuzzi. There was no one else but me in the club. Not even the masseuse.

Impatient and cranky, I was tired of waiting and of being awake. Also of being half-naked for no good reason.

"Svetlana," I said, "if there is a problem, I can come back later."

"There is no problem."

"I've been waiting twenty minutes, and I need a full hour massage, but I have a hair appointment, which you made for me, in forty minutes. I don't want to wait anymore. How about we reschedule." It wasn't a question. I had already turned around to go get dressed.

Just as I returned to the reception area, fully dressed, the masseuse ran in, panting. "I'm sorry. That traffic. They're fixing the roads."

"They certainly are," I said.

I was relieved that he was late and that I was dressed, because the masseuse was actually a masseur, a man, and I'd never had a massage by a man before. I'd sold this trip to my husband as one for research and sentiment and desperately needed wisdom. I knew that the husband would not be especially keen to learn that 5000 miles away from home, his wife lay half-naked while being rubbed in oil by a panting Russian man.

I had my hair blow-dried instead. It took an hour, like a massage — a very long hour. The stylist looked all of twelve years old. But she did an impressively good job of straightening my hair.

Back at reception and ready to pay, I asked Svetlana how much the blow-dry cost. "Two hundred and twenty," she told me.

I churned this for thirty seconds.

"Two hundred and twenty *units*?"

"Yes," Svetlana replied — then followed up with a quick "*No!*" when she saw my face. "Rubles," she said. "Rubles."

That was it. *Rubles*. How much was two hundred and twenty rubles? I didn't know how many rubles made a dollar. I could not exchange dollars for rubles in the United States before I left, since the Russian government did not and still does not allow their rubles to be exported.

I pretended to think about it for another minute as Svetlana and the masseur stared at me.

Finally, helpfully, Svetlana said, "About six rubles to a dollar." I conjured up a thoughtful face, to create the impression I was trying to work out the conversion in my head. Truth was, I was falling asleep right in front of them as I leaned against the counter.

To end my suffering, Svetlana took mercy on me. "About thirty-five dollars," she said.

I paid up, and went back to my room — *for just a second,* I told myself. It was noon, and outside was a lovely day. I had three and a half hours to myself before I had to meet my father, and I couldn't *wait* to go out for a meander.

I looked at one of the down-covered twin beds. I had chosen the one closest to the window, the other one having already become a storage surface. It was covered with information packets, a map of Leningrad, the room service menu, the hotel's alphabetical list of services, my three purses, and an Olympus pocket camera.

I wanted to go out. But my twin bed had a down quilt on it, and down pillows, and a down mattress pad. The room was full of daylight. It was noon, my first day in Russia. I went to the window. The two smoking road warriors must have run out of cigarettes because the street was empty and quiet.

I sat down on the bed. Then I lay down on the bed — *just for a sec,* I told myself, *and careful, don't mess up your hair.*

When I opened my eyes and looked at my watch, it said 3:15.

I jumped up. My father was going to be here in fifteen minutes!

PAPA

I tried to dress thoughtfully. I didn't want to overdress. But I didn't want to underdress either. I was about to meet my father's oldest friends, Anatoly and Ellie, and their daughter, Alla, my best friend once upon a time. Two years older than me, she now had a husband and two children — by Russian standards a *tremendous* number of children. I put on a white denim skirt, a brown V-neck shirt, and low-heeled, strappy sandals.

At precisely 3:30 the phone rang. It was my father. "I'm waiting downstairs," he said.

I hadn't seen my father since our trip to New York the previous summer, when we had first broached the idea of going to Russia together. Out in the street in broad daylight he nodded in my direction, smiled even, and I gave him a hug outside the doors of Grand Hotel Europe. Were these the same doors he had wheeled my baby carriage through when he was smuggling books from his American acquaintance? It had been winter then, cold and dark. Now, the sunlight was very bright.

My father looks a lot like me. If I were a man, twenty-seven years older, a few pounds heavier, smoked, and drank lots of beer, I would be my father. I get my curly hair from him, and my Russian features. I have three-quarters of his memory, half his intelligence and a quarter of his sense of humor. He is of medium height and always dresses extra nicely. He is freshly shaved and smells clean. On this occasion, he was wearing jeans with suspenders and a button-down shirt. As his cousin and my aunt Tania once told me — she who knew my father well, for they had been close growing up — "Your Papa, when he was an adolescent, was always trying to find himself, to reinvent himself. He didn't know if he wanted to be Gérard Philipe or Clark Gable, but he knew he wanted to be someone great and important. And as ever — humor oozed out of his every pore."

Papa studied me silently. Finally he said he didn't recognize me. "What did you do to your hair? Why is it straight? Why are you always trying to be something you're not? And you're not really dressed for the weather, are you? Where is your coat?"

"But it's so warm," I said.

He shook his head.

As we arrived at Viktor's car, my father said, "Get in the back. It's easier for you to get into the backseat. I will sit in the front." It might have been easier for me to get into the backseat, but it was much harder to see anything from the tiny rear window of the Volkswagen.

After we started driving, I casually asked where Fifth Soviet street was, so I would know where to go another day. I felt such regret for sleeping. I could sleep any time. But to walk to Fifth Soviet by myself, on my first day back in Russia — how often could I do that?

Well, now never.

Papa asked Viktor to drive us to Fifth Soviet, so that we could see for ourselves. "Just for two minutes, Viktor, all right?" my father said. "Because we must go to Anatoly's. They're expecting us. They are very excited to see you again, Paullina."

The road was bumpy and in the backseat, I felt quite thrown about. I saw a man in a dress shirt standing on a corner, smoking a cigarette. He looked as if he had nowhere to go. He could've been one half of the road crew jackhammering outside my hotel. Or he could've been homeless. It was impossible to tell the difference. The homeless were well dressed in Leningrad. They looked like normal people in suits. I watched him until the traffic light changed, and we zipped away.

I saw little of Leningrad out of the car's narrow window. But the back of my father's head, his cigarette, and the traffic lights out in front I could see perfectly. While Viktor navigated the streets to Fifth Soviet, my father and I digressed into his reasons for arriving to Russia so late on July 13. Viktor had just picked up him from the airport.

"Papa," I said, "so tell me again why you couldn't meet me any earlier than today?"

"I don't know what you mean."

"Well, you were so adamant that I couldn't come any earlier than today. Even today was too early. Why was that again?"

"I don't know what you mean," he repeated, taking a long drag of his cigarette.

"Uh-huh," I said. "So tell me, how was the World Cup Final *yesterday*?"

Pause. "Fine," he said. "Why do you ask?"

"No reason. Did you enjoy watching it?"

"Very much. Zinedine Zidane was a marvel. I invited some people over to my Prague apartment. France has never won the World Cup before. It was a momentous occasion. If you knew anything about anything, you would have been glued to your television, not gallivanting around the globe."

"So why didn't you just tell me this is what you were up to?"

Viktor was smiling, but my father kept a straight face. He sort of flung his head in my direction, to pretend to look at me. "What?" he said. "I have to report to you now?"

"No, of course not," I said. "Here we are going to Russia, and I thought you were delayed and limited by work …"

"What do you care what I'm delayed and limited by? I told you no earlier than Monday, but you of course don't listen."

"I just want to know how your World Cup Final was, that's all."

Viktor was trying not to laugh as he drove.

*

We stopped at a red light on Ligovsky Prospekt. On the corner was a four-story redbrick building, partially concealed by a tall iron fence and large, leafy trees.

"See there?" my father said. "That was the hospital where we took you after you swallowed a whole bottle of aspirin. You were two. We took you right there. And do you know what you did as soon as we brought you back home? I come into the room and you are standing on our bed, and your mouth is filled with more aspirin! You must have hidden the bottle somewhere, and as soon as we got home, you retrieved it."

I sat back and listened to him.

"Oh, and here? See these cobblestones? This is where I dropped you on your head out of your carriage. Do you remember that?"

"Oddly, no."

"How you cried. We brought you to the same hospital. And you were so scared when the doctors took you from me, you stretched out your arms and cried, 'Papochka, come, let *me* carry *you*.'" He laughed fondly.

Up ahead was a large concert hall. My father told me was the October Concert Hall.

"No, Papa," I corrected him. "That's the Grechesky Concert Hall."

"I can't believe you're arguing with me," he said. "What do you know? It's October Hall."

Viktor didn't help any: he agreed with my father.

"But I know it's Grechesky Hall," I insisted, "because I used to play on the steps over there."

"You might have played there, but you obviously didn't know what it was called," said my father.

I let it go. Seeing the big, beige, ugly building, childhood came flooding back. When I was five, I performed in that concert hall with my kindergarten class. I held a giant red cube in my arms, a cube bigger than I was, and I danced. My mother was in the audience. My father was already gone. He was in prison.

On the weekends, when my mother was cleaning or cooking, she would send me out to Grechesky Concert Hall to play. I would cross Grechesky Prospekt by myself, hoping some other kids would be there. Sometimes there would be, but sometimes there was no one there at all. After all, it wasn't a playground, just a flight of steps.

There was one girl I had really liked. I can't remember her name now or how I knew her, but she was a few years older than I was. She always let me play with her and her friends.

One day she must have noticed I was cold. Was I shivering? Was I blue?

"Are you cold?" she asked. I nodded. And she said, "Oh, my baby!" She knelt in front of me and hugged me to her, and rubbed my back to warm me up, and I remember being stunned by the long embrace, by the comfort of it. Afterward, every time we played, I would tell her I was cold, or hungry, or that something hurt, because I wanted her to hug me again. She reminded me of my friend Alla.

When I was a child, Grechesky Prospekt seemed extremely wide to me. A tram ran through it. Now, as an adult, I saw that the street was really quite narrow. With the sun setting down its length, it looked almost rural.

There were hardly any people on the street. Then as now.

Across from the Concert Hall, on the corner of Grechesky and Fifth Soviet, I saw an olive-green stucco building.

"That's it, isn't it?" I cried.

"Yes, that's our building," my father said. "Listen, don't get too excited. When I came to St. Petersburg last time, I walked by here and the building was closed off. They were doing renovations or repairs. I don't know. It could be anything now. Condos. Business. Anything. You won't be able to go inside. You'll see. I wasn't."

We turned across Grechesky and pulled up outside our old building. We sat quietly for a few moments. Viktor did not turn off the engine, or even put the car into park.

"Well, this is it," my father said. "Do you remember it?"

What a funny question. This building was one of the few things I remembered vividly. He knew that. He was asking to be dramatic.

I was surprised to discover the building was green. I don't remember it being green. But the location of the building, I remembered exactly. Even the address. House no. 3, apartment 4.

I didn't remember it looking so old. The intricate stucco trim was chipped, and the glossy cream front doors hung loose and unevenly on their hinges. They looked as though one hard push would send them falling right off.

"I thought you said they were renovating the building?"

"Yeah, I don't know what to tell you. That's what they said."

From the backseat, I peered out at the cream double doors. I remembered walking through them and going up three flights of stairs.

"Well, we've seen it," my father said. "Ready to get going?"

I didn't answer.

"Or ..." He sounded uncertain. "Or what? Do you want to get out?"

"I want to get out," I said instantly.

Papa looked at Viktor apologetically. "Okay, Viktor? Just for a second."

"Of course." Viktor was unflappable. He switched off the engine.

We got out, and my father looked up. "There are our windows. Over there, on the third floor, on the left. Do you see them?"

I looked up. I felt weak.

It was at that moment that I got a queasy helpless feeling. I began to feel unmoored in a brew of strong sentiment. Looking up at the windows of the rooms where I used to live, it occurred to me then and there that I may have gotten in over my head. Though with undeniable curiosity, I had come mostly as an intellectual exercise. But what if the memories of the life I used to have, memories deliberately untouched by me for all these years, unrelived and unrelieved, turned out to be too much for me?

Frozen, I continued to look up. I remembered those windows as being large and majestic. But they were small and old, with cracked frames.

I didn't know what to say.

"Papa," I finally managed, "didn't you once try to walk along the ledge from one window to the other?"

"Yes," he said, with a sheepish chuckle. "We were celebrating. I had a little too much to drink. I can't believe you remember that."

I walked away from my dad and Viktor to the street corner. This was not how I wanted to see the place where I grew up. Not with Papa standing and smoking, in a hurry to get going. Not with Viktor waiting for us, puzzled and not understanding. Who could explain it to him, anyway? I didn't understand either why seeing two old windows would fill my insides with such anguish.

I would've preferred to come by myself. To cross Grechesky Prospekt as a grown woman, to linger at the Concert Hall, remembering the little girl who tried to find some friends to play with while her mother cooked dinner.

My father came up to me, watching me, waiting for my reaction. I hoped my face was blank.

I stared at the street and my father stared at me.

"Okay?" he said. "Ready to go?"

"Absolutely," I replied, turned and got back into the car.

As we drove away down Fifth Soviet, he pointed to a little park at the end of the street where he used to walk me in the stroller.

"I don't remember that park," I said.

"You were a baby."

Briefly I caught sight of the avenue flanking the other side of Fifth Soviet, Suvorovsky Prospekt. Seeing Leningrad this way, from the backseat of a car, was surreal, as we whizzed away and soon crossed the Neva. It was as if I were looking at the city through the myopic viewfinder of a stranger's camera.

We were driving through a part of town I'd never been to before. That was better. It wasn't hitting as close to home. I focused on looking out of the window onto a deserted treeless street.

To avoid thinking — to avoid *feeling* — I asked Viktor what time the sun set in Leningrad these days.

"Oh," said Viktor, thinking. "Right now it sets, I guess, around nine in the evening."

"Nine?" I was mildly surprised. We had come to Leningrad on July 13 — the day *after* the World Cup Final — so that we could see the famous white nights. In Texas in summertime, the sun sets around nine, and there certainly weren't any white nights in Texas.

"There are no more white nights," Viktor said firmly. "No. It's quite dark by about ten."

The disappointment was a welcome distraction from the other things I was feeling.

As we drove through the southeastern part of town, away from the city center, the buildings got taller and shabbier. We passed balconies filled with hanging clothes, firewood and debris. Nothing had been painted. The windows were rotted out.

"When were these apartments built?" I asked carefully. I didn't want to offend anyone. Viktor might live in one of these buildings. My father smoked and said nothing.

"Some in the sixties, some in the seventies," Viktor said.

I couldn't help but say the wrong thing. "The *nineteen*-sixties?"

"Of course," Viktor said.

Finally my father spoke. "You remember your Babushka and Dedushka's apartment building?"

"Of course."

"It was exactly like one of these buildings."

I didn't believe it. I told him that. Their apartment on Polustrovsky was so luxurious — the dank staircase with the drunk man passed out on the landing notwithstanding.

"I'm telling you, Paullina," my father repeated quietly. "Exactly like one of these buildings."

We turned a corner near an outdoor market; it looked like a harmless rural shopping strip, its tables piled with vegetables. Viktor told us it was a hotbed of drug activity.

Anatoly and Ellie lived near this market on a street called Ulitsa Dybenko. Their street was lined with concrete tenement structures, once painted white, now grimy. They looked like dilapidated city projects about to be demolished. The sidewalks were unswept, the grass unmowed, the trees sloppy. Across the street from the ramshackle high-rises was nothing but fields.

What St. Petersburg needed, I decided, was a community association like the one we had in Stonebridge Ranch, Texas. The association told us how high our grass could grow. It regulated the size and color of our children's play fort in the backyard. Didn't I just get a third stern letter from the association, warning me of severe penalties if we didn't immediately plant shrubs in front of our exposed air-conditioning units? That's what St. Petersburg needed. Foliage police.

First, though, they would need to get some air-conditioning units.

ANATOLY

It took us a few minutes to find Anatoly and Ellie's apartment. Their group of buildings looked discouragingly the same as all the others. My father had trouble locating the right one.

"What street is this?" Papa asked Viktor. "Is this still Dybenko?"

"I think so," Viktor replied. "The tram runs through it, see?"

"Yes, yes."

"Maybe there is a street sign?" I offered helpfully.

"No," Papa barked. "There are no street signs."

We drove around some more.

"Papa, have you been here before?"

"Of course I have, several times, but it all looks the same."

"What number building is it?"

"Thirty-eight, but that won't help. There are no numbers on the buildings."

"Oh."

"Look!" my father exclaimed. "I think that's Ellie on the balcony, waiting for us." We pulled up to a building, got out of the car, and my father waved. The woman on the balcony didn't move. "No, it's not her," he said, shoulders slumping. "But I'm pretty certain this is the building. I'm almost positive."

We thanked Viktor, asking him to come back for us a little later that evening, and then walked up to the front door. My father had his two heavy luggage bags. I carried one while he carried the other.

"Do you know what apartment number it is?" I asked.

"Yes," he said. "Number nineteen." He sounded unsure. The door had no handle, no lock, no hinges — just a vertical metal bar running down the length of it. It almost didn't look like a door, but a metal wall, hermetically sealing the building from the outside.

There was no list of apartment numbers, no names, no doorbells, no intercom. Instead there was a contraption like a giant combination lock. To my surprise, my father seemed to know what to do. He turned three dials on the combination lock on the rebar — one to 0, one to 1, and one to 9 — and pressed a button.

In a few seconds, there was a buzz and the door popped open an inch. Papa grabbed the metal bar and pulled it open the rest of the way. We walked into a tiny, dark, low-ceilinged entrance hall that smelled of (very) old urine. Not that new urine would have been much better.

The elevator was at the top of a narrow stairway. Why did we have to walk up seven steps to get to the elevator? Haven't the Russians heard of the 1990 *Americans with Disabilities Act*? As we climbed the stairs, we had to hold the bags out in front of us: there was no room on the staircase for a person *and* a bag side by side.

As we waited in the gloomy hall for the elevator, I tried to make conversation. "So …" I asked, "Babushka's and Dedushka's building was really like this?" Not hiding my skepticism.

"Almost," my father said. "Theirs didn't have an elevator."

The elevator door opened; my father hopped in, and the door promptly started to shut behind him. I shoved the bag into the doorway, but it kept closing, unmindful of me or the bag. For the next fifteen seconds the door and I engaged in a fierce battle of wills while my father stood and watched with the detached helplessness of a television viewer.

Finally, I won, but it had been by no means a certain victory.

Out of breath, I got into the elevator and asked my father what seemed to me a reasonable question to ask of a man in an elevator.

"What floor?"

At first I thought he hadn't heard me. I was about to repeat myself when he said with a chuckle, "I really don't know."

"I thought you've been here before."

"Many times. But I can't remember the floor."

The number of the apartment was 19. What floor would that be? Using logic and inferential deductive reasoning, what would we in America do?

"Is it on the first floor?"

"No, definitely not."

"Is it on the nineteenth floor?"

"The building has only nine floors."

"Maybe it's the ninth floor?"

"No, they're not on the top floor. I'm sure of that."

The elevator door remained calmly open, as if, now that we were inside, it had no intention of ever closing again.

My father pressed a button.

"Maybe it's eight," he said. "Although I don't think they're up so high."

The elevator creaked up to the eighth floor. The doors opened halfway, then began to close again. I squeezed myself into the gap, through the vise-like grip of the doors, and then pried them open so my dad and his bags could get out, too.

We stood on the small landing in front of three apartment doors, none of which was open.

"This is not the floor," Papa said. Then he walked to the stairwell and yelled. "Ellie? *Ellie!*"

From below us, a woman's voice yelled back, "Yura!"

"Ellie! Where are you?"

"I'm coming down!" Ellie yelled.

We heard footsteps somewhere beneath us, heading farther down the stairs.

"No, don't come down. We're up! Up on the eighth floor."

The footsteps stopped. There was a pause.

"What are you doing up there?" she asked.

"I forgot what floor you're on! What floor are you on?"

Ellie laughed. "We're on fifth."

"Fifth," I said. "Of course."

"Wait, we're coming down," yelled Papa.

On the fifth floor, Ellie was standing on the landing, waiting for us. I hadn't seen her in twenty-five years, yet she looked just as I remembered her. She was blonde and little with the same sweet, small-nosed, freckled, smiling, clear-eyed pixie face. Her arms were open to embrace me.

She showed us into her apartment.

"Where is Anatoly?" my father asked.

"He is getting bread. He'll be back soon."

Ellie gave me a tour of the apartment. It was tiny, much smaller than my family's first American apartment in Woodside, Queens. They've been working all their lives, I thought, and they still live here? But as she proudly showed me her pokey kitchen with its sunny view, I realized with shame that she thought she had done quite well to have such a nice home.

I made a note not to be such a judgmental idiot.

There was a short corridor with two narrow doors. "One is the toilet, the other is the bath," Ellie said. "Do you need the toilet?"

"Not right now."

"I'm going to put my things down and take a shower," my father said. "Is that okay, Ellie? Before dinner?"

"Of course," she said.

My father would be occupying the computer room for the next six days. There was also a living room, a small front bedroom, and a narrow concrete balcony that overlooked Ulitsa Dybenko. I guessed that it had indeed been Ellie who had stood on the balcony and watched us as we pulled up in Viktor's car. She probably hadn't been sure it was us.

When we got to the bedroom, Ellie said, smiling, "Plinka, why don't you stay with us? As you see, we have plenty of room for you. We could give you our bed."

"No, stop it," I said. "Where would you sleep?"

"Oh, we're living at our *dacha* now." Many Russians live at their *dacha* — their summer house — during the warmer months.

"Where is that?"

"Lisiy Nos."

I shook my head. "I don't know where that is."

"Across the gulf from your Babushka and Dedushka's *dacha* in Shepelevo."

"That's where we're going tomorrow, by the way," my father pitched in from the other room.

"Oh, so you're in Karelia?" I said excitedly to Ellie. I planned to set part of my book there. "Papa, how do you say перешеек in English? Is it peninsula?"

"No, not peninsula," he called out. "Peninsula is surrounded by water on three sides, isthmus on two. It's isthmus."

"Oh."

He stuck his head in. "So what two bodies of water surround the Karelian Isthmus? Do you know?"

"Ha! Of course I do," I said, thinking furiously. "Gulf of Finland and Lake Ladoga?"

He laughed. "Why is there a question mark at the end? Are you asking me or telling me? Because *I* know."

I spotted an empty bottle of Lancôme's Trésor perfume on the nightstand.

"Your mother gave me that perfume, when she was here last,"

said Ellie. "It's all gone, but I really liked it. The bottle still smells of it a little."

The floor was warped hardwood. The cabinets, the tables, the red curtains, the bed, the bed stand — were all simple and old. Only the dark wallpaper looked new.

I wanted to say something, anything, so I nodded at the walls. "Nice wallpaper."

"That?" Ellie said dismissively. "Nah. What about this?" She led me back into the living room. There, the wallpaper reminded me of the place I had lived in in England, a former council house. Paper that had once been yellow but was now a sooty gray with cigarette smoke. Paper my first husband and I had spent money we didn't have to remove. Ellie smiled. "It's from Europe."

"Oh," I said. "Europe. Very nice."

My father reappeared, all fresh and washed.

"Did you have a nice shower?" Ellie asked. "Plinka, maybe you want to have a shower today? The water is nice and hot. Have one. Because tomorrow they're turning it off." She chuckled.

"Oh yeah?" I said, chuckling right back. I thought she was joking. "Don't worry. I can have a shower at the hotel." I paused. "When will they turn your water back on?"

"August fifth."

I stared rather dumbly at her. "Three weeks from now? You mean you'll have no hot water?"

"Yes."

"In the whole building?"

"Right. So will you stay? You can sleep in our bed."

Before I could answer, my father interrupted. "No hot water? That's no good. Paullina, I'll have to come and shower at your hotel."

Before I could reply, Anatoly came home.

Anatoly and my father had known each other since 1952, when my father was sixteen. They had known each other ten years before my father even met my mother, eleven before I was born. If it weren't for Anatoly, there would be no pictures of me as a baby. He was the only one in those days with a camera, and even a film camera. He was my official photographer. Every single photo of me as a child was taken by him. If not for Anatoly, there would be no home movies of three-year-old me being stung by a bee while eating watermelon in the Red Cave in the Caucasus Mountains by the Black Sea. If not for Anatoly, there would be no footage of my mother and father meeting and falling in love in a seaside resort town in 1962.

I was dismayed by how gaunt Anatoly was. He was only one year older than my father, but the ragged lines in his face made him look much older. I remembered Anatoly as such a happy, slender, funny man.

He was still funny — and slender. Withered, maybe.

A few minutes later, Anatoly's brother Viktor and Viktor's wife Luba arrived. Viktor and Anatoly were twins.

Viktor's only son, Paul, had left Russia some years ago to study engineering in Princeton, New Jersey. I had met Paul when Kevin and I were living in New York; Paul had come to our house to celebrate New Year's 1995. He was a polite young man of about twenty, very inquisitive. He walked around my entire house, looked at every book on my shelves, pressed every button on my VCR and laser-disc player and TV, crashed my computer, and got hold of my camera. When I developed the photos, I discovered that he had taken pictures not of my kids, or the Christmas tree, or the people at the party, but of an empty cake plate. A dirty fork. My cat sleeping under the table.

I shared this now with his parents, Viktor and Luba. They laughed joyously and said with adoration, "Yes, Pasha is like that. He does the same at our house when he comes to visit. He is always adjusting the color temperature on the TV."

I asked what he was doing nowadays. They told me Pasha had recently married a Russian girl and taken her back to Princeton with him.

Finally Ellie and Anatoly's daughter, Alla, arrived. She showed up with her husband — *another* Viktor — and their two children, Marina and Andrew.

My childhood friend Alla looked remarkably lovely and remarkably as I remembered her. Her hair was short now, but her freckles were the same, her upturned nose, her round eyes, and she was still taller than me. And still two years older. This pleased me: I wasn't the oldest young person in the room. I liked the grown-up Alla immediately. I had liked the young Alla, too. She had taught me how to play cat's cradle and eat watermelon. Every time our parents got together, we were together, which meant we were together a lot. She wasn't a reader like me, but because of that, she was more social and had more friends. She was always the popular one.

Alla's husband Viktor was good-looking in a generic European sort of way; he didn't look particularly Russian. I thought he was our age; when I found out he was forty-four, I was shocked. There was no kidding yourself with forty-four: it seemed so old.

I realized shamefully that I was underdressed and had no hope of becoming overdressed on this trip unless I went shopping. Alla and her husband were wearing suits; the kids were in their Sunday best. Luba wore a dress with stockings and black high-heeled pumps. They had dressed up to meet me, to make a good impression.

I went out on the balcony for some fresh air. Papa was there, smoking. We didn't speak. Though it was supposed to be the suburbs of Leningrad, it didn't look like the suburbs. It looked like the boonies. The sight of rural Russia outside, with its dying grasses and wooden huts and broken roads, was too much for me on my first Russian evening. I needed to continue to believe that our friends were living here well.

We squished around the dining-room table, which was flanked on one side by three chairs and on the other by a low couch, on which three of us would have to sit. I did not want to be one of those people. The couch was so low, I would have to ask someone to pass the food *down* to me. And I didn't like the thought of just my head bobbing above the table. I took a chair.

The food, and there was plenty, was served on Ellie's wedding china. We drank vodka out of crystal shot-glasses and wine out of elegant goblets. For appetizers or *zakuski*, we had herring, crab and rice salad, smoked salmon, tomato and cucumber salad, radish salad, and lots of fresh white bread. I ate as much as I could and had four shots of vodka, each accompanied by a loquacious toast: one to me, one to Papa, one to the hosts, one to the new generation.

Two hours after we had started dinner, the *zakuski* disappeared and were replaced by large dinner plates, on which we were served steamed turkey and boiled potatoes with dill. No one could eat one more bite, yet we all did, and washed it down with more vodka.

"It's very hard for us, Paullina," Ellie said. "Very hard. I get a pension, and we have to live on that. I used to have a good salary when I was working. It's hard to get by on just the pension."

"What about Anatoly? He doesn't work?"

"No, no, he works," she said evasively. "He writes scientific papers, he does research for an engineering company."

"That sounds like a good job."

She was non-committal. "So-so. He hasn't been paid in four months."

To punctuate that, I had a fifth shot of vodka. "Four months?"

"Hmm."

"So why does he keep going to work?"

Ellie shrugged. "What else is he going to do? Anyway, sometimes he goes, sometimes he doesn't."

Ellie said she herself missed going to work.

"Really?" I said. "What was your job?"

It's not that she didn't tell me. She did. Her work had something to do with submarines and traveling all over the world. It sounded important and interesting. But I had had too much vodka, and the words she was saying to me weren't part of my ten-year-old Russian vocabulary. Sometimes I would ask her to repeat a word, but that didn't help me understand her any better. If anything, it confused me.

Maybe splashing some cold water on my face would help. Standing up shakily, I asked Ellie to point me to the bathroom.

She walked me down the hallway.

"Right in here," she said proudly. "If you need to wash your hands, you can go across the hall to the washroom, okay?"

I locked myself in. The little cubicle, three feet by two feet, did not smell fresh. The toilet paper was cheap and rough.

And the flush was not intuitive. There was no handle, no button, no cord to pull. I spotted a series of metal wires. I pulled on one of them several times, and when that failed, I stuck my head outside, where Ellie was waiting in the corridor. She told me to pull the metal wires *up*. The toilet flushed.

When I had finished, I found Ellie in the kitchen, cleaning up. While I helped her, she continued with her story. She told me she used to get paid *a lot*, but since she had retired, her pension was only three hundred and eighty rubles a month.

I did the calculations. "But Ellie," I finally said. "How can that be? That's only about sixty-four dollars."

She shrugged. "Don't you remember how much your mother and father got paid when they lived here? Three hundred and eighty rubles is a very good pension. Your mother used to make a hundred rubles for a full month's work."

"Yes. Yes, she did." I remembered that. I knew that. My mother told me enough times. I wanted to ask how that number translated into today's rubles.

"Ellie, how do you pay for your apartment?"

"No how," she replied. "We don't. We get vouchers. When they pay Anatoly, then we pay rent. We haven't paid in three months."

Back at the table, Anatoly asked me questions about my first novel, *Tully*, the only one of my books so far to have been translated into Russian, and therefore the only one of my books he had read. He wanted to know if the story was true or made up. If it was made up, he asked me how I could make up all those details about Tully, as if I actually knew her.

Anatoly was an aspiring writer himself, as almost everyone in Russia seems to be. His brother Viktor — a poet — kept saying, "Give it to her, go on, give it to her. Why won't you? You have to. Go on. She'd love to read it."

Anatoly would ignore his brother for a while and then snap: "Why do you keep going at me? *'Give it to her, give it to her …'* She is too busy. She is an author. She' got her own work. You think she has time to read it?"

"Read what?" I finally inquired politely.

Proudly Viktor said, "Oh, Tolya wrote a book, too. Just like you."

Anatoly demurred. "Hardly a book."

"No, a book, a book. All right, maybe shorter than Paullina's book."

"*War and Peace* is shorter than Paullina's book," chimed in my father, who had overheard.

"But longer than a short story," Viktor continued.

"A novella, maybe?" I offered helpfully.

"Yes, yes," exclaimed the twin brothers. "A novella!"

Anatoly lowered his voice. "It's about the time many years ago your father and I and Ellie met."

"Oh," I said. "Nostalgia?" As if I knew what it meant to have lived a life and at sixty look back at yourself when you were twenty, full of youth and hope.

"Yes, nostalgia," said Anatoly.

"It's very well written," said Viktor.

"Oh, Viktor," said Anatoly. "It's not up to us to say that. We have an author among us. *Her* opinion is what's important."

"Give it to her, give it to her. Go on."

"She has no time to read it. She is too busy."

"I *am* pretty busy," I said, "but do give it to me. I'll be glad to read it."

"See? What did I tell you? What did I tell you?" exclaimed Viktor. "I told you she'd read it!"

I went back out onto the balcony. There was very little room to stand because it was covered with old chairs, large and small pieces of wood, and dirty chunks of white plastic. My father came out and lit a cigarette. We stood for a minute without saying anything. I went back inside.

*

We had sat for many hours at the table, and the sun hadn't moved in the sky. Every time I went outside, it remained directly above our fifth-floor windows.

After the dinner plates were cleared, I casually asked what time it was. I didn't want to look at my own watch for fear of giving the impression that I wanted to leave.

"Nine o'clock," Alla said.

"No!" I checked my watch. It was twenty past nine. I looked outside again. The sun was still 60 degrees high in the sky. Didn't our driver tell me it was going to get dark around ten?

We ate dessert and drank tea out of china cups and saucers. Alla had made a fourteen inch round cake with whipped cream, fresh fruit and rum. Although we had been eating since five in the evening, in a matter of minutes all the cake was gone.

My father started telling everyone our plans for the next day. We were going to Shepelevo.

After Shepelevo, he detailed our schedule for the rest of the week. Everyone at the table had suggestions.

"You're here to do research on the siege, Plinka," said Anatoly. "You have to go to Piskarev Cemetery, the memorial to the dead."

"We're going there on Wednesday," my father said. "Ladies and

98

gentlemen, I have it all planned out. You're not dealing with an infant. You're dealing with a professional manager of people. I know what I'm doing. Leave it to me."

"I really want to see your hotel room," Ellie said. "It's not every day we get to go to Hotel Europe."

Yes, of course, come.

Alla wanted to try my famous hotel breakfast buffet with blini and caviar.

Yes, of course, come.

Viktor, Anatoly's brother, wanted to show me where the music stores were. "I have a car, too, you know," he said. "Not just your papa's co-worker. I could take you anywhere."

Yes, of course.

Anatoly wanted to stroll with me through the streets of Leningrad and talk about the siege.

Yes, of course.

Ellie wanted to come, too.

Yes, of course, come. How about if we go out to dinner?

Everybody wanted to know when I was going to call Yulia, my cousin. Yulia's father and my father are brothers. I looked at my dad. He was making stern eyes at me and shaking his head a little.

"I'll call her, um, soon?" I said tentatively. He shook his head.

"Do you want to use the phone?" asked Anatoly. "You can call her from here."

My dad stepped in. "Paullina, you should go. It's getting late. And we have a big day ahead of us tomorrow."

I stood up to leave, got my camera and my purse.

"Paullina," my father said, "after Viktor drops you off, don't go walking the streets. All right? Go to your hotel room, relax, get some

rest. Tomorrow we go to Shepelevo. All right? *Shepelevo*, Paullina."
He peered into my face for a reaction.

I widened my eyes. "I know." I cleared my throat. "Papa, does
Viktor *have* to come with us to Shepelevo?"

"What do you mean?"

"I know he is going to drive us, but what is he going to do when
we get there?"

"What do you mean?"

I didn't know how to explain what I meant. "Well, is there some
place for him to go while we walk around, or is he going to walk
around with us?"

Papa thought, smoked. "There is no place. He is going to have to
come with us. Why?"

I didn't know how to answer *why*.

"Papa, Viktor is very nice, but we don't know him. *I* don't know
him."

"So?"

"Well, what if I want to cry? What if we want to cry?"

"Me cry?" He scoffed. "What, are you crazy? And how would we
get there without Viktor?"

"Take public transportation." I perked up. "Like we used to!
Remember?" It was important to me to completely recreate my
Shepelevo experience.

"Take public transportation in Leningrad?" repeated my father.
"You are, you are crazy." He turned to Ellie. "Ellie, my daughter has
gone completely mad."

"Your Papa is right," Ellie said brightly. "Why do you have to go
to Shepelevo? Stay in Leningrad."

*

At ten in the evening I left with Viktor who had returned to take me back to the hotel. He also agreed to drive Alla and her family to their apartment. When we were in his car, I said to him, pointing to the sunlit outside, "Viktor, what do you see?"

"I know, I know," he said, sheepishly. "I don't know what I was I thinking. I got confused."

The white nights were famous; how could Viktor not know that they began on May 20 and ended on July 16, year after year after year? For fifty-seven days and nights, no streetlights were lit in the city so that nothing could detract from the sky and the sun. If someone were to ask me what the weather was like in Dallas in the summer, I would say instantly that it climbed as hot as 105° Fahrenheit, or 40° Celsius. If someone asked me what the temperature was in Dallas at midnight in July, I would say without hesitation, 94° Fahrenheit.

But then I hadn't lived in Dallas my whole life. Maybe if I'd spent a lifetime in Texas, I wouldn't notice the heat any more than Viktor noticed the citrus midnight sun.

Alla, her husband and their two children were squeezed into the tiny backseat of the Volkswagen. They didn't seem so impressed with the white nights either. The rows of tenement houses along the Prospekt of Bolsheviks, which soon turned into the Prospekt of Five-Year-Plans, were dark rectangular giants rising along the wide boulevard, backlit by the sun behind them. Countless satellite dishes hung from their crumbling walls. With different buildings it might have been quite a view. Even with these buildings, it was too spectacular to take for granted.

"Wait," I said to Viktor when we pulled over to let Alla and her family out. "I want to get out for a second. I have to take a picture."

"A picture of what?" Alla asked. "It's only our building."

"A picture of the satellite dishes."

"Why? You don't have satellite dishes in America?"

After I said goodbye to my friend, Viktor and I cruised along the river Neva as the sun set. We neared one of the most famous Leningrad landmarks — Peter and Paul's Fortress.

The Imperial Russians used it as a prison and a graveyard, burying you in a gorgeous ancient tomb right on the premises by the prison walls. The burial service took place in the cathedral, a hundred paces from where you had lived out your miserable days behind bars. The Communists, who didn't believe in God, turned the place into a museum. Only when Communism fell did Peter and Paul's Cathedral become active again as a church. So active that the last Tsar of Russia and his family's remains were going to be interred at Peter and Paul's on Friday, and my father and I planned to attend.

The cathedral's golden spire glowed in the sunshine, its slender gilded reflection shimmering on the surface of the Neva. The fortress stood just inside the Neva delta on a tiny man-made island built by Peter the Great to defend the city against northern invaders, like Finland.

Along the Neva, across a narrow canal called the Kronverk Strait was the artillery museum, which is where we stopped next. I wanted to get a picture of the surface-to-air artillery tank that was aimed directly at Peter and Paul's shining spire.

The picture for some reason looked unfocused through the viewfinder of my Olympus. Before I could utter a "Huh?" I heard a ripping noise coming from the gears inside my camera. I tried again. This time there was a cracking sound. I tried to take a picture but it was no use. The camera had stopped working. What in the world was I going to do? This was the only camera I brought. What a shame. The midnight sun was extraordinary.

Viktor said, "We'll just have to come back another night."

"I'll have to get a camera first," I said, so upset with myself. How many times does one return, after twenty-five years gone, to the city of one's birth? Yet to mark the occasion, I had brought the tiniest and silliest of the three cameras I had at home.

I had a beautiful Nikon SLR, and a decent automatic Pentax with a 38-165 zoom. I didn't bring either of those. Oh no, I brought my ancient weatherproof Olympus, the camera we had bought solely for the purpose of taking with us on vacation with small children, because I couldn't carry my heavy Nikon and two boys and two diaper bags and push the double stroller at the same time. What was my excuse for not bringing the Nikon to Russia? I had been so conditioned to travel *light* because the children were *heavy* that I had come by myself to Russia with *nothing*. No decent clothes, no decent camera.

Quietly we drove along the river embankment, crossed the Palace Bridge, next to the Winter Palace, and made our way down Nevsky Prospekt. In two minutes we were outside my hotel.

"Viktor," I asked, "how serious do you think my father was when he told me not to walk around by myself at night?"

By way of answer Viktor said he would park the car and walk with me. I declined. I had wanted to know if it was safe for me to be alone. I didn't want to walk with Viktor. I wanted to walk alone through Leningrad.

Instead I returned to my room, where I opened my blinds and looked out onto the Italian Gardens. The street was quiet. The trees were covered in shadow. The park was dusky, but the light violet sky above me dispelled the illusion of night.

I spent a long time in the bathroom, taking off my makeup and getting ready for bed. I suddenly remembered my busted camera. From the hotel phone I dialed Anatoly's number, hoping to talk to my dad, but Ellie said he'd already gone to bed.

"Tell him," I said, "to pick me up a half hour later because I need to go and buy a new camera."

Ellie clucked sympathetically. "Are you sure it's broken? How do you know? Are you sure it's not supposed to make a ripping grinding noise?" Finally she promised to give my father the message but not before adding, "What do you need a camera for, anyway?"

I briefly considered calling Texas. But by the time I figured out what time it was there — mid afternoon — I was too tired to talk to anyone.

Still I could not sleep. Images of the day kept loudly intruding in my subdued room, like late-night TV, but I couldn't turn them off. My first day in Russia had come and gone. Turn it off, turn it off. It wasn't what I had expected. What did I expect? I couldn't say. Not this.

I tried to look forward to Shepelevo. I had dreamed of returning there, to my idealized childhood haven, for twenty-five years. I had been dreaming of Shepelevo since childhood — in adolescence, maturity, womanhood. Now we were going back. How did that make me feel?

Happier, I decided, than returning to Fifth Soviet.

But not by much.

I was wrong. This trip was not an academic exercise. It wasn't like the brief research excursion I had made to Dartmouth College, the setting for my second novel *Red Leaves*. Leningrad meant something to me. The crumbled stucco, the window frames as old as Communism, Ellie's wallpaper. On this first day, everything was just a vague thread of pain, but I couldn't grasp its meaning.

I sat on the edge of my bed and stared down at the hardwood floor.

By the time I fell asleep it was after 2:00, the sky a metallic blue, blinds, curtains, windows wide open.

Anatoly's building on Ulitsa Dybenko. July 1998.

My room at Grand Hotel Europe.

DAY TWO

PENTAX

I slept restlessly. I woke every hour or so, opening my eyes and seeing light outside. What time was it? It seemed perpetual dawn.

The Grand Hotel Europe may have been chosen as one of the "Leading Hotels of the World," but whoever did the grading obviously didn't need to wake up in the morning. There was no alarm clock in the room. There was no clock at all, not even on the tiny TV. Because I was getting old and losing my eyesight, I could no longer read the fine gold lines on my analog wristwatch without reading glasses, not even in the white night.

Kevin was my alarm clock. He called at 8:30 in the morning to wake me up. It was 11:30 in the evening his time the night before.

"Can I talk to the kids?"

"Well, it's nearly midnight," he said. "They've been sleeping for three hours."

At 9:00 my father called.

"You are not buying a camera in Leningrad," he said. "What are you, crazy? I loaded new film into my camera. I have a beautiful camera, a Pentax. It's yours for the rest of the trip. You will take it, and you will give it back to me before you leave. Just don't forget to give it back to me before you leave."

"But Papa—"

"That's all. I will pick you up in a half hour. You will be ready, right? I don't want to wait. You have to be ready. I'm not even going to come up."

"Papa?"

"What?" he barked, already done with the conversation.

"I thought you said not to call it Leningrad."

I got ready in record time. What to wear to Shepelevo? I didn't know. The night before, I had found a note on my bed from housekeeping: "Good evening. The temperature for tomorrow, Tuesday, July 14, 1998: 18–21ºC or 67–73ºF. Good night!"

I wore khaki shorts, a chenille short-sleeve white top and over it a sleeveless white tunic. My feet I decided to place into my relaxed-fit sneakers, although there had been nothing relaxed-fit about them on the plane. Perhaps they would be more comfortable in Shepelevo.

I ate my buffet breakfast in exactly five minutes. My father did not like to be kept waiting. I had two *blini* with caviar, fried potatoes with fried mushrooms, and some coffee.

My father was waiting for me on Mikhailovskaya at 10:15. He eyed my short sleeves with disapproval.

"Paullina," he said. "You're not dressed for the weather."

I shrugged. I was fine. It was a cool crisp morning. He was wearing a navy nylon jacket.

"Did you bring a bathing suit?" he asked straight-faced as we walked to Viktor's car. "To go swimming in the Gulf of Finland?"

"I thought you just said I wasn't dressed for the weather?"

"What does that have to do with swimming in the Gulf of Finland?"

"Never mind. No, I didn't bring a bathing suit with me," I said. "Maybe we can buy one at Gostiny Dvor."

Papa shook his head. "Sarcasm does not get you my camera. If you're so clever, where is your camera?"

"Broken."

"Exactly."

But we did cross Nevsky Prospekt to Gostiny Dvor, which occupied a whole city block. Gostiny Dvor is the premier shopping mall of St. Petersburg. It's a sprawling two-story yellow stucco building. It was built in 1765. It looks it. We went not to find a bathing suit, but to buy a camera battery, although what I really wanted to buy was a new camera. My father wouldn't hear of it. "I told you, I'm giving you my camera. I already put film in it."

While my father bought a camera battery, I gawked at the automatic cameras. The lady behind the counter let me hold a Canon. Viktor stood quietly by my side, and whispered as we left, "That's how you know big changes have come to Russia. You think they'd ever let you touch a camera in a store in the Communist days?"

"Probably not," I acknowledged.

"That's right," said my father. "Because they didn't have any cameras."

Reluctantly I took my father's Pentax.

TO SHEPELEVO

The memory of Shepelevo is strikingly real, vivid as the yellow velvet lamp on the night table at Grand Hotel Europe. There is a hammock and there are cucumbers and there is water. I row a boat, I taste clover, and all the smells are right. I learn to ride a bike. I see my first — and only — house on fire. I taste warm goat's milk and warm cow's milk. I catch my first fish. And my last. I try to catch one with my bare hands in a shallow brook by the gulf. I see the sun rise and set. I read *The Three Musketeers*, my favorite book. I break my toe, my first toe-break, on the door frame between my room and Yulia's. I pick blueberries and mushrooms. I kill a hamster — accidentally — by letting him eat old coffee grinds my grandmother had thrown out. I have a fish bone stuck in my throat that no one can get out except my grandfather with his surgeon-sure hands.

Was I ready to see my Land of Oz?

*

We drove merrily. I say merrily, though Viktor seemed to be uncertain of the way, distrustful of the map and my dad's innate and remarkable sense of direction. My father kept telling him which way to turn. Viktor complied, but remained unconvinced.

We were headed for the south coast of the Gulf of Finland. First Peterhof, then Oranienbaum, then Big Izhora, Little Izhora, Lebyazhye, then Gora-Valday, and then at the crest, right before the shore curved — Shepelevo.

Just past Shepelevo a larger town, Sosnovy Bor. The Soviets built a nuclear reactor there in the early 1980s and restricted all access down the coast. That's why my mother did not go to Shepelevo when she visited Russia in 1987. In 1992 the reactor in Sosnovy Bor had a serious radiation leak and was now in the process of being dismantled.

All I wanted to do was look out the window in silence, and daydream, but my father was telling Viktor and me about the Russians who got rich when Communism fell.

Through small bribes, he said, some enterprising Russians acquired Soviet buildings on the cheap in the early 1990s, when they saw what was about to become of Communism. The buildings were cheap, yes, but they were also falling apart. With a few connections and some foreign capital investment, the Russians renovated the buildings, and then leased them out in the new post-Communist Russia. They made millions. Most of this reconstruction was in Moscow but there was some in Leningrad, too.

I half listened.

"Any questions?" my father asked.

"Yes," I said. "Tell me again why we couldn't go to Shepelevo by public transportation?" I so fondly remembered taking the train and bus to Shepelevo. It would take us fifteen minutes on the metro, and then before boarding the train Papa or Mama would buy me a crème brûlée ice cream, the best thing in the world. Sometimes they'd be out, and I'd be forced to get disappointing vanilla. We would take the *elektrichka* — the short-distance train — for forty-five minutes to Lomonosov (now Oranienbaum), where we would wait for a bus that would take an hour to get to Shepelevo. I suspect that today all I really wanted out of the public transportation experience was the crème brûleé ice cream, but I couldn't confess this to my father.

"I'm too old to take public transportation," he said.

But when we were driving through Lomonosov, the train station, a big old yellow stucco building, struck big weepy chords in both of us. "Take a picture for your mama," my father said. "She'll cry."

That's exactly why we should have taken the train and the bus, I thought. I remembered waiting in front of that station with my mother. I remembered sitting on the dusty bench that was still there, just as dusty.

A bus pulled up. It didn't so much ride in as hobble in, as if perhaps one of the tires was blown. The wine-colored paint was peeling and the bus's undercarriage was rusted out. The small, opaque windows were firmly shut. The bus made a reluctant-sounding engine noise.

"Is that the kind of bus we used to take?" I asked.

"This one is worse," said my father.

We bought some drinks in a little shop next to the station. Viktor bought a jar of pickles.

The shop was new, my father said. There had been nowhere to buy anything before; not pickles and certainly nowhere selling Coke and Sprite and Perrier spring water.

"What *did* they sell?"

"Nothing."

We drove on.

"Papa," I asked him, "what am I going to do, how am I going to write about Russia during the war? It was sixty years ago!"

"Write, write," he said. "Everything is exactly the same."

*

"Did the Germans get to Shepelevo?"

My dad told me they did not. They trampled through Peterhof — Peter the Great's summer palace, a rich man's Versailles — from which they stole rugs to line their miserable trenches. Forty kilometers before Shepelevo, they were stopped by the Red Army at Lomonosov, the town we'd just left, which remained in Soviet hands throughout the war.

"Were they stopped because of Kronstadt?"

"Exactly," replied my father, with slight surprise that I even knew what Kronstadt was.

Kronstadt was a tiny island in the middle of the narrow entrance to the Gulf of Finland. It housed a Soviet naval base. From this base, the Soviets bombarded the Germans to the south and the Finns to the north with artillery fire. Kronstadt saved Leningrad.

Just past Lomonosov, on the edge of the Gulf of Finland, Viktor stopped to ask for directions.

Gazing out onto the Gulf, I said to Papa, "I wonder where Kronstadt is?"

He pointed to a bit of land some way out into the Gulf. "Right there."

"Can tourists go there?"

"They can now."

"They can?" I became excited. "I really want to go."

"Paullina," my father exclaimed, sounding exasperated, "you should've come to Russia not for six days but sixty."

Viktor returned and informed us that just a few kilometers up ahead, past a town called Big Izhora, was a border patrol point. Without special permission, no one was allowed through.

"Oh, *koshmar*! *Koshmar*!" said my father. "That's it. Everything fell through, Paullina. All our plans. What a nightmare. What a horror. That's it. Well, it's all over."

We drove on anyway, but slower. For fifteen minutes, my papa continued to lament. "I can't believe it. I asked him if we needed permission. He said, *No, go right ahead, they'll let you through.* I could have gotten permission so easily. *No,* he said, *you don't need it.* Well, that's it now. It's all over. What a tragedy. Nothing to do. Ah, hell."

Who this *he* was, I didn't know and was afraid to ask.

There was no *Let's see what we can do. Let's try. Maybe there is another way we can go.*

No. Apparently it was all over, and *he* was to blame.

The border patrol booth was manned by two young, extremely able bodied soldiers in full uniform with guns strapped to their waists. The gate was a manual one: to let a car through, the soldiers had to push the gate open with their bodies.

The three of us sighed as we parked the car and got out. Slowly we walked up to one of the soldiers, who listened carefully to our pleas to let us pass and then shook his head. My father handed the soldier his business card and said something about coming from America to see his grandmother's grave in Shepelevo.

The soldier looked at my father's passport and his business card. He looked at my passport. He studied each of us, and then shook his head again.

I didn't understand what the border post was for. What border? We weren't on the border of anything. We were in the middle of a two-lane highway, between nowhere and nothing, traveling alongside the Gulf of Finland from one Russian village to the next.

The soldier disappeared to make a phone call. My father shook his head and again mumbled something about some man named Viktor who should have told him about needing permission. I looked at our Viktor, the driver.

"You?" I mouthed silently.

He shook his head. Loudly he said, "Another Viktor who works at Radio Liberty."

"Papa," I asked, "isn't this the road the bus used to go down?"

"Of course it is."

"Well, what's the checkpoint for?"

"How do I know? Viktor, do you know?"

He didn't.

"Nobody knows. Maybe it has something to do with the nuclear reactor in Sosnovy Bor, but probably not. The soldiers themselves most likely have no idea. That's Russia for you."

As we waited for the soldier to return, through the pines I glimpsed the dark waters of the Gulf of Finland.

It was on this highway thirty-three years ago that my mother and I took a taxi to Shepelevo because the hourly bus hadn't come in three hours. I was two. I looked out the window and watched the water appear and disappear behind the trees, for an hour saying only: "Yes Gulf. No Gulf. Yes Gulf. No Gulf. Yes Gulf. No Gulf." My mother told me that my hypnotic repetition of those three words had a barbiturate effect on our taxi driver, who fell asleep behind the wheel.

"Did we stop?" I asked my mother. "Did we stop to let him sleep?"

"Oh no," she replied. "We kept driving."

I'd heard the story many times. It happened on this road, the road we were not allowed on.

And by the way, it wasn't that they weren't letting *anyone* through. Villagers? Yes. Summer residents? Sure. Fishermen? Of course. Drivers with permission? Absolutely. Just not *us*.

Could it really be that our quest for Shepelevo was going to end in failure? I refused to believe it. What if I never got another opportunity to return to Russia?

The soldier hung up the phone, came back and shook his head for the third and final time.

"They won't let you through," he said. "It is very strict. I can't disobey. But if you want, you can go the back way. You can go around. Go back where you came, to the Tallinn Shosse, and take the road through the woods that will connect you back with this road twelve kilometers farther down. Near Lebyazhye." The soldier was serious and unsmiling. The other soldier, in the meantime, a big strapping guy, was unhappily pushing and pulling the two gates open and closed by himself, earning his soldier's pay. As he passed from one gate to the other, he glared at me. I stared back.

We turned the car around and drove back a few kilometers to what we thought was the Tallinn Shosse. Since none of the roads, even the major highways, were marked, Viktor had to stop for directions before we could be sure. He called out to some teenagers walking along the shoulder and asked if this was the Tallinn Shosse. Like they knew. They shrugged and said, "Think so." Great.

We turned on this possible Tallinn Shosse and soon came to an army truck and a red Mercedes parked in the middle of the road at odd angles. The two drivers were angrily gesticulating to each other. Only when we passed did we see that the Mercedes was caved in along the passenger side.

After driving for a few kilometers, we turned onto an unmarked road that led into the forest of tall birches and reedy pines. It smelled good, of pine cones and wet moss and butterflies.

"No," said Viktor. "This isn't right." I wondered how he could tell.

He asked a handful of people. They all pointed him toward the woods up ahead.

Suddenly, there was no more paved road. We were driving on a dirt road, the likes of which I'd never been on. I'm not saying roads like this don't exist in other places. I'm just saying I haven't seen them. Once when I was fourteen, I was taken for a ride on a motorcycle on an unpaved road in Canada. That road seemed as unpaved as a road could get. However, it was like freshly poured tarmac compared to the lunar craters we now found ourselves navigating. This road had potholes every three yards, potholes about three yards in diameter, all filled with muddy water. The holes alternated — one on one side of the road, one on the other. Viktor had to zigzag around them, like a skier on a giant slalom course.

"This cannot be right, Viktor," I said. "This can't possibly be right. Turn back at once."

He continued to drive.

For five kilometers.

After five kilometers I was sure we were going the wrong way. I could not believe the nice young soldier would have told us to take a road like this. He didn't say, *You'll need a four-wheel drive.* He didn't say, *You might have to push your car through the bushes.* He didn't say the dinosaurs had walked through here and left footprints. He said "a road." All my definitions of the word "road" involved asphalt or cement. We had to be going the wrong way.

"Give me the map," I said.

Yet, there it was, a beige line on Viktor's map — ten kilometers long. On the map legend, the color beige stood for "dirt road."

My father cheerfully called it "forest road."

As we shuddered along, I studied the map. Beige lines crisscrossed all over the place.

Feeling nauseated, I put away the map and stared straight ahead, trying not to vomit.

The unpaved road forked in quite a few places. We bore to the right. At one point, Viktor declared we were going the wrong way, turned around, drove back to the fork and went left instead of right.

How he knew which way to go was a mystery to me.

After seven kilometers, we saw a woman by the side of the road. We stopped for her.

"Why do we have to stop?" I asked a little petulantly.

"She'll take us to the highway," Viktor said. "She'll tell us where to go. She looks like she knows where she's headed." The woman was wearing orange knee-high rubber boots, light blue sweatpants, a dirty white long-sleeved shirt, and over it an old ski vest. Every inch of her body, other than her face, was covered by clothing.

She told us she and her two male comrades, standing dumbly nearby, had been picking mushrooms all night. They were heading to the train station, three kilometers away. We put her mushrooms in the trunk, and she climbed into the back seat with me.

When my father asked if we should give the men a lift, too, Viktor said, "They're men. They can walk three kilometers."

As the woman got in, a swarm of mosquitoes got in with her. I saw that her face had been bloodied by insect bites in a few dozen places. And it was a small face.

"What's your name?" I asked.

"Olya," she said, and smiled, flashing all four of her teeth, yellow with black holes, as if the mosquitoes had drilled through them, too. I spent the next three kilometers killing mosquitoes and trying not to look inside Olya's friendly, smiling toothless mouth.

We let her out near the station. She told us our highway was just half a kilometer up the road. My father shook her hand. When he got back into the car, he turned to me. I lifted my eyebrows.

"She has the teeth of poverty," he said.

I said nothing.

Viktor drove five yards, and stopped to ask a group of people where the highway was. Half a kilometer down the road, they told him.

Finally we were back on A-121, and this time there was no border patrol, no gate — just the highway, the pines, and the Gulf of Finland peeking through them.

No Gulf. And now, yes Gulf.

SHEPELEVO

"Papa," I asked, "what is the lake called in Shepelevo?"

"I don't know," he said. "I don't think it has a name. Even your Dedushka never called it anything but the lake. It doesn't have a name, I'm sure."

I looked at Viktor's map. It was called Lake Gora-Valdaisko. Gora-Valday was the town just east of Shepelevo.

"Papa, the lake is called Gora-Valdaisko. It says so here on the map."

"Oh, that's right," he said, as if it didn't really matter to him.

I thought to myself then that I couldn't wait to tell my grandparents when I got back home. It would matter to them. But when I had returned to New York and told them, they said, oh, that's right, as if it didn't really matter to them either.

We had left Leningrad around eleven in the morning and it was now about three in the afternoon. We hadn't eaten, and I hadn't gone to the bathroom. My father and Viktor had twice availed themselves in the woods.

Finally we passed a sign for Shepelevo.

I said, "Papa, where can we get some lunch? Maybe a little Chinese take-out?"

He spun around and glared at me. "Are you joking?"

I wanted to continue with the tease, but thought better of it. "Yes."

He and Viktor were trying to work out where to park. I stared out the window, trying to spot the dirt road that led down to my village from the highway.

There was nowhere to park, although of course I was half-expecting a little paved lot somewhere — next to a convenience store, perhaps. We parked right off the highway, on the grass, by the side of the cemetery where my great-grandmother was buried.

*

I couldn't wait to get out of the car. The first thing I did was smell the air. I closed my eyes and took a breath, the biggest breath of my life, knowing I was taking the biggest breath of my life. I was taking a breath to smell Shepelevo. Inhaling Shepelevo into my lungs was like hitting the right note on the piano. There was only one right note.

When I was a child, Shepelevo was the smell of nettles, of salted smoked fish, of fresh water from the Gulf of Finland, and of burning firewood, all wrapped up in one word: Shepelevo.

As it had been then, so it was now.

Across two continents, a dozen countries, twenty cities, three colleges, two marriages, three children, three books, and twenty-five years of another life, I breathed in and smelled the air. For me nowhere else in the world had quite the same smell. How well I recalled it, how familiar and just right it was. It was as I had wished it — the first thing so far this trip that was.

"Papa," I said, my voice breaking. "Do you think we could photograph the smell?"

He gave me a funny look and then laughed.

*

I walked along the edge of the highway, stepping carefully on the pine needles and dirt. I picked up a handful of both and smelled them. Papa and Viktor were in front of me, heading toward the gate of the cemetery, but I was in no rush. I was getting light-headed from breathing so deeply.

The cemetery was ancient and fairly small, maybe fifty yards across, completely covered by a canopy of oaks and pines. If you didn't know it was there, you'd miss it. Though it had been bitter bright sunshine on the highway and warm, the cemetery was dark and noticeably cooler.

My grandmother had given me very clear instructions regarding her mother's grave. "Somewhere on the right-hand side, toward the back." We had to find it. We could not fail.

The problem was, the cemetery had been expanded in the twenty-one years since my great-grandmother's death. What once had been the back was now the middle. We could tell it had been expanded because the old crumbling fence ended and a new, slightly less crumbling fence began. But we didn't give up: we walked up and down, looking for the back, or the middle, or the front.

We could not find a gravestone marked with my great-grandmother's name. Every once in a while, my father would exclaim, "I think this is it!" But it never was.

When we had walked through all the gravestones on the right-hand side of the cemetery, we started on the gravestones in the middle.

There were three of us, but we didn't trust one another. We kept retracing each other's paths and re-checking the graves. I know Papa wanted to be the one to find the grave. I wanted to find it, too. I wanted to be the hero.

It was not going to be easy. First of all, the majority of the graves had rusted wrought-iron fences around them. We had to open each gate and walk inside to read the name on the grave and then leave, closing the creaking gate behind us. Second of all, about a quarter of the graves were unmarked. That was discouraging.

And third, as I walked through the ragged rows of graves, I became eight years old again. I stopped looking for a name. I was eight, and my cousin Yulia was by my side. We used to go inside the cemetery to look for candy. Where else could two poor village kids get candy in Communist Russia? Graves, of course. There was no candy for the living, but mourners put candy on the graves of their loved ones, with the wildflowers. Yulia and I would walk through the cemetery, pilfer the candy and eat it. We couldn't bring it back home, because our grandmother would kill us. We ate it then and there, standing in between the tombstones, and dropped the candy wrappers onto the ground.

Now, as I walked, I looked for candy on the graves, to see if the old tradition still stood. It didn't. There were only flowers.

My ankles and calves were itching uncontrollably. That was distracting. I was scratching instead of searching. The large Russian mosquitoes were having a field day on my legs. My father and Viktor were covered by clothing; not me. When I checked the back of my calves, I found big red welts. I wouldn't last another five minutes in the cemetery. The insects were sucking out all my blood.

Blood.

I looked at the fleshy space between my right thumb and forefinger. In the folds of the skin, the scar was still visible. Yulia and I had found a piece of broken window-pane glass in this cemetery. Yulia wanted it; I wanted it. She grabbed one side; I grabbed the other. She pulled; I pulled.

I won.

She let go of the glass. Involuntarily, I might add. I was eighteen months older and considerably stronger. The glass slipped from her hands and sliced into the meaty flesh of mine.

My grandmother was not happy with me. Of course it was all my fault. Because I was older and should've known better. Bloody hand and all, I was punished and had to stay inside for the rest of the day.

After we'd walked along the left side of the cemetery, closest to the road, my father said, "We can't find it. It's impossible."

"But Papa!" I said, scratching my legs.

"I know! What can I tell you? We can't find it. There are so many unmarked graves. And maybe your grandmother made a mistake. Maybe she is buried on the left side, not the right."

"We are on the left side."

We walked back to the right side, glancing at the tombstones as we passed.

"We've checked every grave. We can't find it."

"Papa, we can't tell Babushka that."

He looked around. "I have a terrible feeling that her tombstone, because it was unmarked, was torn down and another erected in its place."

"You mean somebody is buried on top of Babushka Dusia?"

"It's possible. It was unmarked. And they're clearly running out of space."

Hunched over, my hand never leaving my calf, I said, "Papa, it's not possible. What would they do with Babushka's casket? It's only six feet under ground."

"I'm not saying they took it out. But look at the uneven ground right here." He pointed under the trees. "It's all messed up. Maybe that's where it was. You can see how crowded it is."

Viktor and Papa stood and looked at the disturbed earth. I couldn't believe that any cemetery, even a village cemetery, would be doubling up. Especially not a village cemetery. The Russian villagers have nothing but their faith. They wouldn't put a body on top of another body.

These weren't mass graves. All the graves in this cemetery were moderately well kept, with iron fences around them, with little gates and benches where visitors could sit. Many tombstones had crosses and photos of the deceased's loved ones. Fresh flowers were everywhere. Sure, there was no caretaker's building. Yes, the grass and nettles were four feet high. But no one would tear down my great-grandmother's grave to bury their own dead on top of her.

Dejected and hungry, we searched again. My effort was hampered by my bare legs. I was lunch for mosquitoes — big, black, ravenous mosquitoes. As I walked through the graves, I hopped and itched and flailed my arms. Now I knew why Olya, the toothless mushroom picker, had been covered up from head to toe.

My father stepped outside the cemetery for a smoke, and as he smoked, he kept yelling to us, "Forget it. It's no use."

But I could not leave. Finding Babushka Dusia's grave was the only thing my grandmother had asked me to do. I was not going to be the one to tell my eighty-seven year old grandmother that her mother was not found, and her mother's grave not brought to order. The sun fought its way through the leafy pines; it was shadowy and dark in the cemetery and smelled of sap and pine cones. It smelled of earth and flowers and mosquitoes. I wasn't leaving.

My father returned, took one look at me, and said, "Paullina, get out of here. You are being eaten. Go now, or you will ruin the rest of your day. Go into the sunshine."

I went out to the highway. My father came out too, for another cigarette. Was he thinking what to tell his mother? Maybe we could lie? We could say we found the grave, say we gave the Likhobabins money to take care of it. My grandmother would never know.

Yes she would. She had a sense. She knew everything.

Viktor yelled something. My father went back into the cemetery, walked over to Viktor, bent over, and then yelled to me.

"Paullina! Come, come! Viktor found it. He found it!"

He had. Viktor found it because he would not give up. While my dad and I were quibbling and rationalizing our failures, he doggedly looked at every last stone. He found it because he, *literally*, would leave no stone unturned. We had passed the grave that turned out to be my great-grandmother's three or four times. It was poor, neat, and at first glance unmarked. But Viktor had stepped inside the little iron fence and searched the ground. Who knows why? He found a dislodged overturned stone plaque that read, "EUDOKIA IVANOVNA PAVLOVA. 1894–1977."

Papa and I stared dumbly at it.

"Paullina was right," Papa said. "Now I *do* want to cry."

What did finding the grave mean to our driver? Nothing. Yet he would not give up. I didn't feel bad anymore about sharing Shepelevo with him.

We took pictures of the grave, commented on how adequately kept it was despite nearly twenty years of no visitors, wondered if it was Yulia who had been taking care of it. My father brusquely dismissed the idea and went to put Babushka's plaque back.

"What do you want to do now?" he asked. He sighed. "I suppose you want to go find our summer house?" That's what he said, but his body language said, *Please can we be done? Can we leave?*

"Of course I want to see our house," I said. "Don't you?"

"All right," he said in a tired voice. "Let's go."

The village of Shepelevo was at the bottom of the hill, down a dirt path just wide enough to fit a car. Viktor drove down the hill. He didn't want to leave his car on the highway. My father and I walked.

At the base of the hill was a cherry tree. Every summer that tree would blossom with aromatic white flowers, filling our entire *dacha* with its perfume. When it had finished blooming, the flowers would fly off the tree like birds. In my memory, it was a giant tree. Now, looking up at it, I saw that with a six-foot ladder, I would be able to touch the top branches.

A few yards farther on, we stopped at a faded blue house.

"This is it," I said.

"No," Papa said. "This isn't it."

There was a number on the house. It said 32.

"This isn't it," he repeated.

"It is, Papa," I said, filled with heartache. "This is it."

I knew why he didn't want this to be it.

It was abandoned. It didn't look like my memory, or like his, I was sure. I knew his memory was at least as sentimental as mine.

The little yard around the blue house was overgrown with long grass and nettles five feet tall. I couldn't see the gate because weeds covered it outside and inside. Where there once was a hammock, there now wasn't. Where there once was a garden, there now wasn't. It was just a shabby deserted *dacha*, and it looked as if no one had been inside it in years.

How could I explain what I felt, looking at house number 32 in Shepelevo, the house where I spent the happiest months of my childhood?

"This isn't it," Papa said again in a reasonable tone, hiding his sadness. "I know, because look, there is a window on the second floor, and we didn't have a second floor. I know this for a fact."

We stood and stared for a long time at the blue house.

"This isn't the house," he repeated. "Let's go find the Likhobabins. I hope they're still alive. They'll tell us which house it was. You'll see I am right."

Viktor stood beside us, not understanding.

I walked stiffly ahead down the dirt road. My father and Viktor followed.

When I was a child, this road I was on felt wide like a thoroughfare. But now I saw that a car could barely drive through without hitting the wooden fences on either side.

The fences were falling down, barely held up by rusty nails. They were older than I was. Broken fence posts lay strewn in the tall weeds by the side of the road.

In one yard, a tall Russian man in a skimpy bathing suit stood watching his son — also naked to the waist — play on a garbage heap.

We asked him if he knew where the Likhobabins were, or if they were still alive.

"Maria and Vasily?" he said gruffly, as if there wasn't much love lost between him and the Likhobabins. "Right there." He pointed to the unkempt two-story building across a dusty common.

"*Still?*" my father said, as if stunned that after twenty-five years the Likhobabins could be living not just in the same village, but in the same apartment building.

"Still. As ever," said the near-naked man, turning his attention back to his son on the trash heap.

We crossed the road. There were no names on the bells. There were no bells, for that matter. Or mailboxes. There was just a single front door leading to a central stairwell.

"I don't know how we're going to find them," my father said.

I was sure they lived on the first floor, but my father didn't trust my memory. Outside, two old ladies sat on a bench in a clearing under the trees.

"Oh, the Likhobabins," they said when we asked. "They're probably by the gulf." And they waved their arms. *Over there.* So we went over there. My father and Viktor leading the way, while I trailed a hundred paces behind.

I couldn't be certain of this, but this was more difficult for me than for my father. I wanted to linger, and he wanted to speed up. He wanted to rush through Shepelevo, so that he could leave it behind again and forget we were ever here.

And there was so much to forget. We were witnessing our past life through our new American eyes. I was crushed by the relentless poverty of it. Except for the smell — the heady, intoxicating smell of childhood. That was still perfect. As ever. But the sight of Shepelevo tore us up inside.

On the way to the gulf to find the Likhobabins, we stopped at the public bathhouse. It was a tiny brick bungalow, closed up because it wasn't Friday or Saturday. The sign on the door — the same as I remembered from childhood — said, "MEN: FRIDAYS. WOMEN: SATURDAYS." Every other Saturday, my mother, my grandmother, my cousin, my aunt and I would go have a communal bath.

We had a half-hearted laugh about that sign, my father and I, then resumed our trek to the gulf. The smell of smoked fish was very strong. We could also smell fresh water. The factory that made the smoked fish was to the left, and the Gulf of Finland, full of fresh water, was ahead. We could already see the bulrushes and the seagull-stained rocks.

Everywhere I looked I saw peeling paint, rotted wood, broken glass, crumbling concrete, rust.

Anywhere there was metal, there was rust.

There was no litter. There weren't any trash cans, either. Maybe there wasn't much to throw away.

The Likhobabins — Vasily Ilyich and his wife, Maria — were by the gulf. They were surprised to see us, although not exceedingly so.

Their sons, Yuri and Alyosha, were both engineers living in Sosnovy Bor, twenty kilometers down the highway. I'd had the biggest crush on Alyosha when I was young. Maria didn't look happy when her sons were mentioned, particularly Yuri. Vasily whispered to my father, "Yuri is not making his mother happy." He didn't give any specifics.

Maria was short and heavy-set. She wore a peasant print dress, an apron, and a narrow-brimmed hat. Vasily wore glasses that made his eyes as large as two moons. Apart from his vision, he and Maria seemed in good shape. They looked older than my father but younger than my grandparents.

"So, what are you doing?" my father asked Vasily.

"The same, the same," the old man said. "Fishing."

Vasily said he would take us to our *dacha*. As we walked, he regaled my father with stories about his cataracts, his cataract surgery, his recovery, and his general health. I saw my father's pained expression and wanted to laugh. My father is mortified by talk of other people's medical histories. He can barely stand talking about his own health. A few years earlier when he'd had kidney stones, he didn't tell anyone in his immediate family except for my mother that he needed to be hospitalized.

I straggled behind as the four of them strolled in front of me. Endearingly, Maria had her arm through Vasily's.

Likhobabin stopped at the blue house, number 32, and said, "This was yours."

I stared at my father with an I-told-you-so face. He pretended not to look at me. We both stared through the fence at the house, the flaking paint, the high grass. Some of the windows were boarded up with rusty nails.

"Okay," my father said eventually and reluctantly. "Well, do you want to take a picture? Babushka and Dedushka would probably like to see a photo of it."

I turned back to the house and said to my father, "See that big window? That's Yulia's bedroom. I ran to that window in 1971, and watched you come down the cemetery hill with Mama on your arm after you returned from the Gulag. I hadn't seen you for three years."

"That Mama was on my arm," my father said, "I have no doubt. She loved to touch me. But we did not come down that hill. We came down the other hill." He pointed to a hill farther away. "You couldn't possibly have seen us."

"But I did," I said. "And Babushka, your mother, said, 'Here comes my son.'"

My father was quiet. "I know who Babushka is. Well, do you want to see it up close? Or do you want to go?"

We pushed open the gate, nearly breaking the rotted wood. The nettles stung my legs. First the mosquitoes, then the nettles. Just like when I was young.

My father tutted at the disarray.

"Who does it belong to now?" he asked the Likhobabins.

"Papa, what are you talking about?" I said. "You know it belongs to Yulia."

"Well, look at it. It can't. No one's been here in years. Maybe she sold it."

"Babushka and Dedushka gave the *dacha* to her when they left. She wouldn't have sold it without telling them."

My father shrugged. Vasily said he had no opinion.

When my grandparents left Russia in 1979, they left the house to Yulia. She abandoned it; that much was obvious.

My dad picked some cherries off the cherry tree and ate them. He gave me five. That was my lunch. Gratefully I popped them in my mouth. They were exquisitely sour.

When I mentioned this, my dad glared at me, as if I had insulted his cooking.

Our *dacha* was a little square box. Breaking through the brambles and the tree branches, we circled the house. At the front door, I stopped. I pulled on the handle, but it was locked. A wooden clock hung above the doorway. My grandfather had made it. It wasn't a real clock; he painted a fake face on it with black ink. The hands perpetually said 1:20. I showed my father, as absolute proof that the house still belonged to a member of our family. My father nodded, which could've meant, *Yes.* Or it could have meant, *Let's go already.*

He instructed me to take some pictures of Dedushka's ruined garden, in the middle of which stood the wooden cucumber supports he had built back in the seventies. If any village garden deserved high praise, it was my grandfather's; after all, it fed a family of ten every summer for ten years. Supplemented by the fish he caught. The fish *we* caught. And the blueberries and the mushrooms we picked. That's all we ate in the summers. There was no meat. There was no chicken. Oh, there were cows. And there were chickens. But to eat the cows would mean no more milk, and to eat the chickens would mean no more eggs. So no meat and no chicken, but eggs once in a while, and milk.

The others stayed in the front yard. Lagging behind, I stopped at a small, shattered window. A window under which I had slept for nine hundred summer nights.

I found a stick, pried open the window, looked inside. Maria Likhobabina suddenly appeared and stood next to me, peering in.

"What are you doing?" she asked suspiciously.

"I don't know," I said. "Just looking around."

She stood and looked around with me.

"This must be the kitchen," she said.

What was this woman talking about?

"This isn't the kitchen." I tried not to sound rude. How could this be the kitchen? There was a bed in there! *My* bed.

There was a bed. The same bed. Not just the same bed, but the same yellow-brown bedspread, dirty now, casually covering the bare mattress. The wallpaper was as I remembered but ripped, stained, dirty. Through the torn paper, I could see the wall. The bare plaster had holes in it. But they were the same walls. My bedroom walls—

"It *is* the kitchen," Maria repeated. "There's the stove."

Oh my God. It was true. There was the stove. I had slept right across from the stove for ten years, yet never realized it was the kitchen. Until now.

"This was my bed," I said unhappily. Why was I telling her this? Like she cared. All she wanted to know was why I was breaking open a window. I wanted to call out to my father. Papa, look. Did you see this? Can you imagine that I slept here? How can that be, Papa? It's all disintegrating before my eyes. I saw D'Artagnan's Paris from this bed, and Oliver Twist's London. I read those books lying on this bed, looking out this window, dreaming a thousand childhood dreams. I saw the world from this bed. Yet I didn't see the stove, didn't see the rotted window frame, barely holding together. I was barely holding together.

"Papa!" I called. "Where is he?"

"He's out front," said Maria. "They're waiting for you. I think they want to go up to the cemetery, back to your grandmother's grave."

I wanted him to see this. But I had a feeling he didn't really want to.

I stuck my head inside the room and took a deep breath. It did not smell like Shepelevo. It smelled of dust and dirt and old papers. On the wall was a painting my grandfather had made of the cat I used to torture when I was eighteen months old. I wanted to take the picture from the wall and bring it back to America with me, and give it to my grandparents. But the painting was sixteen inches by twenty and I had only the one garment bag. I had no room for Dedushka's cat.

Maria stood like a sullen pillar next to me. I wasn't going to cry in front of her. I grit my teeth and shook my head slightly to clear my eyes. Then I dropped my camera through the window and onto the bed.

"I'm going in," I said.

"Why?" said Maria.

"I want to see."

"See what?"

"The rest of the house."

"It's all like this."

"I want to see. I'll only be a minute. You can leave if you want."

She didn't move. She must have been thinking: *They come all the way from America to burgle our houses.* Maria was too old to crawl in herself, so she stayed at the window and watched me take pictures. When I disappeared into the front bedroom, I kept hearing her voice, calling, "Where are you? Are you coming?"

"In a minute," I said.

I took with me my grandfather's gardening and weather journals, and some small pictures I thought might be of sentimental value to him.

In the front room I found a letter that Yulia had written to her small son. The letter read, *"Our dear bunny rabbit, Mommy wants to say sorry to her little bunny for last night. Daddy and I were tired and tense and we yelled a little bit and scared you, and we're sorry. We both love you so much, little bunny, and Daddy isn't going to leave us ever."*

Daddy never did leave them, but Yulia later left *him*, and left her little bunny rabbit, too.

It was hard to leave your spouse in Russia. There was nowhere to go. You lived in a communal apartment. If you shared a room only with your husband and child, you were lucky. If you were unlucky, you also shared the room with your brother and his family. Or your parents. And your great-grandmother.

If you were fortunate enough to work at a good job that let you put your name on a list for a private, non-communal apartment, you might wait years. But if you had connections or if somebody died, you might get a tiny, non-communal apartment for you, your mother, your husband, and your child. Which is what happened to Yulia. She lived with her sick mother and her husband and child in her sick mother's apartment. But if you wanted out, there was nowhere to go. You couldn't move to another city: you didn't have a job to go to. You couldn't go to a realtor and find a new apartment. There were no realtors. You couldn't even fall in love and go to a hotel room: you could not get a hotel room if you were Russian, only if you were a foreigner with a foreign passport and visa, like me.

So when Yulia got disenchanted with her lot in life and fell in love with another man, and wanted out, there was nowhere for her to go. She left her husband and son, and her sick mother, too, and went to live with her lover and his mother in his communal apartment on the other side of Leningrad.

She returned two years later to find her mother nearly dead of renal failure and her former husband ready to go to Canada with his new wife.

He went to Canada. Yulia's mother died. Yulia stayed by herself in her mother's tiny but non-communal apartment with her son, the bunny rabbit. This all happened in the early 1990s.

Had she not been back to Shepelevo in over five years? By the state of things, it might have been longer. The bunny rabbit was probably twelve years old by now. Maybe her memories were not as sentimental as mine. After all, she still lived this life. She could smell Shepelevo any time she wanted to. Maybe the smell of Shepelevo didn't mean to her what it meant to me.

I would have sat down and cried, but there was nowhere to sit. Clothes, books, papers, garbage covered every flat surface: floors, beds, tables, chairs. All of it was covered with trash and dust.

I glanced out the front window, the same window through which I saw my father in 1971, strolling down the cemetery hill, partially obscured by the cherry tree. Now he was standing on the road, talking to Vasily Likhobabin, eating cherries. I understood — my father had no interest in getting inside this house.

Grabbing Yulia's letter, I made my way to the porch, where we ate our family meals, and peeked into my grandparents' room. It was just storage for old trash, although it still had their bed in it and a dresser. I stuck my head into the washroom, a small room off the kitchen porch that housed a basic toilet. This *dacha* had never had running water. The toilet was a wooden bench with a hole in it. Below the hole was a pit, ten feet deep. When I was little, our envious neighbors considered us lucky because we had the toilet *inside* the house.

I heard Maria's voice from the open window. "Are you coming? Is everything all right?"

I returned to my little bed and the window where she stood waiting. "Everything is fine," I said, climbing out. She held my camera for me.

"What are these?" she asked, eyeing the pictures and the notebooks, in a tone that suggested I was about to take off with the contents of her safe deposit box.

"Just some stuff for my grandfather," I said, as the nettles stung my legs.

My father was waiting for me on the road outside the gate. He hadn't gone to the cemetery yet.

"Well?" he said. "Finished?"

"Yes."

We pulled the gate closed behind us.

"I'm going to show Vasily Ilyich Babushka's grave," my father said. "Are you coming?"

"No," I said. "The mosquitoes. I'm going to go for a walk."

My father must have had his own instructions from my grandmother. He was going to give Likhobabin a hundred dollars to take care of the grave. A hundred American dollars was probably twice what Likhobabin earned in a year.

While they went back to the cemetery, I left Maria and walked alone to the outskirts of the village. I wanted to find the field where I used to go and eat clover.

I got lost and I felt lost. Both literally and figuratively, for I could not find that field.

The scale of things confounded me. Nothing was what I knew it to be. The giant pungent cherry tree was small, but everything else was vast and overgrown. Long grass, sloppy bushes, large branches, concrete blocks, tall nettles, rusted pipes, all spread out on the narrow dirt roads. Back when I was small, the roads were wide and the trees tall, and I saw no rust or broken windows anywhere.

When I turned around, I saw Maria, some distance behind me, but still doggedly following me.

Why? I thought. Why? But really I didn't care.

I walked past a tiny wooden house that was missing one wall. Maybe the wall had been burned in a fire; maybe the wood had rotted out. Whatever had happened, the missing wall had been replaced by cardboard. There were two large sheets of cardboard, nailed to each other and then nailed to the rotting wood of the rest of the house. Where the cardboard had gotten wet from rain, it was mushy and crumbling. There was no fence around the house, but there were tomatoes growing in the side yard, and a chicken-wire cage, with some clucking chickens.

I wondered how good an insulator cardboard was in the brutal Russian winters when the temperatures dipped well below freezing, and stayed freezing until April. The cardboard didn't look like a temporary solution. I doubted that the people who lived here left at the end of summer for a warm communal apartment in Leningrad. Once you had chickens in your yard, you were there to stay.

The Likhobabins didn't have chickens, but they weren't going anywhere either. I glanced back. Maria was still behind me.

I walked past a house that was half-burned from ground to roof. Part of the wall had crumbled into ashes, leaving the black charred frame sticking out. The left side of the house was still standing. There was a small window with floral curtains. The curtains parted and a woman's frowning face stared back at me.

I thought about the iron fences around the graves in the cemetery. They were clean and not rusted. If there was money to put nice fences around dead people, why couldn't the fences around the living be repaired? I wanted to ask Maria, but I doubted she knew. My father would just shrug. "Paullina, this is Russia. You want logic, you go back to America."

But the greatest contradiction was this: as I saw the Shepelevo of adulthood — the Shepelevo I was not prepared for — each breath I took reminded me of the Shepelevo of childhood. Unchanged, unchanging, Communism-defying smell.

The smell reminded me of being eight years old, on my rusted bike trying to outrun a truck — and failing. I walked to the place in the road where I had deliberately wiped out, because it was either wipe out or collide with a Soviet truck.

I smelled going to the library and borrowing the same books week in and week out.

Another thing about the new, adult Shepelevo: how small it was. I walked past the cardboard house, past the black ash house, past the spot in the dirt where the truck ran me off the road; I was looking for the house that belonged to Yulia's mother's side of the family, but there was a field and beyond it trees. Shepelevo was over. Before I could say *huh* and turn around, Maria came up behind me.

"You're looking for something?"

I would have liked to tell her what it was, had I known it myself. "Yes."

"Come," she said. "I'll show you Yulia's grandmother's house."

We walked past a rock. I stopped and stared at this rock.

"What?" she asked.

"Nothing." I remembered that rock. Us kids used to climb it and then fight about whose turn it was to sit on top. The whole summer would pass with us fighting for sitting-on-the-rock rights.

"Here's their house," Maria said.

I looked. It was a proper two-story house. It had curtains hanging in the windows. It had no fence, just the grass and bushes.

"No one lives here anymore," she said. "They're all dead." I wondered why the house was better kept than our blue house. Maria couldn't say.

We walked back to find my father. He was waiting for us on the corner. He looked done. Just like me.

"Ready, Paullina?"

"Wait," said Vasily Ilyich. "Don't you want to come in for a minute?"

"Papa," I whispered. "I really need to use the bathroom."

He sighed.

We walked back to the Likhobabins' apartment.

The apartment was small, but extremely clean. Everything looked pre-twentieth century, but it was all neatly organized. The floor was swept, the table empty of debris. There were no dishes in the sink or smoky ashtrays. No old food. No odd pieces of old wood on the balcony, like at Anatoly's place. And it smelled okay.

In their small living room was a couch, a gramophone, and some shelves with books. I stared at the couch.

"I remember the couch," I said.

"Yes," Maria said, "it's the same couch."

"It's nice."

I asked if the gramophone worked.

"We think so," said Vasily Ilyich. "We got it as a gift many years ago. We don't have any records to play on it."

Maria showed me to the bathroom. There was no bathtub, only a toilet and a sink and barely enough room to turn around in.

Although the apartment smelled okay, the toilet did not. I tried to breathe through my mouth. It didn't help. I held my breath. No use. I tried not to touch anything. I started to retch. I saw they had an overhead flush. I used it. It worked. But why the stench? The toilet smelled like it hadn't been cleaned in ...

I left the bathroom, shutting the door quickly behind me, and smiled my best smile at Maria.

"Well, thank you *so* much," I said. "Ready, Papa?"

I was glad when we left.

*

"We will walk down to the gulf now, all right, Paullina?"

"Of course," I said. "I want to see our beach."

"Oh, yes," he said. "I forgot. We'll go there. Viktor, how are you holding up?"

"Fine." He shrugged. "*I'm* fine." He was a good sport.

On the way, we passed a garbage dump that wasn't there twenty-five years earlier. Actually, we didn't pass it: it was blocking our path. We stared at it with dumb disbelief.

We couldn't smell the pines for the rancid stink of garbage. It made my father feel so bad he didn't want to go any farther.

"Papa," I said consolingly. "Where else are the villagers going to throw out their garbage?"

"Where did *we*?" he said. "Forget it. Forget the Gulf."

"Papa, we have to go to our beach. Let's find another way to get there."

He turned and found another way, walking on without a word.

As we walked past the unpainted village houses, I studied their fences. Where the wood had fallen apart or rotted away, instead of whole fence stakes being replaced, patches of new wood were nailed to the old palings, giving the fences and everything within them the appearance of poverty.

I mentioned this to my father.

"No," he said. "It's *actual* poverty."

*

When I was a little girl, my grandfather — my Dedushka — would take me fishing on the Gulf of Finland. I would row the boat out to sea, and we would hook our worms and maybe catch some perch.

After a few hours, around midnight, I would row us back to shore. Dedushka would pull our rowboat onto the sand. He wore knee-high rubber boots. We would walk through the woods to our blue house, number 32. My grandmother would be waiting up for us, yelling at my grandfather for bringing me back so late, although the sun was still up. He and I would be laughing and we'd be hungry. My grandmother would make us delicious fried potatoes with onions. And outside it was light.

In 1973, a few weeks before we left Russia, I went to visit my grandparents. I had just found out that we were not moving to Moscow, as I had been told initially, but to America. My grandfather touched my face and said, "Ah, Plinochka, we are never again going fishing in Shepelevo, you and I."

I was excited about America, but a little sad for him. Trying to find a comforting thing to say, I blurted happily, "Yes, but you still have Yulia. You can always go with Yulia."

He nodded. "Yes. But it won't be the same."

We never did go fishing again.

*

As we neared the beach, we came to a small clearing carpeted in pine needles. My father stopped and said that this was where he and his friends used to meet to drink and smoke and talk. Papa had his memories, too.

The mosquitoes started feasting on me again.

We walked out onto the Gulf of Finland where my grandmother used to take Yulia and me to swim, three times a week, every week for three months for ten summers.

Memory was one thing; what I saw was something else. The beach sand was sparse and mostly covered by long water grasses and bulrushes.

The water in the gulf looked muddy and dark. The brook where Yulia and I tried to catch fish, where we waded up to our knees in muck and weeds, was maybe three feet wide and only a foot or so deep. I remembered it as a rapidly burbling stream.

Was it better to see that it was calm and narrow? Was it better to see that it was shallow, that the rocks were small? I don't know. I preferred my unsoiled, pristine memories.

"What a nice sea," Viktor said. "How lucky you were to have this."

Ten seconds later, my father said, "I'm going back," and disappeared into the woods with Viktor close behind him. Five seconds later, I heard him calling me: "Paullina, Paullina."

I didn't want to go yet. I stared at the water. A young mother and her daughter stood in the sea about a quarter mile out. The water came up to the woman's knees. It had always been shallow. The girl was diving and splashing about. The echo of her laughter blew like a breeze over the water.

And through it, I heard, "Paullina ... Paullina ..."

Then, more insistently: "PAULLINA."

I stared at the peaceful water, the cattails, the lily pads. "Paullina ... *Paullina!*"

"I'm coming!" I yelled.

I caught up to my father.

"Why are you lagging behind?" he said. "We have to go."

We walked up the hill to the highway, crossed the road and followed a narrow path next to the railway tracks to Lake Gora-Valdaisko. By the side of the lake, my father took off his nylon jacket, his long-sleeve shirt, his undershirt, his shoes, his socks, his trousers and dove into the water.

I perched on top of an overturned rowboat, and Viktor gave me a pickle from his pickle jar. I gratefully accepted. Papa swam. Viktor kept talking about something. I couldn't listen.

The lake was peaceful.

As my father was drying himself off, he said, "Oh, to swim, Paullina! You really should have brought a bathing suit."

I shivered. It was about 55°F.

"I used to row right across this lake when we lived here," I told Viktor. "We rowed across to the other side to pick blueberries."

Viktor looked across the lake. "That's a long way."

Yes, it seemed far, even then. It was about a mile across. It was far. In memory and in real life.

We left.

We walked back to Viktor's car, climbed in, drove away.

I turned back to glance at Shepelevo. I saw the white smokestacks of the fishing factory rising above the trees. Rolling down my window, I inhaled the air one last time.

"Roll up the window, Paullina," Viktor said. "They're promising rain."

I rolled up the window.

A few miles down the highway, we saw a woman by the side of the road selling blueberries. She didn't have a sign or a stand. She was just sitting by the road with a ceramic jug. Had we been going faster, we would have missed her.

Viktor said, "Want some blueberries?"

"No," I said.

"No," my father said.

But then I remembered the five cherries I'd had for lunch, and the pickle by the lake. I remembered rowing my whole family across the lake to go blueberry picking.

"Yes."

Viktor stopped the car and we approached the old woman. My father didn't come.

"How much for the blueberries?" I asked.

"Thirty rubles." About five dollars.

"With the jug?" I asked.

"No, the jug is mine."

I exchanged a glance with Viktor. "So how am I supposed to take the blueberries home?" Where were the cute little baskets, the ones you saw at every farm stand in America? "I'll give you thirty more rubles for the jug," I said.

The old lady shook her head. She wore a kerchief over her gray hair. "I can't."

"Fifty more," I said.

Sadly she shook her head. "Don't you have a plastic bag in the car?"

"Blueberries in a plastic bag? They'll get mushed. We'll have blueberry jam by the time we get to Leningrad."

"I think they'll be all right," Viktor said quietly.

I turned to the old lady. "A hundred rubles for the jug."

She looked at her jug, looked at me and said, "Darling, don't you think I want to sell you the jug? I do, I'd sell it to you. But where am I going to get another one? I won't be able to pick any more blueberries. I'm sorry."

"Oh," I said. "I understand. *I'm* sorry."

We found a plastic bag in the car and bought the blueberries. I put a few into a plastic cup and the rest in the plastic bag, which we stored in the trunk.

"Well," said my father once we were back on the road. "How are they?"

I tasted them. "They're okay," I said. "They're a little under-ripe."

"They're not under-ripe," he said. "That's what they taste like."

"But they're sour," I said. I remembered the Shepelevo blueberries as juicy and sweet. "They don't taste like American blueberries."

Viktor and my father laughed. "You're a fool," my father said. "American blueberries are grown on a farm, not in the woods. Or they're grown in Chile."

We drove back to Lebyazhye, where we had turned into the main road and had dropped off the mosquito-eaten, mushroom-picking Olya, and then quaked through the potholes for ten kilometers.

Viktor said we were lucky it hadn't rained, because then these holes would be filled to the brim with water, and passage would be *really* impossible.

I looked at the potholes, which at the moment, it was true, were only *half* full of sloshing liquid mud. I closed my eyes to rid myself of the holes. I wanted to see what image would rise up.

My childhood bed rose up. The bed near the wall with the ripped wallpaper. The little bed with a pillow and a blanket. Me lying in bed and looking out the window and seeing the sunrise. The window was open. I smelled Shepelevo.

WASHING THE CAR WITH THE GULF OF FINLAND

I sat up with a jolt. Viktor had suddenly stopped the car. We looked to be on the outskirts of Leningrad. My father was vigorously sleeping. While he slept, Viktor got out a white bucket and a brush he must have carried for such emergencies. Maybe he didn't want his wife to know where he had been.

I rolled down the window. "Viktor, what are you doing?"

"I'm going to clean the car a little," he replied. "It will only take fifteen minutes."

I rolled the window back up and watched him jump over a short stone wall and walk down the rocks to the gulf. Beyond him I saw the Kronstadt naval base in the distance, in the open sea. I tried to imagine the sound of artillery as the Soviets barricaded in Kronstadt bombed their own coast for three years to prevent the Germans from taking the island. I was sitting right in the line of fire.

When Viktor returned with his bucket filled with gulf water, I rolled my window down again.

"Viktor, but didn't you tell me it was going to rain?"

"Yeah," he drew out. "What do they know? Often it doesn't rain."

I rolled the window back up.

To pass the time I wrote in my journal and stared out onto the road. Once in a while a bus would pass. No bus looked less than half a century old. The buses came in three colors: burnt yellow, dreary olive and faded maroon. The wheels had no hubcaps and rattled, not having been aligned in decades. The buses lurched. Where the paint had peeled off, they were rusty. The windows were small and rectangular: seven on one side, six on the other.

Viktor continued to fastidiously wash the windows of his vehicle. After he got behind the wheel, he said, "I couldn't drive a car in the city that looked like *that*."

I became certain he didn't want his wife to know what he had been up to.

My father woke up. It was 6:40 in the evening.

We passed an *elektrichka*. Rather it passed us. It was army green and looked brand new as it sped by.

"Papa, so how come that train is new and green?"

"What do you mean how come it's green? The Russians built a new train."

"Huh. No new buses, though."

"They can't do everything at once, Paullina," he said.

We passed some graffiti in English that read, "Punk's not dead." It was scrawled on a deep yellow stucco building, next to a sign that read "Magazin." *Magazin* meant store. What *kind* of store, the sign did not specify. Just *store*. The building looked abandoned, yet the *magazin* was open.

We stopped by an ornate Russian Orthodox Church. As I got out to take a picture, the skies began to stream down. It got dark. I quickly dived back inside the car.

Pulling away from the curb, Viktor said, "See how lucky we were that the rain held off just long enough for us to get off that dirt road."

"Yes," I said. "But not lucky enough for it to rain before you washed your car."

"When did you wash your car?" my father asked.

"When you were sleeping, Yuri Lvovich," replied Viktor.

We drove a little farther, then stopped at a tall obelisk. A sign announced: "This is the farthest point of the front in defense of Leningrad during World War II, 1941–45." I got out and walked through the rain to the stone pillar and took a picture. The Gulf of Finland was across the highway. If the rain hadn't been falling like a curtain over the gulf, I was sure I'd be able to see Kronstadt.

We continued on, down a bleak, treeless boulevard.

"This is the Prospekt of Veterans," said my father.

"Uh-huh."

"Don't you remember? Yulia used to live here with her mother."

"Shall we go and visit her?"

My father said nothing. I wanted to talk to him about Yulia and his obvious reluctance to meet up with her, but I was too exhausted.

With tired fascination I stared at the famous Kirov Wall, which surrounded the Kirov Works Factory on the southern outskirts of Leningrad. Despite war, despite siege, despite hunger, despite all the odds, for four years the Kirov Works produced tanks for the war effort. Production slowed down when the factory was bombed nearly to the ground by the Germans, whose bombers were stationed a kilometer or two away from it at Pulkovo Heights, but it never stopped. The Soviets built a new factory under the camouflage of the ravaged old one, and churned out 200 KV-60 tanks a month.

Originally, the Kirov Works were called Putilov Works. But in 1934 Sergei Kirov, Stalin's right-hand man, was assassinated. Many say this was done on Stalin's direct orders. Although this has never been admitted or confirmed, it was an open secret among the intelligentsia of Russia and proof in the pudding was the Soviets renaming half the city in his honor, to cover up the tracks of the head of state of a civilized country murdering his most trusted lieutenant. After the cover-up everything became Kirov this, Kirov that.

As we drove, my father told the story of how the Soviets took a big, beautiful gilded iron fence from the Winter Palace and transported it to the Kirov Works. They wanted to set it into the ground so that the workers could marvel at it and be inspired by it, but it was much too heavy. So they ditched the project, and the poor fence was abandoned.

"Why didn't they take it back to the Winter Palace?" I asked.

"Too heavy to move."

"But they moved it once."

"That's how they found out it was too heavy to move."

"So where is it now?"

"Lying on its side somewhere, rusting."

It was still raining when Viktor dropped us off at Grand Hotel Europe. My father told Viktor to go home, although Viktor didn't want to leave us. I think he wanted to make sure Papa got back to Ulitsa Dybenko safely. We made plans to meet at ten the next morning.

Papa came upstairs with me to my room. "Nice room," he said, walking around. "Is there a bathroom?"

I showed him the bathroom. "This is not a bathroom," he said. "This is Ellie's whole apartment."

While he was in the bathroom, I checked my hotel voicemail messages. There was one from my three-year-old son. "Mommy … Mommy … just calling to see how you were …"

I sat on the bed, head bowed, and looked at my hands. Did I have time to call home? What time was it there? I tried to figure out the time difference, but an image kept intruding: Yulia and me, walking on tiptoes on the railroad ties in Shepelevo, carefully avoiding the pebbles between ties because if we stepped on them, we would lose. Lose what? Lose, that was all.

My father, meanwhile, was appraising my shoe collection, which was arranged in pairs on the carpet. "Paullina! You said you had no room in your suitcase for T-shirts for my friends, but look at all the shoes you brought!"

I looked. "What? It's not that many," I said. "One pair of shoes for each day I'm here."

He shook his head disbelievingly. Damn. Now my dumb shoes would end up as a story around the dinner table with my father's buddies.

For dinner we went to the dimly lit Caviar Bar. I didn't want my father to worry about money, so I told him dinner was on me, a sort of belated birthday present.

Approvingly, he took out his pack of Marlboros.

"Papa, what are you doing?"

"What?" he exclaimed. "There is no smoking here?"

"Papa," I said to him in condescending dulcet tones. "It's a *restaurant*."

When the waitress came, he asked if he could smoke. She looked at him as if he had just asked if he could *eat*.

"But of course," she said in condescending dulcet tones.

All I wanted for dinner was black caviar and *pelmeni*. My father ordered salmon roulettes and sturgeon with onions and mushrooms.

"We'll share, all right?" he said. "You get the caviar and *pelmeni*, and I'll have the salmon roulettes and the sturgeon, and we'll split it."

I agreed.

His roulettes, with smoked salmon, dill sauce, shrimp and red caviar, were to die for. He allowed me one tiny bite. He didn't even taste my poor man's caviar.

As we ate, my father talked and I listened. I'd had plenty of practice. Both my parents are similar in this way; only the subject matter is different. They talk and I listen. I know, I know — you wouldn't think it from meeting me, because I seem like a talker — but it's only because I was trained by the best. Around my family, my whole life, I sat and listened.

Tonight, I was glad to let my father do the talking. I was tired. We did not talk about Shepelevo. Like not a word.

In between a double vodka and a beer chaser, my father told me stories about World War II. He tells very good stories.

He talked about Stalin's unheeded warnings — all one hundred and ninety-four of them — to his Communist colleagues about Hitler's planned invasion of Russia.

He talked about Hitler's impassioned speech in response to Roosevelt's diplomatic one, which my father said made him realize that Roosevelt was a politician but Hitler a madman. A madman who sent ten million German boys to their deaths on a point of principle.

"What was the principle, Papa?"

"The principle?" he asked, as if surprised by the question. "Why, that German supremacy was all, of course. That Aryan supremacy would be achieved at all cost."

Then he started talking about the final solution, how it undermined Hitler's war effort and in the end cost him the war, because so many of his resources were fed into the extermination machine.

"Instead of transporting arms and weapons and soldiers to the Eastern front, he transported Jews to Poland. It cost him the war."

"I'm surprised," I said, "that he didn't build more concentration camps in Germany."

"He built them," my father said, "where there was least resistance." He paused. "And the largest number of Jews."

He spoke at length about the madness of World War I, fought over a misunderstanding over nothing, a war that was continued twenty-one years later to the cost of half of the world's young men.

As soon as I brought up the U.S. Civil War and the casualties America had suffered in it, he lit a cigarette and changed the subject: to his impending retirement to Hawaii.

"Does it scare you, Papa, retiring?" I asked. "You've worked for so many years."

"In America, Munich, and Prague, altogether twenty-five. I will have worked two months short of twenty-five years for Radio Liberty. My whole American life. Does it scare me? Well, what do you think? But —" and here he shook his head, and lit another cigarette after a long pause. "There is no other way. I have to go. Your mother won't have it any other way."

"She says you should work, make more money," I said teasingly. Actually, my mother really did say that. She said, "I tell him to keep working, but all he wants to do is to leave that place. His sanity is at stake, Paullina."

"Your mother's sanity is at stake, Paullina," my father said. "She needs me. So I'm going."

After his retirement in early August we were all meeting up in New York for a couple of weeks before my parents flew out to Hawaii. I tried to convince him to drive cross-country to California instead of flying, so he could stop over in Texas and visit me, see my incredible new house.

He declined — not for the first time. His health wasn't good, he said. There were a million other reasons why he wanted to go straight to Maui and get himself in order. Then, with renewed vigor, once he was well settled into his retirement, he and my mother would consider traveling around the mainland.

"There is so much of our beautiful country we have never seen. I can't wait. All those western states. Your mother of course wants Las Vegas." He rolled his eyes. "I'll get fly-fishing in Montana, she'll get Las Vegas. Everybody wins."

Remembering what my mother had told me the day before I left for Russia about Maui's red dust, I tried to prepare him.

"Maybe Hawaii is not the paradise everyone thinks it is," I said cryptically. "Maybe there are problems you haven't seen yet."

"What kind of problems?" he asked incredulously, suspiciously.

"You'll be all alone with Mama. That's one. When was the last time you did that?"

"In Prague."

"And how did that turn out? Exactly. On Maui there's also wind. Have you considered that it might be windy?"

He waved his cigarette in my face. "I'm going to make Maui my permanent home. Your mama and I are going to have a wonderful time. We don't need anybody else."

"What about fishing?"

"There is plenty of fish in the ocean, Paullina."

"What about your garden?" Gardening and fishing were what my father loved best. Just like his father.

"I won't garden. I don't know if you've noticed, but I'm not a young man anymore."

"Yes," I said. "Your own father, who *does* garden, is not a young man either. He just turned ninety-one."

"Yes, well. Maybe when I turn ninety-one, I'll garden too."

He then proceeded to tell me, aside from ocean fishing and *not* gardening, what he *was* going to do every day on Maui. I found this to be the most amusing part of our evening discussion. Him laying out on the table a strict regimen for his and Mama's daily life. He would get up at seven and before coffee or a cigarette he would walk down to the ocean and go for a swim. He would come back, have his coffee and cigarette and make himself and Mama a beautiful breakfast. Then he would head to the market to buy fresh fruit for lunch and something for dinner. In the afternoon, he and Mama would browse the shops and swim. He would have a short nap at four, before dinner and his sunset stroll to the ocean. In the evening they would watch baseball and movies.

But Papa, I wanted to tell him, nowhere in this daily schedule do you mention wiping red dust off the furniture.

He must have smoked fifteen cigarettes as he spoke of his plans.

For dessert I drank too-sweet tea and ate passable tiramisu. For dessert my father had another cigarette.

*

One Saturday when I am eight and my dad is home on weekend leave from his post-Gulag exile in Tolmachevo, he and I go out, just the two of us. It takes us a long time to get where we are going. He takes me by bus and by tram to the remotest part of Leningrad, to the borough of Kirov, past the Kirov Wall, not far from the soccer stadium where his favorite team, Zenith, plays.

In the borough of Kirov there is a movie theater, and every once in a while, on Saturdays, this movie theater shows American movies. What a treat! That particular Saturday they are showing The Wizard of Oz.

We get to the theater at noon.

The movie isn't starting until four.

There was no way to check the movie times. Russian newspapers do not carry that kind of information; certainly there is no one to call.

My father says, "I'm sorry. Let's go home."

"Papa, please!"

"Plinka," he says. "What are we going to do here for four hours?"

I shrug my shoulders. Like that is my problem.

He looks around. "There is nothing for us to do." There really isn't. The theater is in the middle of a concrete industrial park. There are no gardens, no trees, no playgrounds, no bars, no stores — naturally.

The sun is shining.

"Plinka!"

"Papa."

We stay.

We stay for four hours.

Finally we are inside, and the movie starts. Imagine my rank disappointment when it is in black and white. I am crushed. If we wanted to see a black and white movie, we could have stayed home and watched another war movie on television, or gone to the theater on Sixth Soviet. I fold my arms.

Then Dorothy lands in Oz.

She opens the door of her fallen house, and through the narrow opening I see joyous, vibrant color. Oh the elation.

When I glance at my dad, he is smiling. As if he had known all along.

*

"Paullina, do you want to go for a walk?" It had stopped raining, but it was cool. I did not have a coat.

"Sure, Papa." It was 11:20 at night. We had just emerged from the restaurant.

Wearing his navy nylon jacket, he glanced at my short-sleeved shirt.

"Are you going to be cold?"

"Absolutely not," I said, hoping the light was too dim for him to see the goosebumps on my arms.

We strolled in the wet dusk down Nevsky Prospekt toward the Neva.

I was not terribly impressed by Nevsky Prospekt. Oh, I know that the famous Russian writer Nikolai Gogol wrote in 1836 that there was "nothing finer than Nevsky Prospekt," but I wondered if he had ever been abroad. "At least not in St. Petersburg," Gogol had added. Even then I had to disagree, having seen the Neva embankment with its glorious bridges in the fiery midnight twilight. When Gogol finally got down to the details of what precisely was so "resplendent" about Nevsky Prospekt, he mentioned "how spotlessly clean its pavements were swept."

I'll give him that. It *was* swept pretty clean.

But otherwise there was something utilitarian about it: wide and treeless, it lacked the atmosphere of Paris, Amsterdam or London. The French built boulevards like nobody else in the world. Amsterdam (like Leningrad, a city built out of the swamp) was lousy with trees and canals. (Leningrad has as many canals as Amsterdam. The difference is in the greenery.) London's stucco houses gleam wet white — when you can glimpse them through the thousand-year-old oaks. Why had London come through the Blitz with its ancient trees still standing, while Leningrad had hardly any remaining? Had people burned the oaks for fuel? Fifth Avenue held the promise of Central Park. Even Rodeo Drive had palm trees. What did Nevsky Prospekt have to offer?

Well, for one, it offered me a walk with my father on a summer night.

A young woman, long-haired and distraught, approached my father, sticking a rose in his face and asking him if he would like to buy it for his young woman. My father stopped walking and said, "This is not my young woman. This is my daughter." If he thought that would put her off, he was wrong. The girl stared at me, then at my father, as if she couldn't comprehend what he had just said. Maybe she was trying to find a family resemblance. Maybe she thought he was lying. Slowly she offered the rose to him again. I kept walking, as behind me I heard my father repeat, "This is my daughter. One does not buy roses for his daughter." The girl persisted. When I glanced back, I could tell that my dad, at a loss for words, was about to lose his temper. Our lovely long-awaited walk down Nevsky Prospekt was being ruined by a dimwitted flower girl. I ran back, stuck myself brusquely between him and the girl, and said, "No! But thank you." Taking hold of my father's arm, I dragged him away. She trailed behind us for half a block with a rose in her hand until we crossed Moika Canal and lost her.

Nevsky Prospekt buckled at the Neva and Palace Bridge. To the left of the bridge stood the slender-spired Admiralty building. To the right of the bridge, on the embankment, sat the Winter Palace, with its famous green stucco and Russian Baroque façade. Just behind the Winter Palace was the enormous and sprawling Palace Square — the Palace's backyard, so to speak.

"Paullina, you've seen Palace Square, right? You remember it? Let's go. This is one of the best spots in the city," my father said. That may have been, but I was exhausted.

We turned right on a short, narrow street called Bolshaya Morskaya. We were the only ones walking. Ahead of us I saw the Arc of the General Staff Building, and through it Alexander's Column in the middle of Palace Square. Beyond it glowed the Winter Palace.

"Well, what do you think? What do you think?"

I thought it was dark. The sky was cloudy. There was no sun. I could barely place one foot in front of the other.

"It's incredible," I said.

Crossing the Palace Square as if we were in *Doctor Zhivago*, as if Warren Beatty were about to storm the Winter Palace to help the Bolsheviks take power in *Reds*, we came out onto the Neva embankment.

"Look at this river," said my father, his voice full of yearning. He lit a cigarette.

What was he yearning for? I didn't want to ask him and ruin his moment. He was feeling things; I just wished I knew what they were.

After we passed the palace, my father stopped on a bridge over a small canal emptying into the Neva. "This is the Winter Canal Bridge. The canal separates the old Palace from the new Palace. Here, Pushkin's Liza fell to her death, in his story *The Queen of Spades.* Do you remember that story?"

"Of course," I said. "You named both your daughters for that story."

He laughed. "That's right. Liza and Paullina."

We stood and stared at the rippling water. "Well, let's walk along the Moika," my father said. "Then we better head back. It's late, and it's a long way."

"If you say so." How many more times in my life would I have a walk like this with my dad?

"Look at the Neva, Paullina," my father repeated. "Isn't it so beautiful?"

The night bleached out what the eyes did not want to see. The night was God's denial. So there was nothing to stop me from saying, "Yes." And meaning it with all my heart.

It was after midnight and there was no one on the streets. On Moika Canal we passed Aleksandr Pushkin's house. Pushkin is the greatest of all Russian poets; his poetry is the embodiment of the soul of the Russian people. Pushkin wrote the poem *The Bronze Horseman*, having been inspired by the monument to Peter the Great that Catherine the Great commissioned in 1792.

I stopped and touched the door to Pushkin's house. "Papa, I really want to come back here another day."

"Yes, because we have infinite time," my father said, without stopping.

After Pushkin's house, we crossed Griboyedov Canal and came to stand in front of the place Tsar Alexander II was slain by revolutionaries in 1881. In his memory, a glorious cathedral was built called *Spas Na Krovi* — Church of the Savior on Spilt Blood.

The church was closed.

"I really would like to come back *here* another day."

"Paullina, you cannot do everything."

"I don't want to do *everything*," I said. "I just want to come back *here*."

The sky was darker than it had been yesterday and the clouds obscured the setting sun. But at midnight it still looked like dusk in New York on a summer evening.

We were walking more and more slowly. By the time we got to my hotel, we were barely inching forward.

I attempted to get my father a taxi in front of Grand Hotel Europe, but the bell captain talked me out of it, saying it would cost a prohibitive amount, so much that he didn't want to tell me how much.

"I don't want to frighten you," he said.

"Frighten me."

Shaking his head, he told us to go to the corner of Mikhailovskaya and Nevsky and hail a cab from there.

"Be sure to negotiate before getting in," he added.

We did as he said. My father walked up to an idling taxi.

"How much to Ulitsa Dybenko?"

The driver appraised my father. "A hundred rubles."

"Done."

"Nice negotiating," I said.

Before he got in, he asked me to call Anatoly and Ellie and tell them he would be arriving in twenty minutes. He told me to ask one of them to go downstairs and wait for him, because he did not want to wrestle with the front door in the dark.

"Sure, I'll call them," I said. I forgot as soon as I got back to my room.

I remembered after I ran my bath. When I called, Ellie answered. "He's already here."

My father was going to be pleased with me.

Before I got into the bath, I called my grandparents in New York. Babushka picked up the phone.

"Babushka," I said, "you can't talk, you can't say a word, because it's costing me five dollars a minute to call you, but I just wanted to tell you, we found Babushka Dusia's grave."

My grandmother started to cry.

"You think it's Yulia? You think Yulia is taking care of it?" she asked with hope.

I thought of our decrepit blue *dacha*.

"Not sure, Babushka. But the Likhobabins will take care of it now."

I fell asleep in the bath. At one point I closed my eyes, and when I opened them again I was still in the water. I had made it too hot to soothe my aching joints. When I crawled out, something was hurting, breaking me up inside.

I slept with the windows open, the light from the dawning sky streaming in.

Lake Gora-Valdaisko. I rowed across it every summer in that boat. My dad is in the water.

The room on Fifth Soviet where I grew up. I shared this room with my parents, my aunt and uncle and my cousin Yulia.

DAY THREE
Wednesday

MARBLE PALACE

I hadn't talked to my children since I left New York. I missed them. It was hard to believe it had only been three days and not three years.

The time difference meant that when I woke up at eight in the morning, it was eleven in the evening in Dallas, and the kids were sleeping. When I came home at one in the morning, it was four in the afternoon Dallas time, and the kids were napping.

When I told my grandmother that it was costing me five dollars a minute, I didn't really know. I just picked a number out of my head and said it for emphasis. In the morning I checked the rate card by the phone.

It had cost me EIGHT UNITS A MINUTE to call her.

Once I got over the initial shock, I didn't mind the phone call to *her*; it was worth it. But when I called Kevin, I told him that from now on he had to call me, because otherwise the phone calls were going to put us out of our new house before our first mortgage payment was due.

It took me an hour to get ready. I was achy and slow.

For breakfast, I had my usual buffet of blini with red caviar.

Before I met up with my dad, I went to a room off the glass mezzanine, labeled *Business Services*, and inquired about a computer.

The helpful blonde behind the desk told me it would cost me FIFTEEN UNITS per hour. "Would you like to book the computer now?" she asked. They only had the one.

I looked around. There was no one in the room.

"Is there a need, um, to book?" I inquired.

"Oh, yes, we get quite busy. Especially if you want two hours. We can book now if you want."

I booked for the following day at eight o'clock in the morning. When else could I sit down and write? But I felt I needed to. The few scribbled pages at the end of the night just weren't enough. Too many things were filling up my day and my head. I didn't want to forget any of it.

My father must have struggled with getting up himself, because he was quite late, picking me up at quarter past eleven. I waited a long time for him on the street.

He met me with our driver Viktor and another man, whose name was of course also Viktor. He was Viktor Ryazenkov, a dark, bearded, neatly dressed colleague of my father's from Radio Liberty's bureau in Leningrad.

When my father introduced us, he said, "Paullina, this is the infamous Viktor who forgot to tell me about the guard post on highway A-121."

Viktor R. looked sheepish. Then he kissed my hand.

I smiled. "Viktor, do you think it could have anything to do with that nuclear reactor spill in Sosnovy Bor in 1992?"

Raising his voice, my father exclaimed, "This is six years later! Why are they letting people go the back way if they're trying to keep outsiders from Sosnovy Bor?"

"You tell *me*, Papa," I said. "I'm just asking the questions here."

We had planned to head down to Piskarev Cemetery and the Siege of Leningrad Museum. But my father told me the first thing we had to do was go to the Marble Palace with the two Viktors to get press accreditation for the Romanov funeral on Friday.

"It won't take but a minute," my father said.

*

The words *Marble Palace* meant nothing to me until I walked inside and saw the wide gray marble stairs leading up to a hall on the third floor. When I saw the stairs an instant feeling rose up in my heart, an unpleasant, hazy recollection. Something had happened on these stairs.

That's impossible, I thought. I've never been here before. But the emotion remained: a vague discomfort, a disturbance. I poked it a little, turned it around, and saw that it resembled fear.

Fear? Looking at the stairs was making me afraid. I couldn't move.

I heard my father's voice. "Paullina, let's go, why are you always dawdling?"

Dimly an old memory relit: my young teacher had fainted here. I saw her fall down, saw her crumpled body on the marble stairs. I was so small, I didn't understand what fainting was. I had never seen anyone faint before. I thought she was dead.

In twenty-five years I had never thought about the Marble Palace. I'd forgotten I had ever been here.

I looked at the steps again. I saw the cracked marble under my old brown shoes as I climbed the stairs in my brown uniform and white apron. Every year on January 21, my school would go to the Marble Palace to commemorate the anniversary of Lenin's death.

We would climb the stairs and stand in the great big marble hall, listening to songs and speeches about Lenin.

The Neoclassical palace was completed in 1785, renamed the Lenin Museum during Communist rule, and after 1991 changed back to its original moniker. The Marble Palace now contained a permanent exhibition about the Romanovs. When I came with my dad, the palace was in the process of being restored. Either that or it was in chaotic disarray. Restoration and disarray look remarkably the same in Russia. The same peeling paint, the same chipped stucco, the same dirt and dust and rotted window frames. And outside in the courtyards, the same haphazard clutter.

On the third floor I caught up with my father in a vast rectangular room with forty-foot ceilings, thirty-foot windows, marble floors and marble columns. The Marble Room. It was grand yet shabby. In one corner, a crowd of people milled around a table and a bulletin board. In another corner, another confused cluster of people stood dumbly. No one was directing traffic, so at random, we joined the group on the right. After standing for five minutes, we moved to the group on the left. Five minutes later, we asked the person ahead of us what we were waiting for. He shrugged.

We asked another man. He didn't know either. We were all here to get an accreditation for the Romanov funeral, but no one knew the procedure.

Viktor R. went off and came back five minutes later with some information.

"We have to stand in the line to the right until we reach the table. We give them our name and then we go to the line on the left to take our photo."

"And then?" Papa asked.

"Then we go to the third line in the middle to get our accreditation pin." This mystical third line had not been formed yet.

We waited for ten minutes. The girl behind the table, giddy with knowledge and self-satisfaction, told us we had been standing in the wrong line. "Before we take your photo, you need to give your name to the girl over there," she said pointing to the girl sitting directly next to her.

"Can we just give her our name now?" I said. "She is sitting right here."

"No!" the first girl said. "You have to stand in her line. You give her your name, and she will look it up in her logbook to verify that you have filled out an accreditation application."

My father turned to Viktor R. "Have we filled one out?" he asked, not at all sure that we had.

Viktor R. nodded. "I filled it out for all of us last week."

Resentfully we shuffled off to stand in the other line.

"I got my press pass here yesterday," Viktor R. said. "There was nobody here. It took fifteen minutes. Today is the deadline. That's why everyone is here."

"So why are you here if you already did yours yesterday?" my father asked.

"Why, to help you out, Yuri Lvovich."

For the lack of anything to do, I read the notices on the bulletin board next to us.

"Now why," I asked no one in particular, "couldn't we have a small, *tiny*, notice regarding the procedure for accreditation? I'm not saying anyone should remove these long letters from members of the Romanov family to the media that no one besides the really bored is tempted to read. God forbid. I'm saying, right *alongside* the Romanov letters, couldn't we have even a little handwritten note about what we are supposed to do?"

Viktor R. shrugged. My father didn't answer, preferring to wait with the hangdog look of someone who had waited in Soviet lines for the first half of his life and was quite prepared to do so again.

Finally we were at the front. After giving our names, we shifted over to the line on the right to get our pictures taken. In the forty minutes we had been there, the crowd had swelled appreciably. Many more people now tried to muscle their way straight to the photographer, without realizing they first had to give their name in the invisible line right next to the photographer.

After we got our pictures taken, we moved *all* the way over to the cluster on the left.

I say *cluster* because *line* is too orderly a term.

We noticed several people handing over fifty rubles at a time to the teenage-looking clerks giving out accreditation cards. Wondering if we could just buy an accreditation and get out of there, Viktor R. asked what the money was for.

Apparently it was a form of bribe called a fine. It worked like this: Yes, today is the absolute deadline to get the press pass, but if you are strapped for time and want to come and get your accreditation tomorrow, it will cost you fifty rubles now and in cash. Then you can come back any time you want.

At last we got our photo IDs and left quickly, taking the wide gray marble stairs two at a time. On the landing, an enterprising woman had a table of books about the Tsars. I bought a book about Nicholas II and some St. Petersburg postcards. A man appeared and loudly informed the seller she couldn't sell merchandise on the stairwell. "I don't know who told you you could, but you can't. Move immediately."

When we walked outside, we stood in the courtyard for a few minutes, as my father smoked.

"Paullina, pay attention," Viktor the driver said. "See this statue? It's a very famous equestrian statue of Alexander III."

"Oh?"

"Paullina, do you remember?" my father asked. "It stood for many years on Insurrection Square near Fifth Soviet?"

"Insurrection Square?"

"Yes," he said impatiently. "Where we used to catch the metro."

"Oh, that Insurrection Square."

I looked at the statue again, trying to jog my memory.

"What was in this courtyard before?"

"Lenin's armored car."

"Where is that now?"

"In the scrapyard," replied my father, still smoking.

Changing the subject, I asked, "So what do I wear to the funeral?"

"How would I know?" said my father. "Viktor, can you get us inside the church?" He turned to me. "Because otherwise, I guarantee, we will see nothing. Mark my words."

"No, no, Yuri Lvovich. That's not so," said Viktor R., promising nonetheless he would make a couple of calls and try to get my father and me inside.

"Forget me," my father said. "Just get Paullina in. She has to see it. She is the writer."

"I don't want to go without you, Papa."

"Forget me. Do you have a black dress at least?"

My stare was his reply.

"Didn't I tell you to bring a suit?" said my father. "What do you think that meant?"

"I thought it meant bring a suit. So I brought my best suit. My best, *taupe*-colored suit."

Papa waved his hand at me. "What can I tell you? I brought a black suit —"

"You told me it was blue."

"It's dark blue. So dark it can pass for black. Can your taupe suit pass for black?"

"No."

"No. Of course not. That's why I'm going to be inside the church and you will be out on the cobblestones. You'll look good, though."

"I will go and buy a black dress," I said. "My hotel has a boutique. I'm sure they sell a black dress."

Viktor R. told me not to buy anything until tomorrow — the day before the funeral — when he would find out for sure if we could get inside the church. "I don't know if I can do it. It's only big enough for three hundred people, and political leaders are coming from all over the world. I'll try."

"Oh," I said. "Political leaders from all over the world? It's a big deal, then. Is Yeltsin coming?"

Viktor R. shook his head. "No. Yeltsin is not coming. There is a lot of controversy over this whole funeral thing."

"Yeltsin is not coming? What controversy?"

"Well …" Viktor R. looked at my father, who took a deep puff of his cigarette and shrugged as if to say, *I'm tired of talking about it.*

"The controversy is — well, the Communists did kill the Romanovs."

"Yes, but Yeltsin didn't personally kill them."

"He might not have killed them, but he did order to demolish the Ipatiev House in which they had been murdered. It was burned down one night in the seventies."

I had heard something about that. "So, who will greet the international political leaders?"

"Yeltsin is sending Lebed," my father said. Aleksandr Lebed was the governor of Krasnoyarsk, a region of Siberia.

"The Archbishop of the Russian Orthodox Church is very upset," said Viktor R.

"Because he wants Yeltsin to go to the funeral?"

"Well … it's more complicated than that."

I glanced at my father, who was studying his cigarette. Turning back to Viktor R., I asked, "What's complicated? Yeltsin is not going. The Archbishop is angry."

"No, the Archbishop is angry because Yeltsin is permitting the Romanovs to be buried at Peter and Paul's. It was a museum for seventy years, you know. It's not a sacred enough place to bury the martyred Tsar and his family."

"But it's a church."

"The Communists had made it secular. The Archbishop wants the Romanovs to be buried in a church in Ekaterinburg."

"That's why he is upset with Yeltsin?"

"No," Viktor R. said patiently. "He is upset with Yeltsin for not going to the service. He figures if the Romanovs are going to be buried in a godless place like Peter and Paul's, the least a Party flunky like Yeltsin can do is pay his respects."

"Oh dear," I said. "So will the Archbishop be at the funeral?"

"Of course not," Viktor R. said. "He is not going. I told you, he doesn't think the Romanovs should be buried in a church."

"But didn't you just say …?"

"*If* they are going to be buried anywhere, they should be buried in Ekaterinburg, where they were murdered. But he doesn't think they should be buried at all."

"They shouldn't be buried?"

"No," said Viktor. "The Archbishop wants them to be canonized, as do many people. If sainthood is bestowed upon them, they cannot be buried. They become holy relics."

"How long does canonization take?"

"I don't know," said Viktor. "Ten, twenty years."

"Ladies and gentlemen!" my father exclaimed. "Please can we go? I'm tired of this."

We all piled into Viktor's little Volks.

My father announced that he was hungry and invited the two Viktors to have lunch with us. "My treat," he said. "It's not every day your boss buys you lunch."

The two Viktors heartily agreed.

The Marble Palace sits on the north side of the Field of Mars, named no doubt for its Parisian peer, the Champs du Mars. The Field of Mars is a park about thirty acres in size, used as a training and parade ground for the Soviet military. In the middle of it burns an eternal flame in memory of the heroes of the first 1917 Russian Revolution.

As we drove past the Field of Mars, my father said to me, "If you only knew how much of my youth I spent here with my friends. What great times we had. Yes, it holds many memories for me. See the eternal flame in the middle of the field?"

"Yes. It's beautiful."

"Late at night, my buddies and I used to cook a shish-ke-bob over that flame," he said. "And wash it down with vodka. Ah. Those were the days."

*

We found a café called Laima for lunch. I had come to Russia looking forward to some of my favorite Russian food: mushroom and barley soup, *pelmeni*, caviar. At Laima they served hamburgers, hot dogs, and chicken. If I'd wanted a burger I could have gone to a Wendy's back home. They offered a few Russian dishes. I ordered Brussels mushroom soup and salad Olivier.

The *Brussels* in the title meant my mushroom soup was *cream* of mushroom, which was so *not* what I wanted, while my salad Olivier was just ordinary potato salad. I glanced longingly over at Viktor the driver's actual potato salad, which for some reason looked better.

"Take it," he said. "No, really. Go right ahead."

"I couldn't," I said. "I really couldn't."

I took it. It was better. Viktor ate mine.

While we sat at Laima, we planned the rest of our day. Rather, my father planned the rest of our day, and we ate and listened.

First, he said, Viktor R. could go back to work.

"Very kind of you," Viktor R. said.

Then our driver Viktor would take us to Piskarev Cemetery, where victims of the Leningrad blockade were buried in civilian and military graves.

"Then —" he broke off, turning to me. "Well, what do you want to do then? Do you want to go to the Hermitage Museum and to the Siege of Leningrad Museum? We can go to the Hermitage for an hour, but then Viktor can drive us to your old school and then he can drive us —"

"Whoa, whoa, Papa," I said. "What do you mean, 'drive?' I thought we were going to walk?"

He paused. "Walk from where? From Piskarev? Are you crazy? Do you know how far it is?" The other two men smiled at this. "It's on the other side of the city."

"No," I patiently went on. "I thought we agreed that Viktor was going to drop us off at the record store, and then we would walk to my school and to Fifth Soviet?"

Silence at the table. My father sighed theatrically. "All right, Viktor. You will take us to Piskarev, and then you will drive us to the record store and there we will say goodbye. We will walk to Paullina's school and then to Fifth Soviet. Afterward we will take the metro to Anatoly's place and have dinner —"

"Whoa, whoa, Papa," I said. "I didn't know we were going to Anatoly's for dinner. Didn't we *just* have dinner there?" I said that, but I really couldn't recall *exactly* when we had dinner at Anatoly's. It seemed a long time ago. But I didn't want to have dinner there again so soon. There was too much to do.

Papa shook his head. "We have to go to Anatoly's," he said. "You don't know the pressure I'm under. They want you to come and stay in their apartment. We have to go." By way of enticing me, he added, "Ellie made blueberry pie with the blueberries you bought yesterday."

"She did?"

"Yes. And borscht."

"Also with my blueberries?"

"Don't be fresh. She thought borscht was your favorite soup."

"Did you tell her I prefer mushroom barley?" I said, finishing up my inadequate cream of mushroom.

"You're lucky you're being fed at all," my father snapped. "Can you even afford to eat in Texas?"

The Viktors chuckled. There is nothing my father likes more than an appreciative audience.

"We simply have to go, Paullina," he said. "They made us borscht. Ellie has been cooking all day. Also they're going to show films of you when you were a baby, and of your mother when I first met her. Don't you want to see them?"

"All right," I said.

"They really want to do this for us."

"I said all right."

Viktor and Viktor sat and smiled.

After lunch, Viktor R. went back to work, and our driver Viktor drove us north to Piskarev.

THE OAK LEAVES OF MOTHER RUSSIA

Piskarev Memorial Cemetery is located on the Prospekt of the Nepokorennykh. The Avenue of the Unconquered.

The wide prospekt was empty as we parked by the curb. It was Wednesday, middle of the week. People were working, not visiting cemeteries. I just expected to see more life. I came to see more of it. What about the people who didn't work? Mothers with babies? Old people?

The cemetery was surrounded by a five-foot-tall stone wall. On the other side of the wall lay a tranquil green pond, with an island in the middle and benches all around. A few people sat on the benches. A few others walked on the tree-covered paths.

Once we were inside the gates I instantly saw that this was not the Arlington Cemetery in Washington D.C. or the St. Laurent Cemetery of Omaha Beach.

There were no white crosses here.

There were no separate graves here.

The cemetery was laid out in a large rectangle about the size of a football field. We stood on a hill overlooking this landscaped field. Directly in front of us burned an eternal flame.

"Did you cook shish-ke-bob here, too?" I asked my father jokingly — and immediately saw by his horrified face that he had not.

It was one thing to cook meat on the memory of Communist revolution, it was another to burn it on the flame of the holy dead of war.

In the far distance, across from us at the end of the cemetery, rose a statue of Mother Russia, holding oak leaves in her hands. Before her, rectangular grass-covered mounds spread out, thirty feet wide by a hundred feet long.

This cemetery was a mass grave.

Five hundred thousand people were buried here, casualties of the blockade. Twenty-five thousand people per mound. To distinguish between civilian and military victims, each mound was labeled: a red hammer and sickle for civilians, a red star for the military.

Bodies were brought here for burial starting in 1942. The war ended in 1945, but the cemetery didn't open to the public until 1960.

I motioned for my father to come down with me to the grave sites, but he showed no inclination to do so. He kept milling around the two square white concrete buildings at the gate. I walked back to him.

"I'm looking for the Siege of Leningrad Museum," he explained.

I told him that according to my map, the Defense of Leningrad museum was located elsewhere. Viktor disagreed. "I came here with my school," he said. "It's here."

"Okay," I said. "Papa, why don't you come down to the graves with me?"

"No," he said. "You go. I'll wait for you here."

I stood near the eternal flame. It was a beautiful day. It was breezy, about 60°F and brightly sunny.

I slowly walked down the forty steps and through the graves, keeping my eye on the statue of Mother Russia. She held out her hands to me in mercy and judgment. I walked slowly because the air, the very atmosphere, was charged differently than anywhere else I had been to. Besides oxygen and nitrogen and carbon dioxide, there was something else here. It felt heavier, quieter, more ominous. There was a numinous quality to the air. History, death, the angels, the war, suffering. The red tulips in the flower beds around the graves. The air wasn't light; it wasn't diaphanous. It was thick with death — paralyzed with death — and in the quiet stillness, what cried out was the violence of this death by starvation, by utter indifference. We died and we didn't want to die, the voices from the graves whispered. We wanted to live like you, walk through a pretty park maybe. We wanted to feel the summer sun on our faces, but we weren't as lucky and we died a pitiful death, and we're still here.

That's what I walked through: anguish and desperation and a desire for life. No wonder I was walking slowly. I stopped before I got to the end. It was too much.

As I turned back, something clicked inside me. *I had been here before.* With my grandmother. I was staying with her while my mother went to visit my father in the Gulag. We walked a long way to get here from the bus stop. My grandmother played a word game with me to make the time pass. I was maybe six.

With the graves laid out like hills, the past remained present. This was no usual walk in the park. No peace was to be found strolling among these dead. It felt as if all 500,000 souls still ceaselessly paced the promenade, keeping the past alive, and I stumbled upon them accidentally, like the blind into a wall. I could almost hear them screaming. *I didn't want to die. I was young like you. I loved, like you. But love and youth weren't enough to keep me alive. Here you are, six years old, walking with your babushka among us. You're playing a game and you are hungry and tired. We surround you with our suffering, a suffering you've never understood and cannot ease.*

I found a bench. I sank down, and saw my father. He was motioning to me from the top of the stairs; faintly I heard his voice. He didn't come down to me. He called for me through half a million dead souls.

"Paullina, Paullina ..."

I got up and walked to him.

"We found the museum," he said. "Are you all right?" But he didn't wait for my reply. He had already turned around and was walking toward the square white building.

He and Viktor found a way into the museum, housed in the two white structures, Part One and Part Two. Inside Part One was a thirty by thirty foot room, all gray concrete and darkly lit. Barely lit, I should say, to convey the mood of doom.

It took my eyes a few minutes to adjust to the darkness.

Along the walls, poorly lit words and photographs told the story of the siege of Leningrad.

I stood, sickly fascinated, in front of one panel of glass. Behind it was the very thing I had struggled to imagine on the Aeroflot flight here: the bread ration given to the Leningraders during the first terrible winter of the siege.

It wasn't 125 grams of a crusty loaf. It wasn't 125 grams of a bagel. It wasn't even the cold stale roll I had been given on the plane. It was 125 grams of a dark, porous, unhealthy-looking substance. The moment I saw it I knew it wasn't real bread. Now I knew why. The flour was cut with glue and paper and wood shavings before it was baked. There wasn't enough flour in Leningrad to give two million people 125 grams of rye or pumpernickel each.

Four ounces of this bread a day. Military personnel received eight ounces. They were defending the country. They needed more.

Manual laborers got six ounces. I looked closer. My son Misha drops more than that on the floor every morning as he sucks the cream cheese off his breakfast bagel. Kevie rejoices in feeding twice that to the dogs at every meal.

I couldn't move away from the bread. My father tugged at my sleeve.

"I can't go yet, Papa," I whispered.

He pulled me away to read Hitler's instructions to his Army Group Nord on the demolition of Leningrad by hunger. Then he pulled me away to read the diary of a young girl named Tanya Savicheva, whose entire family had died in Leningrad, leaving only her alive. "Only Tanya left …" she wrote in her last entry. "Только Таня осталась …"

She died too, in 1942. Now my father was the one who had to look away.

We moved away from Tanya Savicheva, from Hitler, from bread, and began studying a mercifully abstract map of the siege. A tall, thin old man stood next to me. He was silent for a moment, and then he started to speak.

His name was Yuliy Yulievich Gneze. He was seventy-six years old. At nineteen he had been a Red Army soldier fighting to defend Leningrad. When Stalin finally decided to open a second front in Volkhov, in December 1941, Gneze was transferred there to attack the Germans from the rear. On the map he showed me the places where fighting had been the most severe. He showed me why and how the Germans always sought out the highest positions from which to systematically mow down the Soviets. There were two such places around Leningrad. One was Pulkovo Heights, in the south, from where the German artillery bombed Leningrad streets for three years. The other was a place east across the Neva near the Volkhov front called Sinyavino Heights.

"Have you ever heard of Nevsky Patch?" Gneze asked me.

I shook my head. Viktor, who had been standing nearby grunted knowingly. My father, who knew everything, had long walked away from us.

"The Nevsky Patch was the slaughterhouse of Leningrad," Gneze said. "I was nearly sent there. But I was lucky: they sent me to Volkhov instead. No one who went to Nevsky Patch came back. No one."

"But finally …" I said.

"Finally, we pushed the Nazis out of Russia."

Gneze was of German descent himself. He wore a little cap and in his hands he carried a loaf of bread. He told me that after the war he always lived close to this cemetery, and whenever he went out to run errands for his wife, he came here just to walk through the museum and around the graves.

Having been through those graves, I was stunned to hear that anyone would willingly walk through them. He must be looking for someone — brother, father, mother?

"I don't have anybody," he said. "They're all dead. Except my wife. I come here just to walk through the graves. To remember."

Gneze was touched to learn that I had come all the way from Texas to research a book about the blockade.

"I wish I had known you were here," he said. "Are you going to be here again? Because I have so much material at home about the blockade."

As we left the museum, Gneze walked out with us, following us to the second building. He asked if I could wait, and he would run home and get me some books on the blockade.

"I have been saving them for years and never knew why. Maybe this is just the occasion," he said.

"Keep your books, Yuliy Yulievich," I told him. "You should not part with your memories."

"My memories I will not part with," he replied. "But if the books can help you, it's worth it."

The second building was better lit. Instead of death, it focused on vanquishing the enemy.

I asked Gneze if the Russians and the Germans exchanged their wounded and dead. As per the rules of the Geneva Convention. He snorted at the suggestion.

"Maybe in Europe," he said. "But not in Russia. No. It was not that kind of war."

My father came over. "Okay, Paullina? Done?"

"Yes," I said reluctantly, and we all stepped outside into the blinding sunshine. As we walked to our car, Gneze stayed by our side.

"See this pond over the cemetery wall? I'll tell you something about the pond."

I waited.

"When the Russian army collected the dead bodies for burial, they didn't know what to do with the German corpses," Gneze said. "At first they were going to burn them or let them rot where they fell, but in the end they couldn't. They took pity. The Russians dumped all the Germans in one spot and covered them with earth. Later, the city decided to fill the space with water, and it became a pond. That's the pond you see here."

"Oh," I said.

"Isn't that funny?" Gneze said. "Benches all around, pedestrians strolling by, speaking softly so as not to disturb the dead." He chuckled.

"Paullina. Ready to go?" my father said.

"Where are you going?" Gneze said, as if he wanted to come with us.

"Today, to the place we used to live," I replied. I could see he lost interest. "But tomorrow, we were thinking of going to Lake Ladoga. To the Road of Life, you know?"

"Of course I know," he said. "Personally I recommend Kobona, on the other side of the lake."

"I think it might be too far for us."

"It's worth it. It's got a great museum."

"Oh yeah?" I said, watching my father slowly walk away. "Is Schlisselburg worth it?"

"Schlisselburg is a must. You cannot go to Lake Ladoga without seeing Schlisselburg. It's incredible there. And it's got the fortress island, Oreshek, that stood against the Nazis for a year and a half. You must go to Oreshek. No matter what."

"We'll definitely go," I assured him.

"There is a wonderful museum in Schlisselburg. Not a museum really, a diorama. It opened recently, it's all about the breaking of the blockade. It's not far from there to Nevsky Patch. Or to Kobona."

"We'll try," I said, knowing what my father would say.

"Goodbye," said Gneze, shaking my hand. He had a firm, hard handshake, like my Dedushka.

This time *I* followed *him*. He was already down the forty steps, marking his time through the graves with the loaf of bread and his hat in his hands, half a cemetery in front of me. As I focused my camera on him, he turned around and stared at me. I took a picture, but I didn't want to get any closer. I waved. Without waving back, he turned around and proceeded down the path.

As we climbed into Viktor's car, I looked around for some public transportation. There wasn't any.

"Viktor, where are the buses?"

"Oh, they stop at the Square of Courage," he replied.

"Where is that?"

"About a forty-minute walk from here."

You would think a bus could be re-routed to the gates of the cemetery, so that the veterans could come and pay their respects —

but no, nearly sixty years later, the old soldiers, the tourists and the six-year-old girls still had to walk forty minutes.

"Where do you want to go now?" my father asked.

I was raw from Piskarev, but my father was already on to the next thing. He knew there was plenty more ahead. He was saving his emotional strength.

I looked at the map.

"See here," I said, to no one in particular. "My map says the Defense of Leningrad Museum is off the Field of Mars, not far from the Marble Palace."

"Oh, *Defense* of Leningrad," said Viktor. "You should have said that's what you meant. Defense is different from *Siege*. We can go there another day."

"That man also mentioned there is a nice museum in Kobona."

"Paullina!" exclaimed my father. "Be serious. How much are you prepared to do?"

"Everything."

"That's what I am afraid of," said my father. "Viktor, let's drive past Smolny Sobor. It's beautiful, plus I used to work there."

"What's Smolny Sobor?" I asked.

"It's a church."

"You worked in a church?"

"Well, it wasn't a church under the Bolsheviks." My father chuckled. "The Bolsheviks loved the religious buildings. The Smolny was the headquarters of the Communist Party in Leningrad."

"So what did you do there?" I asked. "I know you didn't work for the Communist Party."

"No. But when I was a lawyer, I went there to present my legal briefs."

"Inside the church?"

"No, in one of the adjacent buildings. I'll show you. The church was used as a warehouse for document storage."

"Oh."

Smolny was once a brilliant (now faded) blue-and-white Baroque convent, designed by the Italian architect Rastrelli, who seemed to have designed most of Leningrad. Viktor parked the car, and we stood in the open square in the front of the church as tourists filtered in and out.

"Isn't it something?" my father said. "Ey? Isn't it?"

It was certainly something. Would the camera hide Smolny's peeling paint? Yes, if the shutter was softly focused and we stood far away.

"This is one of the most beautiful churches in Leningrad," Viktor told me. "It's a major tourist attraction."

That made it all the more unseemly. Couldn't the city paint the dang thing? I nodded, wondering why my father saw the beauty, why Viktor saw the splendor, while I saw only the degraded splendor.

I was no less sentimental than my father. I wanted it to take my breath away, too. I came to Russia wanting nothing less. But instead I was getting things I had not bargained for. I was getting spirits in a cemetery, and no toilet paper in the toilets, and no toilets, and rusted fences and cardboard walls and people living in partially burned down houses. Papa was getting Smolny.

"Did you like being a lawyer, Papa?"

"It was certainly ironic," he replied. "Me defending the factory from workers' complaints." Indeed it was ironic: my dad, the most ardent anti-communist around, working for the government, since all factories were government-owned.

"Do you see that street over there? At the end of that street was my jail."

Something stirred inside me. "Your jail? What's the name of the street?"

"Shpalernaya. We called the jail Shpalerka. Take a picture for Mama of me with the street in the background. It'll just kill her."

I pointed my camera at my father and Shpalernaya Ulitsa, but childhood got in the way of the viewfinder. I couldn't see the present clearly. All I saw was the past.

"Is this where I came to visit you with Mama that one time?" I asked.

"Yes," he said. "This is where you came with Mama."

THE BLUE SKY

"Daddy, why is the sky blue?"

"Because God made it that way."

"Why did God make it that way?"

"Because he liked the color blue for the sky."

"Daddy?"

"Hmm?"

"Why is the grass green?"

"Because God liked the color green for the grass."

"Daddy, why didn't God make the sky green and the grass blue?"

"Because a green sky would look stupid."

"Why didn't God think a blue sky would look stupid?"

"Why don't we ask Mommy when we get home?"

"Why would Mommy know something you wouldn't?"

"Because Mommy knows everything Daddy doesn't."

"Like what?"

"Like why you are the most curious little girl in the world, and now I know why Mommy doesn't go for walks with you."

"Are you the most curious daddy?"

"No. Why?"

"Because Mommy doesn't go for walks with you either."

*

I am a little girl. Cheerful and curious. I have a mommy who loves me and a daddy to whom I am everything. And he is everything to me. He plays wild games with me. He throws me up in the air so high I think I might never come down. Mommy yells at him for throwing me up high like that, but he does it anyway. Behind her back, he does it, and then we laugh because it is our secret, our world. He is the one who takes me for walks. He buys me ice cream and takes me to the movies. I go everywhere with him. When he goes into a pub to get himself a beer, I wait outside. Mommy stays home and cooks dinner.

Suddenly Daddy disappears. Mommy takes me to kindergarten. She brings me home. We eat dinner alone and go to sleep alone. There are no more walks. Mommy sends me outside to play by myself.

This goes on for nearly a year until one Saturday in April. Mommy and I take a walk. It's a misty and miserable Leningrad afternoon. She holds me by the hand. She doesn't talk, and I don't talk.

We walk for a long time and come to a big gate, like a fortress. Mommy rings the bell and a man opens the gate for us. We walk in. She squeezes my hand, but I have no feeling. I am not nervous or scared or shocked. I am numb.

Mommy holds my hand tight and then a man in uniform leads us through a dark, smelly yard and we come to a hallway with gray walls. It doesn't look like anything I have seen before. I don't care. I know I won't see it again.

Finally we stop walking. The man unlocks a door and shows us into a room. It is a tiny cubicle with dirty beige walls and a naked light bulb hanging from the ceiling. The man tells my mother to wait, and leaves. The room is empty except for a chair, my mother, and me.

After a while we hear footsteps. The door opens. A guard comes in. He is big and not friendly. Then another guard comes in, with my father.

Daddy doesn't look like I remember him. He looks tired and unshaven. He comes to me and hugs me very tightly. I remember that. How tightly he embraces me. Then he sits in the chair and pulls me onto his lap and tells me not to be scared. I wish I could tell him that I'm not scared, that Mommy is scared and he should be telling this to her, not me, but he keeps on. He tells me he will be home soon and that we will go for walks again. He keeps telling me not to be afraid. He talks to my mother a little bit. Soon the guard, who has been watching us, says time is up. Mommy hugs me because she thinks I am going to cry. But I'm not thinking of crying. I'm thinking of nothing. My daddy has tears in his eyes. When they take him away, he looks back at us, and then the guard closes the door. In a few minutes a man comes to show us out, and my mother takes my hand again.

I am five years old.

After that, my mother and my grandparents tell me Daddy has gone on a business trip. They say he will be back soon. My mother goes to visit him two more times on this business trip but doesn't take me. I stay with my grandmother. During one of those stays, she takes me for a walk to Piskarev Cemetery.

I turn six and then seven.

I don't ask about this business trip. Is his business so important that I have to be walked to kindergarten by my silent mother every day? I stop listening to adult conversations. God forbid I should overhear anything. God forbid I should overhear he isn't coming back.

But he does come back — when I am nearly eight and about to start first grade. I am in Shepelevo, it is naptime, around four in the afternoon. I am lying on my little bed reading when I hear my grandmother exclaim from the kitchen, "There comes my son!" I run to Yulia's room and look out of her window and see my father and mother walking, arm in arm, down the hill from the cemetery.

He comes back just the way I remember him.

Not as I remember him in that room with the chair and the naked bulb, but as I remember him in the days before he left, clean-shaven and smiling.

I never cried for my father. I never shed a tear for his absence, but I have tears in my eyes in Shepelevo. I am so happy he is back. I jump up and down on my bed, nearly hitting my head on the ceiling, and then he comes to me, and I still remember hugging him tight enough to break his neck, and my mother standing next to us, patting me on the back.

SHPALERKA

My father was arrested in August 1968 during the Prague spring, when the Soviet Union invaded Czechoslovakia. He spent a year in the Shpalerka jail awaiting his mock trial. He was tried and convicted in three days and sentenced to two years' hard labor in Mordovia labor camp, south of Moscow.

Once, already in the States, when I had expressed regret for my father's suffering, my mother sent me a poem by a Russian writer, Anna Akhmatova, who elevated to high art the abandoned woman's suffering as she waits near the prison gates to give a package to her lover, who's in jail.

"That is me, Paullina," my mother wrote. "And whatever your father might say about it, it was I, not he, who stood at those prison gates, while he sat happily in jail. It was I, not he, who stood near the iron gates to give him a package. How quickly he forgot that."

Another time, when I was twenty, my mother told me, "When we left Papa's prison, you were squeezing my hand. We walked all the way home, and you didn't say a word. Usually we can't shut you up, but that day you walked silently. It rained all the way home."

He and I looked at the gates of this jail now, and my father said, "Yes, this is where you came to visit me with your mama and your babushka."

That shocked me. Babushka came, too? I have no memory of her on that day. None.

"She wasn't in the room with us, was she?"

"Of course she was."

Go figure. I couldn't find her in my five-year-old soul. How unreliable memory was. Yet how indispensable.

The building looked like a typical four-story Leningrad office block.

"They thought they were being so clever," my father said. "Making it look like an office building. It's a façade. Like so much of what they do. It's just pretend windows and pretend doors, as ramshackle as everything else on the street. Behind the fake windows is the prison yard and the cells. Right in the middle of town, next to Smolny Sobor, not far from the river. Nothing is as it seems."

At the rear of the jail were the KGB headquarters, he told me, housed in a Bolshevik-era building, a concrete atrocity of no redeeming cultural or architectural value. But then what did I expect of KGB headquarters? A Byzantine sensibility? Perhaps a statue of David out front?

He told me that when he was in labor camp, he didn't have any sugar for two years. He hoarded the tea my mother brought for him so that he could give it to his friends on his last day in the camp.

"No sugar, huh?" I said, glib, tired, in need of some female facilities.

My father looked at me meaningfully.

"You understand nothing," he said. "That was nearly the worst thing."

Was that the *worst* thing? I wanted to say. No sugar?

He was right. I understood nothing. I lived without him for five years. Three when he was in prison, and two when he was in exile. But I did have sugar.

During the war they didn't have sugar. No bread, no potatoes, no meat, no milk, no sugar. When Leningrad's food storage warehouses burned down in September 1941, and ten tons of sugar blackened and melted into the earth, the city people panicked, but they could not foresee the terror to come. They could not foresee that two months later, one cup of that black earth would be selling on the black market for a hundred rubles.

Silently we got back in the car.

We were driving again, still driving, eternally driving. We drove to my school, number 169. My father didn't want to get out of the car. But he did.

He directed me to take a snapshot of this, to take a snapshot of that. "Why are you so far away? What are you taking a picture of? Take a picture of this."

And I will put the snapshots in the family album: snapshots of my school with broken windows and its dirty empty yard; the paint coming off; the sign out front: "No walking your dogs here."

"Take the picture of the 'no walking your dogs' sign," he said. "Why are you so far from it? Take it up close. Take a close-up of it."

I did as I was told.

"Is this how you remember it?" he asked me.

"Yes."

But the answer was no. I remembered it full of kids. Kids climbing trees, yelling at one another, running. Did I remember the bars on the windows? No. Did I remember the broken windows? No. The yard was large and empty now, so forlorn, so sad. I was here long ago. I spent only two years at this school. But it was at this school that I learned my first English phrase, prophetic in retrospect: "Take a pen."

*

In the yard, a tarp covered the playground equipment for summer break. I didn't know for certain that there was still a children's slide under the tarp, but there used to be. During recess, we would climb up and down this slide, up and down. I climbed up one afternoon and fell two meters down, straight on my back. My mother had to leave work early and take me to the clinic in the redbrick hospital near Fifth Soviet. The doctors took an x-ray of my head because after I fell, I leaned my head in its white hat against a dirty wall. The nurses saw the black smear and thought I must have landed on my head.

The x-ray showed, unsurprisingly, that the head was fine.

The back really hurt, though. When we got home, we ate dinner, and then I sat at my desk and read, and my father lay on my bed and watched me. Every time he saw me slouch, he said, "Sit up straight. Haven't you played enough games? Sit up straight."

I sat up straight. My back really hurt, though.

It still hurts.

*

"I fell off that slide," I said to my father as we stood in the yard.

"What slide?"

"Remember I fell and hurt my back?"

"Not your back. You don't remember anything, do you? It was your head."

Shaking *his* head, he turned to Viktor and said, "Now I understand why she doesn't remember anything."

Shaking *my* head, I said to him, "Papa, go and stand over there and let me take a picture of you looking at the front doors of the school."

"Why?"

"Can you just go do it, and then I'll tell you?"

Reluctantly he went to stand under the shade of the trees as he looked onto the double doors. He lit a cigarette. "What was that all about?"

*

One morning my father, who takes me to school the few Mondays he is home from exile, is mean and I am mad at him. So as we are walking to school, I tell him that the school has a new rule: parents are not allowed inside. They have to leave their children at the front door and go.

"Really?" asks my father.

"Absolutely," I say.

When we get to the schoolyard, I say a quick goodbye and run up the steps, leaving him outside in the courtyard. I know he stands and watches me go in. What I don't know is that he stands and watches all the other parents go up the stairs and inside with their kids.

That evening, my mother says, "Why did you tell Papa parents weren't allowed inside the school? He stood there, the poor thing, and wondered why you said that to him."

"I was mad," I say, my spirits deflated.

I am eight.

*

"What did you do that for? Why a picture here?" he said.

"Don't you remember?"

"Remember what?"

I told him.

He didn't remember.

I remembered though. Nights I can't sleep, when I lie in the dark and think of all the people I haven't called and all the people I haven't written, the image of my father springs up, fresh and raw, standing in the schoolyard, watching all the other parents go in with their kids.

"Will you forgive me?" I said.

"I have no idea what you're talking about," he said. "Have you seen enough? Can we go?"

*

Afterward, Viktor drove us to the record store. We wanted to buy some Russian music CDs.

I was becoming pretty frustrated.

"Papa," I said, "I need to get out of the car. I can't be in the backseat anymore. I can't see anything. I need to walk through Leningrad."

My father sounded exhausted, "Why can't you look out the car window?"

"Papa, I'm writing a book about World War II. There were very few cars in Leningrad then. Maybe I should just have my heroine spend the entire siege driving around Leningrad? Could she fall in love in the backseat, too?"

"But Paullina, you're writing fiction," Viktor said. "Can't you *imagine* getting out of the car and walking?"

"Yes, Viktor, but I need to see what I'm going to be imagining. At a slower speed than thirty miles an hour."

"Viktor can slow down," said Papa.

"Papa!" I said. "We *have* to walk to Fifth Soviet."

My father shook his head. "But we already went there on Monday. You want to see it again? Why?"

I threw up my hands.

My father turned to a smiling Viktor. "What can I do, Viktor? She wants to walk everywhere."

We got out on tree-lined Kirochnaya Ulitsa that ran alongside the leafy Tauride Park. Papa told me the street used to be called Ulitsa Saltykov-Schedrin. We used to walk here all the time when I was small, he told me.

SHINE, SHINE, MY STAR

Papa let Viktor go home, and we went into the record store and argued without much conviction about who was going to buy the Vysotsky CD. There was only one, and we both wanted it. My dad let me have it. I think he was just too tired to fight.

We walked through the streets. It was 4:30 in the afternoon, sunny, warm, and plenty of other people were out, too, just like us. Well, maybe not quite like us. Less tired, less cranky, less hungry.

No, just like us.

My father was a reluctant raconteur and a reluctant pedestrian. We barely spoke and he walked slowly.

On Grechesky Prospekt, we walked past the October Concert Hall. My father was right. It *was* called October Hall. Now that we were walking, not driving, I could read the signs.

On the far side of October Hall was the redbrick hospital where I was born, where I had gone for aspirin poisoning, and where I had x-rays taken of my head.

When we neared the front doors of our dirty green building on Fifth Soviet, my dad mumbled that he didn't want to go inside. He repeated that the last time he had come to St. Petersburg and tried to go in, the doors were closed because they had been renovating.

He didn't know what was inside now. "It could be offices, it could be condos, I don't know," he said, lighting a cigarette. The implication was whatever it was, he didn't want to see it.

I looked at the faded pink double front doors hanging unevenly on their hinges. The building didn't look renovated to me. Leaving him to smoke, I walked through the passageway to the courtyard inside.

Many Leningrad buildings were built in a rectangular or square shape around a central courtyard, as homages to Rastrelli. They were miniature, ignoble imitations of the Winter Palace. Some courtyards had gardens; most were just garbage dumps.

Our courtyard on Fifth Soviet did not have a garden.

In the courtyard's favor, the surrounding walls were of deep yellow stucco and the sunshine hit them just right for me to recall playing in the yard as my mother cooked dinner upstairs. I looked up, counting three stories, and saw our kitchen window. It was open. A man, working on his overturned car in the yard next to the garbage, looked up from his work for a moment and stared at me indifferently.

Back on the street, my father was still standing in front of the front door, smoking.

"Papa, I want to go in."

"Go ahead."

"Come with me."

He shook his head. "You don't understand, Paullina. All the things you want to remember, I want desperately to forget."

He lit another cigarette. I went inside.

There was no renovation. The same torn by time concrete stairs I remembered from childhood greeted me, the same peeling dark-green paint on the walls. There was a dank smell of urine, at once familiar and repugnant.

As I stood at the foot of the stairs, the faded black and white details of my memory turned to color. Shepelevo had always been a myth to me, but Fifth Soviet was reality, then and now.

I trudged up the stairs and became seven years old again.

There is no Papa, just me and Mama. She lets go of my hand, and I walk up the stairs holding the railing. I see the window in front of me on the first floor, my mother ahead of me. I see the dinner she is about to cook for us. We have been alone three years; two more years of silence stretch out in front of us.

It was almost too much for me to walk up to the third floor. I climbed the stairs slowly, as my mother had, carrying the weight of her desperate life to floor 3, apartment 4, while I trailed behind her.

*

I stopped on the landing in front of our apartment and stared at the old brown door. It was just as I remembered it. How could that be? It was twenty-five years ago. It couldn't be the same.

Once, after my father has come back from prison and is living in exile in Tolmachevo, my mother picks me up from school. We come back to our apartment, but when we get to the brown front door my mother can't find her keys. It is a communal apartment — someone could let her in, but they won't have the key to our rooms. She says we have to go and get the keys from Papa. We don't eat dinner that evening. Instead, we travel one hundred and twenty kilometers. We spend a long time waiting for the train. We see Papa for barely five minutes, get the keys from him, and leave. It must have taken us five hours to get to Tolmachevo. Even then I am suspicious of my mother's key story. Papa won't be home for his regular weekend furlough for two more weeks, and I know my mother misses him. I suspect she made up losing the keys just so we could go to Tolmachevo and see him for five minutes. But what do I know? I am only seven.

I pulled out my camera and focused it on the door, but the flash on the Pentax wasn't working properly. I changed the f-stop on the lens to allow more light and pressed the shutter release button.

The glossy brown door opened and a man walked out onto the landing. He eyeballed me, perplexed.

Finally he said, in a measured tone, "Why take a picture of the door?"

I told him I used to live in this apartment long ago.

"Good," he said, locking the door behind him.

I told him I had come back to Leningrad from America.

"Good," he said again, and started for the stairs.

I stayed on the landing, the camera in my hands, looking at the door and at him. He walked down only a few steps before he turned back to me with a sigh.

"Would you like to see?"

"Yes, please," I said, my shoulders hunched in miserable reluctance. *Please don't let me see.* All I once wanted to remember I now wanted to forget. But I knew, *knew* I could not come to Leningrad and not see inside the apartment where I was raised.

As he was opening the door, I remarked, "Looks like the same door."

"It *is* the same door," he said. "Same lock, too. Do you still have your key?"

I laughed half-heartedly. "No, I do not have my key. I don't think I ever had a key."

"That's too bad," he said. "You could've walked right in."

Inside, a woman stood inside the sunny kitchen, drying a mixing bowl with a dishtowel.

"Svetlana," the man said, "I brought a young woman from America who wants to see the apartment."

Svetlana immediately stopped drying the bowl and rushed to me.

"Plinka!" she exclaimed. Her hands still wet, she took my hands into hers and told me how good it was to see me. I had never met her before. An attractive, heavy-set woman in her forties, Svetlana had been living in the apartment for only five years with her husband, Volodia, the man who had let me in.

"What rooms did you live in?" she asked me.

I told her the rooms all the way at the end of the corridor.

"Oh, of course, you must be the Gendler girl."

"Yes."

"Ina has your rooms now."

Svetlana turned to her husband. "Where are you going, Volodia?" she said tearfully. "Stay — please."

He shook his head. "Must to go to the store," he said, and left.

A minute later the long-suffering Volodia returned with my father trailing behind him. My father looked like I had felt coming into the apartment: miserably reluctant. We were rubbernecking, that's what we were doing. We were in my dad's Mercedes, flying by on the interstate, and there was a wreck on the road, with three ambulances. We were ashamed for slowing down, but couldn't help ourselves.

The apartment was built in a style reminiscent of the railroad apartments built in Queens, New York, in the early 1950s. It was a long, narrow corridor with rooms to the left and right. It had nine rooms altogether, along with two kitchens — one in the front, one in the back — two toilets and two baths.

During the heyday of communal living, before World War II, forty people lived in these nine rooms and shared these two toilets. When we lived here in the sixties, the number of people had been reduced substantially by death, imprisonment or, in some cases, both. We shared the apartment with about twenty other people. Our rooms were at the end of the corridor. We were lucky. We had two rooms joined by a narrow hallway in which we could sit and have dinner. Many families had only the one.

The building must have been more than eighty years old. My great-grandmother Anna received the rooms at the end of World War I from the borough residential agency amid mass confusion following the Revolution of 1917. My great-grandmother was so crafty, she somehow received the whole apartment: nine rooms, two kitchens and two toilets.

Clearly it was too much, and soon other people started moving in. My family managed to hold on to the two rooms at the end. My paternal great-grandparents lived in one room, my grandparents in the other with my father and uncle.

During World War II, my paternal great-grandfather died in evacuation, and my grandmother's mother, my Babushka Dusia, who is buried in Shepelevo, was homeless, having had her house recently burned down by the Germans. She came to live on Fifth Soviet with her son-in-law, my dedushka. After the war, she stayed, since there was nowhere else for her to go. In the 1950s my great-grandmother Anna died, so there was a little more space for the remaining five people, my grandparents, my great-grandmother, and my father and uncle.

In 1962, when my parents first married, they lived separately: he on Fifth Soviet, she with her father across town. If you ask my mother about this short period of her marriage before I was born, she'll say, "Yes …" in a voice filled with nostalgia. "That was the happiest year of my life."

Soon after they were married, however, she became pregnant with me (don't ask me how), and my grandparents applied for their own private apartment, to make room for the newlyweds with a baby on Fifth Soviet. They were given one in September, and I was born in November.

After my birth, my parents and I lived in one room on Fifth Soviet, my aunt and uncle and their baby, Yulia, in the other.

Four years later, my uncle got an apartment of his own and wowza, I had my own room. But then my dad started holding secret meetings with his anti-Communist friends in my room while I was away in Shepelevo. Not *so* secret, as it turned out. The KGB had been stalking my father for years. He was arrested, and my mother had a room to herself, I'm sure for the first time in her life.

I said to Svetlana, "We would love to see our rooms. Do you think that's possible?"

A slender woman in her fifties with bobbed black hair tinged with gray came toward me, and took me by both hands. "Plinochka, oh my God, I heard you had come, look at you, I can't believe I'm seeing you. Remember me? I'm Ina."

I didn't remember her.

"Ina!" I said. "Of course. Did you live here with us?"

"Of course! Don't you remember? I lived with my mother and my daughter in this room next to the front door." She pointed.

"Of course," I said, recalling nothing. She was still holding my hands. "Where are you living now?"

"We live in your old rooms! We were sad to see you go, but when you left we applied to the regional committee and got your rooms! We were so happy."

"Have you been living in them ever since?"

"Yes!" she said, beaming. "Come meet my daughter. Surely you remember my daughter. She is your age. She has a daughter herself now, Sophia. She is four. They are living with me at the moment. Come, come and meet them."

I glanced at my father, who was looking profoundly ashamed.

"Do you think we can see the rooms?" I asked Ina.

"Yes, of course! Oh I wish I knew you were coming, I would have cleaned up. You will pardon the mess."

My father started to apologize for the inconvenience we were causing.

"What are you talking about, Yuri Lvovich? We are so happy you came! Is this your first time back in Leningrad?"

When my father said it was his third time, Ina tutted. "And you never came to visit? Tsk. Tsk."

As we walked through the hallway, we had to hold on to the walls. The narrow corridor was poorly lit and the floor was uneven. Two bare light bulbs burned in the hallway. *Just like before.* Winter coats were hung by the dozens on hooks in the wall, even though it was July. Where else were the residents going to hang their winter coats? There were no closets. The dirty wallpaper hung torn off the wall.

We stopped at the gray door that led to our rooms.

I said to my dad, "I don't remember the doors being gray."

"There's a lot you don't remember," he said.

"Gray?" said Ina, chortling a bit. "They're not gray. They're white. They just haven't been washed in a while. I never even noticed. Come in, come in. Please excuse the mess."

I couldn't walk in right away.

*

My father is coming home from an afternoon at the park. He is reading the newspaper. When he is almost at our door, our neighbor Tonia Morzhakova calls out to him.

"Yura! Where is Paullina?"

"Right here," replies Papa.

I am swinging upside down from the crook of my father's arm. He is holding me absentmindedly by the legs, hidden behind his newspaper.

*

"Plinochka, are you coming in?"

The first thing I noticed about our old rooms was the tall ceilings — so tall that they managed to diminish the narrowness and shortness of the hallway itself. The ceilings were pockmarked with water damage stains.

My father leaned over and whispered, "I used to sleep in this hallway, when I would come back too drunk and didn't want to disturb your babushka and dedushka."

"What do you mean, sleep?" I whispered back. "We always had a table here." Like the table that was there now.

"Shows you what you know," he said. "There used to be a couch here. Not a table."

"Excuse us. Excuse our mess," Ina kept saying.

My father kept apologizing for intruding.

The little hallway was tiny. All the furniture was different. I didn't like that. The wallpaper was different too, but the water stains on the ceiling, which resulted in the plaster breaking and falling off — now that was the same.

I stared at the hallway table long enough to remember sitting down and eating dinner there alone, while my mother was in the kitchen.

*

I'm eating my macaroni with butter, and I start to cry. Mama runs in from the kitchen: What, what?

I don't want to die, I say.

Oh, honey, you won't die. You're so young, you have your whole life, you're not going to die.

She pats me on the back and leaves.

I eat my macaroni with butter. A few seconds go by. I start to weep and yell, Mama, Mama. She runs in again. What, what?

I'm going to die, I say. I don't want to die.

You won't die, she says, less patiently. You're going to live a long, long life. You won't die. You're a baby. Now eat your food.

She leaves.

I eat my macaroni with butter. A few seconds go by. I cry again. Mama, Mama.

She runs back in.

I don't want to die, I yell.

She wallops me on the head. Stop your nonsense, she yells. Eat your food. You're not going to die. I told you.

She leaves.

I'm five.

Papa's gone.

*

"Which room was yours, Paullina?" Ina asked.

"This one," I said, pointing to the door. We walked in.

It took my breath away to see how narrow my room was. The walls were covered in red wallpaper and the big wooden furniture made the space seem even smaller.

Everything was immaculate aside from the bed, which was not made. Ina apologized profusely as she rolled up the bedclothes and stuffed them under the bed.

My father had already left and gone into the kitchen but I stood dumbly by the door, trying to see how we could have fit a double bed next to the wall when the room was clearly only seven feet wide.

The window had a deep sill and no shutters.

While Ina rushed around cleaning up the mess that didn't exist, her daughter, who had absolutely nothing to say to me, stood and brushed her daughter Sophia's hair so that I could take a picture. What I wanted to do was look away. Look away, look at something else, as I had been doing for a quarter century. What relief not to think, not to remember, not to stand and pretend it was all right. I smiled at Ina who was searching my face — for what, I didn't know. For sentiment? For happiness?

"You like the wallpaper? It's new."

"I like it very much."

We went into my parents' old room and I stood by the same door handle I grabbed as a young girl of two, when I could barely reach it.

My father, who had come back, obligingly agreed to take a picture of me all grown up by the door, my hand on the handle.

He couldn't get his camera to work.

"Maybe the battery is dead," he said.

"Papa, I just put in a new battery yesterday, remember? Shepelevo?"

"Well, you've done something with it, then." He pushed the flash down and took the picture without it. The shutter snapped.

"Oh, so it works without the flash," I said.

"Yes," he said impatiently. "Paullina, you have to know how to use the camera. The flash won't work without sufficient light."

Ina and her daughter stood politely to the side.

"Wait, let me understand. The flash needs *light* in order to work?"

"Yes."

"So in darkened conditions such as this room, the flash won't work at all?"

"It's a very sensitive camera," he said.

"Clearly." I turned to Ina. "Ina," I said, "the rooms have been redecorated."

"Yes, you like it?"

"Very much. But the furniture is different."

"Yes!" she said proudly. "It's from Europe."

"Ah. What did you do with our old furniture?"

"Sold some," she said. "Gave the rest to my parents. They still use it."

"Let's go into the kitchen," my father said. "*Please.*"

The kitchen was outside the gray door.

It had warped linoleum, bare dirty walls and bare bulbs. I went to the open window and stared down into the courtyard. I saw myself, five years old, playing. I could hear my mother calling me. Often there were no other kids there and I played alone.

The kitchen had no cabinets, so all the aluminum pots and pans were piled on a few shelves. Where did they keep their dry goods? Where was the refrigerator? There wasn't one.

There was an old stove.

"Papa, is this the same stove we had?"

He shrugged.

"The same, the same!" said Ina.

I leaned closer to him. "You think the pots and pans are ours, too?"

He looked down at the torn linoleum.

"You remember the pots and pans?" Ina asked.

I stared at my father. He stepped away from me, looked out the window, and said, "Paullina, we have to go."

"You sure?" Ina asked.

"Papa," I said. "Do you remember the carp?"

Lightly he laughed in spite of himself, pointing to the middle of the kitchen floor.

"Yes," he said. "He was right here. I remember. He was in your bath."

My father says to me, "Come here, Plinka. Come, I want to show you something." He is smiling. I smile too.

"What?" I say, already excited. His enthusiasm guarantees my own.

He leads me into the kitchen, on the floor of which stands my small bathtub. In this white enamel tub I see a fish, large and alive. It fills up nearly the entire tub. It is swimming. It is trying to swim away. The fish is black and shiny, and distressed.

"What is that?" I ask my smiling father.

"Carp," he says proudly. "Carp."

We eat the carp for dinner. It is delicious.

As we stood uncomfortably in the middle of the kitchen, I noticed a pungent smell. I tried to ignore it but was finally forced to admit it came from the half-open door of the lavatory. Despite the wide-open window, despite the warm breeze from outside, the odor was excruciating. You could not breathe through your nose. You would retch.

"You're right, Papa," I said. "Time to go."

He said he had to make a stop first. I looked at him with deep sympathy.

When he came out of the lavatory, I could see by his face that he wished he had waited.

*

With Ina talking into our backs, we walked down the hallway to the front door.

In the kitchen, Svetlana stood by the table, her hands up to her wrists in a mixing bowl full of ground beef.

"Stay, please, *please*," she said. "I am making you stuffed cabbage."

"You have *pelmeni*?" I asked. It was hunger talking. My father gave me a shove.

"You like *pelmeni*?" said Svetlana, quickly washing her hands in the sink. "I will make you *pelmeni*."

Papa glared at me, apologizing again. "No, we can't, we really can't, we have dinner plans."

"Please," she said.

"We really can't," said my father.

Not giving up, Svetlana poured us each a shot of cognac and we drank it on empty stomachs. We hadn't eaten since the Laima café. Was that even the same day, the mushroom soup from Brussels and Viktor's salad Olivier?

"Then come back another day," Svetlana said as she poured my father a second glass while I declined. "Come back and have dinner with us. I'll make you anything you want. When are you leaving Russia?"

"This Saturday," my father lied. We were actually leaving on Sunday.

"Plenty of time. It's only Wednesday. Come back tomorrow, or Friday," she said pleadingly.

"We'll try," my father said. Which is what he says when he knows it will never happen.

Svetlana wrote down her name and phone number.

Holding my hands, she talked passionately into my face. "Oh, my poor life, my poor, poor life. I lived in St. Petersburg, Florida, you know. I lived there for five years. I have many friends there."

"Why didn't you stay?" I asked.

"Why didn't I stay?" She rolled her eyes and clucked her tongue. "Because. Husband here." She said the word husband as if she were saying the word *prison*, or *rats*.

"I would love for you to get something to my friends in St. Petersburg, a letter, a little package. If you come back, I will get it all together. Please."

Squeezing her hands, I said, "You can't mail them the letter?"

She shrugged. "I could, I guess, but it would be so much better being delivered by you."

People in Russia, even those who have been to America, even those who have *lived* in America, have only the vaguest notion of distance. To them, the 1600 miles between New York and Dallas, or the 1100 miles between Dallas and St. Petersburg, Florida, is just a drive away, a day trip. We were all in America, and that was the only thing that mattered. We were all in the same place.

"So what kind of an artist are you?" I asked.

"I'm a singer," she replied, unable to hide the pride from her face.

I thought of a song I would have liked to hear, the song in the soul of every Russian. "Do you know, 'Shine, Shine, My Star?'"

Svetlana, standing barely a foot away from me, put her hands on her heart, opened her mouth, and in a gorgeous operatic voice began to sing "Shine, Shine, My Star."

"Shine on, shine on, my only star
My star of love eternally
You are my sole and chosen one
There'll be no other one for me …"

After the first verse, she broke down and cried.

My father stood by my side, not bothering to hide his ashen face.

I hugged her, he shook her hand, and we let ourselves out the brown door.

Trudging down three flights of stairs was harder than the climb up, which had been full of youthful anticipation, at least on my part. Having seen was more terrible than having remembered. Now there could be no more facile forgetting.

*

When my mother went to Russia in 1987, she visited the Fifth Soviet apartment. She spent a long time telling me *all* about it. Yet now, after being inside, it was as if she hadn't told me a thing.

My mother didn't tell me about the floor or the walls, about the size of the rooms or the heart-wrenching decay of it all. She didn't tell me about the stench from the toilet.

She told me she sat down and had tea with the Morzhakovs, who lived in the room adjacent to ours and who had since died. Morzhakov had turned informant for the KGB, my father later told me. ("Don't you remember how the year before I was arrested he took to his bed with a cold that lasted a year? He lay with his ear against the wall and listened in on all my meetings.") Because of Morzhakov, the KGB collected enough evidence to send Papa away to Shpalerka for a year, Mordovia for two years and then exile for another two.

That's what my mother told me about in glorious detail — having tea with the man who had spied on my father.

*

We walked in silence down Fifth Soviet, and then turned left on Suvorovsky Prospekt. I wanted to walk past my old kindergarten on Sixth Soviet, but I saw my father was close to collapse, so I didn't ask. It was a beautiful sunny evening, around six. The sun was slightly past zenith in the sky. Both of us writers, speakers, my father and I were out of words.

After we bought some film for the camera, we started to talk a bit. About the proliferation of stores and how hard the Russians tried to be like Westerners; how much more there was now than when I was young, how now you could buy film anywhere, even on Suvorovsky, just like in the West. I listened, but I was thinking about our apartment.

"Papa, when was our building built?" I asked him as we made our way to the metro. "I guess it had to have been before the war, because Dedushka lived there?"

"And his mother when she was a young woman," said my father. "It was built in 1857."

"No, stop it."

"It was meant to last a hundred years."

"Stop it."

"Now you know."

"What about the bathrooms?"

"Same," said my father.

"What about the kitchens?"

"Same," he said. "Floor, same. Walls, same. Maybe the wallpaper was different then. I don't know."

We walked down Suvorovsky.

"It's the same toilet we had when I was little," I said.

"Forget *you*," my father said. "It's the same toilet *I* had when *I* was little. The same overhead chain that barely works. It barely worked when I was growing up. It barely works now. Yes, that's right. It's not all about you. It's not just your apartment. I was born in that apartment, raised in that apartment, was a father and a husband in that apartment. It was the first and last place I lived in Russia until we left when I was thirty-seven."

"But, Papa," I asked quietly. "Why the smell?"

"Why the smell?" he said, exasperated. "It's the smell of Communism. The toilet belongs to everybody. That means nobody cleans it."

We couldn't talk about it anymore. I couldn't think about it anymore. The northern sun shined bright on the gray and cream daub of the Suvorovsky buildings.

I was doing the New York City thing: looking for a yellow cab. I would have gladly paid two hundred rubles to have a man, any man, take us to Anatoly's. Although what I really wanted was to find a park, a bench, and sit. I wanted to not move and not speak for three hours. Then I wanted to get up and walk past my Fifth Soviet building again, and touch it. And then I wanted to go back to Grand Hotel Europe and use the toilet in my Art Nouveau room and go downstairs to the glass mezzanine and have a sandwich and a cup of tea. I wanted not to speak to anybody for the rest of the evening.

But human nature is such that even when everything hurts, we find ways to cheer ourselves up. I started goading my dad into going into one of the restaurants and having some *pelmeni*. The signs in the windows of the cafeterias all read, "WELCOME! PLEASE COME IN! HOT DELICIOUS PELMENI, AND CHEAP!"

"Papa," I teased, "come on. We'll go in and have some. They're hot and delicious. And cheap, too. Then we'll go to Anatoly's and pretend we're hungry."

I was half-kidding, but my father said, "I can't pretend like that. I wouldn't be able to eat a bite."

But he brightened, and right before we got to the metro station, he himself pointed at a cafeteria advertising HOT DELICIOUS PIROZHKI and smiled.

We took the metro at Insurrection Square, where there once stood a statue of Alexander III. Now the Tsar was in the courtyard of the Marble Palace, and there was an obelisk to the blockaded Leningrad in the centre of Insurrection Square.

As we were going down the escalator — and going down and going down and going down — my father said, "This is why Russians will never be number one in anything."

I was confused.

"Look how deep they built the subway. Do you know how much money it cost them to build it this deep in the ground?"

"Probably less than what it cost them to make it all out of marble," I replied.

"Nonsense. Marble is child's play compared to how much it cost to build it this far down. And they only did it to make it into a potential bomb shelter. They thought for sure someone was going to attack them."

"Well, someone did, didn't he? Hitler attacked them."

"Yeah? And how many Leningraders did this subway save?"

"It wasn't running yet during the war, was it?"

"No. It was being built. It was a bomb shelter, I'm telling you. They came all the way down here and starved to death."

The escalator *was* taking us a long way down. It was like descending into Hades, six hundred feet into the ground. It was three times as long as the Central Line escalator at Holborn Station on the

London Tube, and the Holborn escalator is notorious in London for being the longest in the city.

It took us eight minutes to snail to the bottom. I wanted to take a picture to show Kevin, but my father wouldn't let me. He was afraid I would be arrested.

Arrested?

"Stop it," he said. "Come, and stop it."

I didn't take the picture.

We had no idea where to go on the metro. Not he, and certainly not I. Without purpose we stood, while I inhaled the fantastic familiar smell of the Leningrad metro, a warm tunnel wind mixed with marble and metal, blowing around in a cavernous space. Exactly as I remembered, only more so. The New York subways or the London Underground did not smell this way. The D.C. metro did a bit — it had the cavernousness and the tunnel wind, but not the marble.

Yet every time I ride down the New York City subway escalator, I inhale deeply, as ever hoping for the smell of Leningrad.

Tentatively we approached a broad, harsh Soviet-looking woman who told us which two trains to take to get to Ulitsa Dybenko.

By the time we were on a train we could barely keep upright, yet there was nowhere to sit. Rush hour. The body odor coming from the blank-faced, bleak-faced Russian commuters was oppressive and pervasive, almost like the toilets.

While I strap-hanged, I marveled at how much of Russia for me was defined by smells. Good smells, bad smells — of spring, of water, of jasmine and lilac, of metro and toilets, human sweat, old alcohol. Why couldn't Russia instead be defined by the poetry of Russian writers? Or by food like herring and smoked fish? Or by the

Russian language heard everywhere? Or by the strings of a plaintive balalaika?

Russian people returning home from work looked no happier than New Yorkers returning home from work. Across the continents, weary people looked the same. In Russia, they got paid less and smelled worse.

DZHUBGA, 1962

As we got off the train, my father said, "We should buy Ellie some roses." Out in the street, we walked over to an old woman selling flowers by the side of the road. The roses were three dollars each. They came wrapped in newspaper.

Most of the paper's black newsprint found its way onto my father's hands in the twenty minutes it took us to walk to Ellie's apartment. The first thing my father did once we were inside was wash his hands under cold water. The hot water had been turned off. I ran to use the facilities — for the first time since Grand Hotel Europe in the morning. It was 7:30 p.m.

Having acquired a little perspective, Ellie's toilet was nicer than any I'd been to so far except for the hotel's. It seemed *clean*. The water flushed. It didn't smell *so* bad.

I had lived my entire childhood in an apartment where the toilet smell was so terrible that, twenty-five years later, I couldn't bring myself to go into it. If I had to, of course, I'm sure I would have. Eventually I would stop smelling the stench as I cooked dinner on the stove a few feet away. Human beings can, and do, get used to worse than that. But in the confined space of Ellie's bathroom, thinking of everything that Soviet human beings had to get used to over the last seventy years filled me with a grief I could almost not bear. Because I now knew the difference.

Obsessively I scrubbed my hands with soap under the cold water. Someone should shout from the ramshackle rooftops, *We are still living.* We have such little time on this earth, we are not going to get any brownie points for suffering. Couldn't we have just a *little* comfort?

With clean hands and an empty bladder, I looked around Ellie's apartment and realized that their home was nice! There were fresh flowers in a vase, the wooden floor was polished and smooth. They had comfort.

It was quieter than the first night. It was only my father and me, Ellie and Anatoly, and it was lovely. We devoured leftovers from the previous dinner.

"Is it still fresh?" I whispered to my father, but he shushed me, so I ate. The two-day-old food was served at room temperature, on Ellie's best china.

She'd also made a delicious borscht and, with my Shepelevo blueberries, an extraordinary blueberry compote and a graham and meringue blueberry pie. My father and I ate non-stop until nine.

My father also smoked, and in between cigarettes kept trying to plan the next three days.

"Comrades," he said, standing before us at the head of the table, as if we were having a managers' meeting. "We have to very seriously think about what we are going to do tomorrow, Friday, and Saturday. We have only three days left."

Stuffed and tired, I said, "I thought tomorrow we were driving up to Lake Ladoga to see the Road of Life?"

Anatoly said, "You should see Schlisselburg too, it has a fascinating island fortress. Oreshek."

"She wants to do everything," my father said with a great sigh.

I nodded. "The man we met today at Piskarevka, Yuliy Gneze, told us we must go to Schlisselburg. He also told us we must go to Kobona, the town across Lake Ladoga. Apparently it has a great Defense of Leningrad museum."

"Paullina!" my father exclaimed. "Maybe you'd also like to go to Stalingrad, to see their museums?"

"No," I said. "But I would like to see Nevsky Patch."

"What about Crimea by the Black Sea?"

"Seriously, Papa."

"Paullina! You, seriously. We have no time for this. Friday, as you know, is the Romanov funeral. That will take up the whole day."

"A funeral that lasts all day? All right, fine, but we still have Saturday."

"No, we don't have Saturday," my father mimicked me, quite agitated. "Saturday we must go to Karelian Isthmus to visit my friends."

"No! What friends?"

"Radik Tikhomirov," my father replied. "And his wife, Lida. You remember Radik, don't you?"

I was pretty agitated myself. "Vaguely. Doesn't mean I want to see him."

"They want to see you."

"So? Why?"

"Why, why. They do."

"We have no time. Is it going to take the whole day?"

"Yes."

"Papa! No. We can't spend a whole day with someone named Radik."

"There is more. Your dedushka wants us to go visit his friends at their summer *dacha*."

"What friends? What *dacha*?"

"The Ivanchenkos. Nikolai Nikolayevich and his wife Valya. You probably don't remember them."

"You're right about that. I don't. Why do we have to go see them?"

"Because they remember you."

"Papa, we don't have time."

"Paullina, Dedushka will never forgive us if we don't go and see his friends."

"Oh my God. Okay, fine, we'll go see *them*, but forget Radik."

"I can't. Radik will never forgive *me*. It's completely impossible. Paullina, you don't understand —"

He broke off. Still standing at the head of the table, he lit a cigarette. "You remember Radik's son, Korney?"

"Yes, he was my age. There is a picture of us standing by the doors of some museum."

"That's right."

"I don't remember Radik, though. Was he the one who was in labor camp for eight years?"

"No, that was someone else."

"Great. Is Korney going to be there?"

"No," Papa said. "Korney is dead."

Silence.

"He died at twenty-two of acute alcoholism," my father said. "Don't say anything to Lida or Radik when you see them. It may be difficult for them."

"Was he their only child?"

"Yes."

"*May* be difficult?"

My father continued. "We have to think about what we want to do very carefully. We have a lot to accomplish and only a few days to do it. Let me ask you in all seriousness, do you *really* want to go to Schlisselburg and Lake Ladoga?"

"Where some of the greatest battles for the defense of Leningrad were fought? Where the Road of Life began and ended? Papa, yes. That's why I came here. To search for a story. Remember?"

"Okay, okay," he said. "But you did see a lot at the Piskarev museum."

"It's not the same."

"I was afraid of that. Fine, we'll go. But we have to go to Karelian Isthmus on Saturday. We have no choice. No one will ever talk to me again, do you understand, if I don't bring you to them."

I sighed desperately. "Fine."

"Paullina, have some more pie," Ellie said.

"Paullina, tell me about Tully," Anatoly said. "When you wrote about her, did you write her from life, or did you make up the things that happened? Because it read very true, and I can't imagine — I don't know, maybe I don't know you very well — but I've known you since the day you were born, and I can't imagine your imagination is that vivid. Is it, Paullina? Did you make it all up? I can't believe that."

"Oh, believe it," said my father. "Of course she made the whole thing up. Anatoly, she is the best liar we know. You should have heard her excuses for cutting school half of her senior year."

Ellie said, "Plinka, do you want some more pie? How about some tea?"

"Papa," I asked, "who is this Radik, and why does he care if he sees me or not?"

Ellie leaned over to me and whispered, "I'll tell you about Radik later," with a meaningful arch of her painted eyebrows.

After dinner, Alla arrived with her husband, Viktor, to watch the ancient home videos of our vacation in Red Schel, in the Caucasus Mountains in 1967, the year before my father was arrested.

We were all eager to watch the films, but there was too much sunlight still streaming from the window. Although it was after nine in the evening, we couldn't see the projection screen. We decided to draw the red curtains and close all the doors. That helped some, but the sun was still very bright. We waited an hour and after ten began.

There I was, a four-year-old child on a mute, slightly speeded-up film reel. Swimming in the Black Sea. Imitating my best friend Alla. Alla and I sat next to each other on the couch and laughed.

"Plinka, look how funny you were," she said. Casually dressed, she seemed a lot more comfortable with me than she had been on Monday night, as if she now knew she didn't have to put on airs.

I said, "What I want to know is, why did my hair look like a boy's? Why couldn't my mother let my hair grow out? Yours was so long and pretty. And look at me."

"Oh, no, Plinka! You were so cute."

There I was eating watermelon, sandwiched between Alla and a boy. I thought the boy might be Korney, Radik's son. I glanced over at my father. Blinking he watched the screen and said nothing. On the screen, I was crying. A bee had tried to lick the watermelon juice off my chest and stung me. In the next shot, my mother stood near a well. She wore two little girlish braids, and no makeup. She looked younger than I am now. I tried to calculate. My God, she *was* younger than I am now. I stared. *Much* younger. She was twenty-seven. My father stood near her smoking, fixing something to eat, talking. He was only thirty-one. He was also younger than me. I couldn't watch them.

That was all there was of me. Thirty-three seconds of a celluloid child, proving I once existed in this other world — a world that was more than just smells.

Finally, the film reel we'd been waiting for. My even younger father on vacation in Dzhubga, a resort north of Sochi on the Black Sea in July 1962, with eight of his best friends. The camera was Anatoly's. My father was twenty-six. Nine of them playing volleyball and practical jokes. Anatoly sleeping on the beach. As we watched we teased Anatoly about his capacity to sleep anywhere, even as a young man.

"Were you already married then?" I asked him.

"Yes," Ellie snapped.

"Why didn't you go to Dzhubga with them?" I asked her.

"Because," she said. "I was home with Alla. She was a baby."

"So Anatoly went without you on vacation?"

"Yes." She squinted her eyes with bitterness. "He did that all the time. All the men did that."

Seeing that I had touched a nerve, I turned back to the screen, where someone had filched Anatoly's clothes. He woke up, and was not happy. We laughed. Ellie's face showed grim satisfaction.

I leaned back and watched my father swim in the Black Sea. My handsome, thin, dark-haired young father, unmarried, childless, happy.

Dzhubga. July, 1962.

Before marriage, before pregnancy, and — unfathomably — before *me*. I found it hard to watch my father living what seemed to be a joyous existence before his new life began. He didn't even know yet that his new life would take the form of an exquisite twenty-two-year-old exotic-looking girl, sitting with her own friends on the same beach, laughing at nine boys playing volleyball.

Dzhubga. 1962. They met there, fell in love in the space of a week. They married two months later. My father had been engaged to someone else. That evaporated when he met the fresh young woman full of life with high cheekbones and cropped hair.

It hurt to see my mother. She was so beautiful, giggling with her friends in their little bathing suits, watching the half-naked boys, not having fallen in love with my father yet.

I watched my father *moments* before he fell in love with my mother. An unbearable suspended-in-eternity moment. How could Anatoly have even known what he was filming? The camera was just merrily rolling along, recording for all the world and me what most never get to see — the instant her parents fell in love with each other. The instant I became possible.

My mother sat in a chair on a porch. One of my father's artist friends was painting her portrait. She couldn't sit still; every few moments her youthful face exploded in animated happiness. My father stood on the wooden steps of the porch, smiling back, watching her watching him. Before everything. Before she thought her whole life was a failure as she wiped the red dust off her furniture on Maui and complained about the Hawaiian sun.

"Look at my wife," my father said. Even in the dark, I could see his eyes, misty and twinkling. "Paullina? Just look at your mother."

"I'm looking, Papa," I said, looking at him looking at her.

The day after my young mother had her portrait painted, the group of them went to a dance, and afterward my father and mother

The apartment building on Fifth Soviet where I was raised.

Feast at Anatoly's. From left, Viktor (Alla's husband), Alla, Papa, Ellie, Anatoly, Viktor (Anatoly's twin brother), Luba (Viktor's wife).

Anatoly's building, one of thousands built by Khruschev in the 1960s to improve the Soviet standard of living.

Our *dacha* in Shepelevo. From left, Vasily Likhobabin, Papa, me, Maria Likhobabina.

My "bedroom" in Shepelevo that was actually once a kitchen.

The Gulf of Finland in Shepelevo where Yulia and I swam every day in the summer.

The Likhobabins with my father in Shepelevo.

The front door to our Fifth Soviet apartment building and the passageway to the interior courtyard.

Our communal kitchen, just as we left it in 1973.

The stairway in the Fifth Soviet building, unrenovated since the Bolshevik Revolution.

The Fifth Soviet corridor gives whole new meaning to the phrase "revolutionary floor tile."

The beginning of the Road of Life across Lake Ladoga. The truck tire tracks are part of the memorial.

Yuliy Gneze standing between mass graves in Piskarev Cemetery.

What 125 grams of bread baked with sawdust and cardboard looks like.

With Papa on Catherine Canal on Lake Ladoga in Schlisselburg. Behind us is Oreshek Island, instrumental in the fight against the Germans in World War II.

Kirochnaya Ulitsa (previously Ulitsa Saltykov-Schedrin), the street where my characters Tatiana and Alexander met. The yellow buses remain unchanged since the war.

With Papa at the Romanov funeral in the courtyard of Peter and Paul's Cathedral.

Our driver Viktor with my father.

Flanked by Lida and Radik Tikhomirov outside their *dacha*.

Eating vanilla ice cream on a bench in the Summer Garden. They were out of crème brûlée.

The final photo of the trip, of Papa and me at Radik's *dacha*.

My new house and flowers in Texas.

dove off a mystical boat into the Black Sea, swam alongside each other at night, and the rest as they say is history.

But before the night swim in the sea, on this porch my mother sat, unable to keep still, unable to keep herself from smiling — at the artist, at the beach, at my father, not quite in love with him yet, but completely in love with being young and beautiful and alive.

How terrifying, how mesmerizing to see that moment.

My father got up to smoke. He kept coming back into the room, and every time he came back, he asked the same thing. "Well, was your mother beautiful? Was she beautiful? What do you think? She was like a goddess, wasn't she? So beautiful."

"She wasn't bad," I said.

"Wasn't bad?"

Everybody laughed.

My father nodded. "Wait till I tell her you said that. Just wait. I'll tell her in America. She won't talk to you for a decade."

"Plinka," Ellie said, "your papa tells me you want to photograph the smell in Shepelevo."

I glanced at him, shaking my head.

"And what *were* you writing," she went on, "while your papa slept in the car on the way back from Shepelevo?"

I stared at my father. He went out on the cluttered balcony to smoke.

So my father had asked Viktor, who had seemed too busy washing the car to observe anything, what I had been doing while he slept. And my father had deemed it important enough to pass along over a glass or four of vodka.

"What were you writing, Plinka?" Ellie repeated. "Were you writing about Shepelevo?"

"Yes, Shepelevo," I replied carefully.

"Yes," said Anatoly. "Your papa said you were very affected by Shepelevo. Is that true?"

"If he says so."

I wondered how long it would take him to turn this afternoon's trip to Fifth Soviet into a story.

As it turned out, just one more cigarette. He returned from the balcony and promptly told everyone how Svetlana had begged us to stay and eat her freshly made *pelmeni*.

"Stuffed cabbage," I corrected.

"And you should have seen the apartment," he continued. "In all this time, nothing has changed." He described the unevenness of the floors, the sagging of the walls. He stopped before he got to the toilet. Instead he recounted Svetlana's operatic singing.

He had so obviously been looking forward to *telling* the story of her singing to us. He told us colorfully, and we emoted colorfully. Ellie teared up. Anatoly made loud clucking noises. I shook my head. Like any good storyteller, he embellished the truth, and like all good listeners, we embellished our emotions. And then we all had another shot of vodka.

As we talked about 1962 and Dzhugba and 1963 and my birth, the subject naturally segued into one of my father's favorite topics: the Kennedy assassination. I was born two weeks before the President was assassinated. In Russia, any time someone remarks on the year of my birth, the next sentence always takes us to Kennedy and Oswald.

Thirstily downing his vodka and shaking his head, Anatoly turned to me. "Your father," he said, lowering his voice with incredulity, "thinks Oswald acted alone."

He glanced guiltily at my father, who tutted and went out to smoke.

"We used to argue about this all the time," Anatoly said. "I think he got tired of arguing."

"That would surprise me," I said. "Papa loves to argue. Especially when he's right."

"You think he is right?" Anatoly asked in the same hush-hush conspiratorial tone.

"Yes," I said. I wished I smoked, too, so that I might go out onto the balcony and have three seconds in the white night air with my father. We wouldn't have to talk about Oswald. We could just smoke.

With his brother and his wife listening raptly, Anatoly said, helped by another shot of vodka, "Yes, but …" he trailed off, shaking his head. "It's the head reeling *back* that stymies me," he said. "If he was shot from behind, why did his head snap back?" His brother clucked and nodded, thoughtfully pulling at the strands of his gray beard.

"Oh my God, you're not *still* talking about that!" my father said, back inside the living room.

Apparently when my father interviewed Mikhail Gorbachev a few years earlier for Radio Liberty, Gorbachev told my dad he had been keeping a major secret that he would take to his grave.

Anatoly thought this secret was about John F. Kennedy. He was certain that there was a conspiracy to kill Kennedy, and that Gorbachev knew the truth.

I looked excitedly at my father, who waved us all away and went back out onto the balcony. When he returned, he said, "So you think Gorbachev would know something like this and not tell?"

"Not tell *you*," corrected Anatoly.

"Not tell *anyone!*" my father said. "Anatoly, you can't keep quiet about what your wife is cooking for dinner, and here is a man who would *die* before he would talk about the second most traumatic event of the twentieth century?" He sat down and poured himself a glass of vodka. "The *first* being the murder of the Romanovs. Which is a perfect example of the point I'm making. The Romanov executioners couldn't keep quiet for *two months*. Knowing the very future of Bolshevism was at stake, *regardless*, they started vomiting up their stories over vodka, then keeping diaries, then writing books, then making full confessions on their deathbeds. All within a decade. The killing of the Romanov family was the first act of political terrorism in the twentieth century, that's why it was so monumental. And nobody could keep quiet about it. But about Kennedy, you think Gorbachev would keep quiet?"

My father said all this as if he had proven his point beyond any doubt, but Anatoly looked at him defiantly and said, "Yes."

Alla picked up on the Romanov thread. "Yuri Lvovich, why do you think there is such fascination with the Romanovs?"

"Why?" he said. "Because they were a family that was slaughtered, that's why. The Communists didn't kill a political leader, they didn't kill the Tsar. They killed a *family*. That's why."

"Papa, come on," I said, pepping up a bit. "Yes, the Romanovs were a family, but that's not why there is such fascination. They weren't killed because they were a *family*. They were killed because they were a *royal* family. He was the Tsar and she the Tsarina and their son the heir to the throne —"

"There was no more throne!" my father bellowed. "Nicholas abdicated. There was no more throne, no more Tsar! There was just the family."

"You think if the Ivanov family was killed by the Bolsheviks, anyone would care?"

"Who the hell are the Ivanovs?"

"Exactly."

Alla looked a little sorry she'd brought it up. "Plinochka, is it true you might be going inside the church for the funeral service?"

When Ellie heard that we might get inside Peter and Paul's, but that I didn't have a dress, she disappeared into another room.

I took the opportunity to say to my father, "Papa, only dead monarchs are entombed in Peter and Paul's Cathedral. The remains of an ordinary family would not be buried there."

"Hurry up, Mama!" Alla yelled to Ellie.

Ellie reappeared, holding in her hands a folded black garment.

"You can wear this," she said to me. "Just give it back, okay? Don't take it to Texas with you."

"Don't worry," I said, slowly unfolding the dress. It could have been worn by Ellie's great-grandmother, and probably had been. "You really don't have to do this."

"Why should you go out and buy yourself a dress to wear just once? It's absurd. Take it."

"I don't know if it will fit."

"It might be a little big. But so what?"

"You're right. Thank you so much."

Before I left with our driver Viktor, who had come back for me around midnight, my father said, "Tomorrow we go to Schlisselburg, God help me. I want Viktor to pick you up first and then come to get me. Ulitsa Dybenko is on the way."

*

I fell asleep on my back with the blinds open, the sun streaming in. Still fully dressed, my earrings in, shoes on my feet. I fell asleep because I couldn't write. I couldn't write about my day, about Fifth Soviet, about Piskarev, about Yuliy Gneze and his Volkhov front and the loaf of bread in the crook of his arm. I couldn't write about my ravishing joyous mother, as I had never known her.

I fell asleep, too tired even for dreams.

My mother in Dzhubga, 1962, when my father met and fell in love with her. She is twenty-two.

DAY FOUR
Thursday

YULIA

I only *thought* I was too tired for dreams. When I woke up it felt as if I hadn't gone to sleep at all. It felt like I had been reliving the same exhausting moment over and over throughout the night. What that moment was I could not say. It involved either mountain climbing or arduous linguistics. Or both. Or it might have been swimming butterfly-style in the Dead Sea.

I dragged myself off the bed, got myself out of my crumpled clothes and into the shower. It was eight in the morning. At eight-thirty, room service came: a tablespoon of black caviar and five tough little pancakes.

The phone rang. It was Kevin.

"Your mother called me ..."

"Why?" I said. "Papa hasn't called her and she was frantic?"

Kevin hemmed and hawed. "She called because she wanted to let you and your father know she might be having gall bladder surgery. The doctor thinks she has gallstones."

"Oh, for God's sake."

"I know. It's terrible."

"No, that's not it. When would the surgery be?"

"I think she's in the hospital now. I can't be sure, I could barely understand her. Something was wrong with her speech. They're doing more tests today, but I think then she's having the surgery."

"Of course she is. I thought you said she said they don't know if it's gallstones?"

"They *think* it's gallstones."

"She's having surgery because they *think* it's gallstones?"

"I know. It's terrible."

"No, that's not it. Mama didn't want Papa and me to have this trip in the first place. Now I'm going to tell him she is about to have surgery and he'll be upset for the next three days. Which is exactly her intention."

"Paullina, you have to tell him."

"I know, I know. But what if it's a false alarm?"

"You've got to tell him."

"I know. But, I mean, really."

"She says she hasn't felt well for three months."

"Try eight years. Oh, but during the six lousy days we're in Russia, that's when she decides to go get her gall bladder checked out? Why not in the three months before?"

"I have no answers. She is *your* mother."

*

We talked for too long, and then I didn't have time to walk the three blocks to Malaya Konyushennaya, the street on the embankment of Griboyedov Canal, to drop off my film: nine rolls so far.

Viktor picked me up promptly at 9:30, and together we walked along Griboyedov to the photo store. It was a crisp, brilliant morning. As we walked, Viktor told me about the apartment buildings Ellie and Anatoly (and my grandparents) lived in.

"They were built during the Khruschev era," he told me, "in the early sixties when the secretary general decided that each and every Soviet citizen was entitled to a living space of seven square meters. He authorized construction of hundreds, maybe thousands, of these tall, boxy buildings. They're called Khrushchyobi."

"But Viktor," I said, "we lived five of us to seven square meters. That's not what he intended, was it?"

"Communism," he said, shrugging.

I fell quiet.

"Speaking of Communism," Viktor said, "President Yeltsin has decided to drop in on the Romanov funeral, after all."

"Oh. Is that bad for us?"

"Well, not bad, but getting inside the church is now impossible. Heightened security. No one is going to let you in, no matter how much you spend on a black dress."

I laughed. "So no need to buy one, then?"

"You can still wear Ellie's, I suppose."

"I could, yes," I said slowly. The dress was four sizes too big and a foot too long. "I do have my suit, though."

We dropped off the film and walked back to Viktor's Volkswagen. We picked up my dad at Anatoly's at 10:30.

Anatoly was still home, wearing his robe.

"Ellie," I whispered, "is he not going to work today?"

"He hasn't decided," she said.

"Oh."

"He doesn't get paid for it anyway. He'll see how he feels."

Ellie asked us to come and have dinner with them again tonight. My father mumbled something indistinct, and Ellie didn't press further.

Before we left, Anatoly said, "Plinka, have you called Yulia yet?"

I hadn't, of course, but my father came to my rescue by saying, "She'll call her tonight."

In the car, he said, "Do whatever you want, Paullina. You can call her, invite her to dinner. Whatever you want. We have only a few days left. Tonight we might be back late. But you have tomorrow night, Friday." He shook his head. "I don't recommend it. If you want to see her, I won't come with you. It's too uncomfortable for me. I'll just go back to Tolya's."

Yulia was my father's brother's only child. But then we left Russia, and my uncle left his wife and Yulia, and got himself a new wife who had a child of her own. This new wife was intensely jealous of Yulia, and so my uncle abandoned Yulia and severed his bond with her. Consequently it became very difficult for the rest of the family to speak to her because she wanted from us what we could not give her — either an explanation or an intervention. My uncle could not and would not be shamed. So it remained from 1977 to 1998, broken and not right. My father did not like this kind of mess. He could barely tolerate messes of his own making. But to be confronted with the child of his brother, so needy, so questioning, was more than he could bear. He hardly wanted to step foot into our Fifth Soviet apartment. Yulia was like that apartment ten times over.

I understood. I let it go.

"Papa, what about taking Anatoly and Ellie out to dinner? We talked about that on Monday."

"Monday?" He repeated the word *Monday* as if I had said *nineteenth century*. "Again, Paullina, you cannot do everything."

We found the highway to Schlisselburg without once asking for directions. I thought this was a good time to clear my throat. I may have been able to drop Yulia, but I could not drop my mother.

"Papa, uh, I spoke to Kevin this morning. He said that Mama called him yesterday —"

"Yes?" He sat up straighter.

"Have you, um, called Mama yet?"

He grunted. "No."

I didn't think so. "Well, Kevin told me that Mama may have gallstones, and that she might need gall bladder surgery. I don't know how to say gall bladder in Russian. How do you say gall bladder in Russian?"

He sank down in his seat and became less interested. "I don't know," he said.

"Well, whatever it is in Russian, Mama might have it, and she might need to be operated on. She is waiting for the test results."

"Okay," was all he said.

"Mama asked Kevin to tell you, in case you called Maui and she wasn't there. She's not there because she's in the hospital. She didn't want you to be worried."

"Okay," my father said. "I'll try to call her."

We said nothing more about it, and soon my father became animated again, this time about the quality of the highway to Schlisselburg.

Highway 105 impressed Papa, who spent most of the forty-five-minute ride to Schlisselburg discussing what a similar well-built, four-lane highway could do for Russian civilization if it spanned the five hundred miles between Moscow and St. Petersburg instead of the seventeen miles between St. Petersburg and Schlisselburg. He said he wished he had some way to explain to the Russians that if they built a road like this between Moscow and St. Petersburg, they would transform Russia. He said if he weren't retiring, he would make a radio program on this very subject.

I wanted to mention that the Chunnel, the tunnel under the English Channel, took the British and the French nearly the whole of the twentieth century to build, and the sea at its narrowest point between Dover and Calais was only seventeen miles wide. So perhaps he was expecting too much from the Russians. Instead, I said, "Maybe there is no money."

"But there's money to throw into the military? Billions of rubles to throw into the military."

"Maybe the Russians don't want the enemy to march up the highway between its two major cities. Its *only* major cities."

"Maybe," my father said, "it's nothing but short-sightedness. Well, what do we expect? Seventy years of Communism will do that."

At the Neva, almost at the point it flowed out of Lake Ladoga, we drove across a bridge called Mariinsky and headed into Schlisselburg.

My father was right about one thing: why they built a highway to Schlisselburg was even more unfathomable once we saw Schlisselburg. It lay on the eastern bank of the Neva at the crest of the river's source in Lake Ladoga. The spot was propitious; the town was not.

Some wretched tenement buildings under a canopy of oaks, a desolate outdoor market, one cafeteria that was closed because it wasn't quite lunchtime. The only church in town was housed in what looked like an abandoned 7-Eleven building. "House of Prayer" the sign read. It didn't even have a cross on it. It could've said "House of Pelmeni."

There was nowhere to park and no one to ask directions to the ferry. From Schlisselburg there was supposed to be a ferry to the island fortress Oreshek. But there was no one to ask, and no signs for the island, or the ferry, or for the blockade Diorama Museum.

Bewildered silence fell inside our car. We were amazed Schlisselburg was like this, my father most of all. Viktor was least surprised, though even his pupils widened. As for me? After seeing Fifth Soviet, how could anything else surprise me? My father must have been recalling Gettysburg, Fort Sumter, Omaha Beach — places where storied battles had once been fought and were properly memorialized.

Not only had the greatest battle of Leningrad's siege been fought on these shores, but the nine-hundred-day Nazi blockade was broken here.

The dewy river shimmered and flowed beyond the oak leaves, a testament to the past, a path to the future. But there was still nowhere to park. Or buy a map, or get a sandwich, or ask a question, or buy a trinket. While my father and I complained, Viktor, with his usual equanimity, parked on the uncut grass and strolled to the banks of the Neva to find a ferry schedule.

I took a picture of a monument to Peter the Great. I had to beat my way through thick brambles to what had once been a clearing. Peter stood on a pedestal, looking proudly onto the underbrush and weeds. You couldn't see the river for the trees. I took one picture.

Viktor returned with a ferry schedule, and he and my father studied it like it was the Dead Sea Scrolls. My father looked worried.

"What's the matter?" I said. "Is there no ferry?"

"No, there is," my father slowly replied. "But the times are no good."

"Let me see." I glanced at the schedule. "The boat leaves at noon. It's now eleven-forty. Perfect."

"Yes, but the boat doesn't return until 2:25."

"So?"

"I'm not going to spend two hours on some island, Paullina. Not when we have so much to do." My father had worked out our whole day in his head, and it did not include two hours on an island, not even the island that saved Leningrad. He cleared his throat.

"Ideally what I'd like to do is take the noon boat to the island, and come back on the 12:25. That gives us about a half hour. Now *that's* perfect."

"Papa," I said incredulously, "how can we do that? The boat takes seven minutes just to *get* to the island. We wouldn't have a half hour. We'd basically get off and get back on again. Maybe we should just stay on the boat."

"*Paullina*," my father said with feeling. "You cannot do everything. You just can't. We have to choose. We can go to Oreshek, but then we can't go north to the Road of Life on the lake."

I stood my ground for a moment. "Why can't we do both?"

"Maybe you'd like to go to Kobona, too?"

"Yes."

He turned to Viktor. "Viktor! See what I mean? What to do?"

Viktor studied the schedule, trying to accommodate everybody. But my father, soon-to-be-retiring-or-not, was still his boss. I was only the boss's daughter.

We didn't go.

Getting back in the car, we drove down a dirt road to another grassy knoll and parked. Instead of taking the ferry, we took a walk on a narrow strip of grass between two canals. The first canal was built by Peter the Great in the 1700s, to protect trade ships and fishing boats from the heavy storms that often plagued the lake. But it wasn't sufficient, so Catherine the Great built another canal in the 1800s.

A mere two hundred meters separated Oreshek from the ten-foot-wide shore of Catherine's canal. Before the Bolshevik Revolution of 1917, the island was a Tsarist prison. It happened to be the prison where Lenin's brother Alexander Ulyanov was hanged in 1881 for conspiring to kill Alexander III. After the revolution, the prison became a museum, and in the spot where Ulyanov died, an apple tree was planted in his honor.

When the Germans occupied Schlisselburg and nearly the entire southeastern bank of the Neva during World War II, they perched on the narrow bank between the two canals, dug their trenches, and shelled the island. Schlisselburg remained in German hands until 1944. The Russian soldiers in Oreshek were supplied and replenished by the Red Army. Oreshek remained in Soviet hands.

But all that history warranted no more than twenty minutes, according to my father; any longer was too much. I was full of regret as we strolled down the strip of land that had once been the German front line. Meanwhile my dad spent the thirty minutes of our walk discoursing at length on the inadequate money-making capabilities of the Russians.

It was hard to argue with him. In the last fifty years, Schlisselburg had remained largely ignored by vacationers and tourists. The town was run-down in a typical Russian fashion, and the glorious lakeside coast, which anywhere else in the world would have long ago become developed and prosperous, lay fallow. In seventy years of rule by the proletariat for the proletariat, the Soviets had not even paved a road in town, except for the highway to nowhere.

My father and I discussed two other canals we had seen with our own eyes: the intercoastal waterways flanking the state of Florida, one on the Atlantic Ocean, one on the Gulf of Mexico. Yes, one could argue there were one too many nightclubs on the Gulf of Mexico, a few too many luxury yachts. But these excesses of Western civilization did not detract from the appeal of the coast. You could get a drink, breathe in the salty air, go for a boat ride, buy a new bathing suit, cluck at the magenta sun beyond the palms.

Here in Schlisselburg, alongside the historic Peter Canal, a potholed dirt road led to nothing. At the apex of a most magnificent view — the Neva opening up into a breathtaking oceanic expanse of Lake Ladoga — lay an ancient closed-down scrap-steel yard and nothing else. No houses, no cars, no shops, no people strolling.

On Catherine Canal a few old rowboats were moored. A squalid hut here and there showed us that some fishermen lived close to their boats. One of the huts had a caved-in roof.

"What happens to the huts when there's a storm?" I asked.

"Take a guess," replied my father.

"How could the Germans have entrenched on the land strip between the canals?" I asked. "How would they get there from across Peter Canal, anyway? Did they swim?"

"It was *winter*," my father said with a disdainful snort.

Oh, yeah. They just walked across the ice. "Okay. But the blockade lasted three years. What about in the summer? How did they get back and forth?"

"If I had a million dollars," my father said, "I would buy all this land. Heck, probably for a lot less than a million. I would buy it all."

"Well, you don't have a million dollars."

"But if I did," he said, "can you imagine? Can you even imagine what this would look like with some Western money? What a waste. Isn't it, Paullina? Isn't it, Viktor? A waste?"

"A waste," I agreed. "But what about the Germans?"

"They had boats," said Viktor. "They rowed across the canal."

"Where did they get the boats from? They didn't bring boats with them from Germany, did they?"

"No," my father said. "They stole them. From the fishermen."

We took a few more unenthusiastic pictures and left, my father all the while lamenting the Soviet lack of initiative.

One last time, I looked at Oreshek Island across the water. With its battered fortified walls, it was a baffling anachronism. It was as if Oreshek was *meant* to look exactly as it had in 1943. As if perhaps Schlisselburg was, too.

As if perhaps this was by design, not neglect. As if it was left as it had been then, in memoriam.

I thought of Shepelevo. I thought of Fifth Soviet and Gostiny Dvor. Had everything been left the way it had been, in memoriam?

"Paullina," my father said, patting my back. "Look at the Neva. It's something, isn't it? Just look at it."

I looked at him, smiling. "You like this river, don't you, Papa? You love this river."

He nodded ruefully. "Did you know the Neva is one of the fullest rivers in the world?"

"This I did not know."

"In spring, when the ice melts, you should see it. You think all is well — you're smelling the daffodils, looking forward to the lilacs — and then, boom, the ice on Lake Ladoga melts, and great icebergs float down the river to the Gulf of Finland. You should hear the noise."

"The noise of the icebergs?"

"Yes. For weeks it sounds like cannons going off, until it is all carried down into the gulf."

"Cannons?"

My father nodded. "Every single year the Leningrad spring sounds like war."

IN STORIED BATTLES

We went back to the car and Viktor drove us back to Mariinsky Bridge under which the Diorama of the Breaking of the Siege of Leningrad was located.

We parked by a tank. God forbid we should take the time to go near it. I gave it a cursory glance — a placard said its name was "Breakthrough" — and hurried to catch up with my father, who was calling me. "Paullina! For once, stop dawdling! Come on." Glancing back, I saw fresh roses lying on the tank's treads.

Ours was the only car in the parking lot adjacent to the museum. There was grass growing through the cracks in the asphalt, which was surprising considering the museum opened only a few years ago in 1994, on the fiftieth anniversary of the lifting of the blockade. Four years later the weeds were already winning.

The museum looked tiny and uninviting from the outside. It was just a low–to-the-ground dark-gray granite building. Above the doorway were inscribed the words, "Breaking of the Leningrad Blockade."

Inside was even more uninviting, all somber and slate-cold.

The entire museum was one room. Two ladies sat at a desk inside the front door.

"Would you like to go in?" one of them asked.

"I suppose," I said. "What's in here?"

"Why, the diorama, of course. Have you not heard of our diorama?" She lifted her eyes to the slate ceiling as if to God. "Wait until you see. That will be five rubles, please. Each."

I looked around and couldn't see a thing except for a dim blue light emanating from the center of the room behind the girls.

As I paid, I whispered to Viktor, "What's a diorama, anyway? And why so dark?"

We walked toward the blue light.

"It's dark," Viktor said, "so that nothing will draw your eyes away from it."

*

I stepped up onto a platform and before me opened up the ragged shores of the Neva in the pre-dawn hours of a bitter winter morning.

I was looking at a life-size panorama of the river in which actual objects and figures were set against a painted backdrop.

The objects were tanks, trenches, guns, artillery. The figures were Russian soldiers charging across the Neva ice, singularly to their deaths but collectively toward the liberation of Leningrad.

A stout Russian woman with a laser pointer appeared and began telling us about what happened on the banks of the Neva for six days in January, 1943.

She talked slowly, stopping frequently. At some point, two other visitors had arrived: a Finnish woman and her translator. I realized it was for the translator that our lecturer stopped every few sentences, and as she stopped, the scene she was haltingly painting — the ice, the blood, the fire and Oreshek up in smoke — burned itself into my heart.

"For six days," the lecturer said, "the Soviet troops attacked the Nazi defenses across the Neva at Schlisselburg."

My eyes wide and my mouth wider, I stood mutely, staring at the expanse of the river in miniature. My father and Viktor stood slightly behind me.

"Look over here," the lecturer said, pointing across the Neva. "We were trying to unite our northern Leningrad front with the Volkhov front. Neither Leningrad nor the Red Army could endure another winter like the winter of 1941–42 when millions of civilians and soldiers starved to death. We needed to cross the river, remove the Germans and unite the two fronts. It wasn't easy. The Germans were well entrenched and well fortified. But it was break the blockade or die. We had to succeed at all cost. At whatever the cost."

Another pause for the Finns. The Finnish woman didn't look particularly impressed by what the translator was telling her.

"This was not the first attempt to break the blockade," the lecturer resumed. "Do you see these bodies over here?" With her laser she pointed to the mass of bloodied forms lying on the ice a little downriver. "Half a kilometer away on the frozen Neva, six hundred bodies lay as a testament of the failure of the first attempt to break the blockade, just six days before, on the sixth of January."

Pause for the Finns.

Turning to my father, I whispered, "Six hundred is a *lot*."

"Shh," he said with a slow blink. "And listen." I turned back to the diorama, and behind me I heard his quiet voice. "It seems like a lot, I know, considering that on the first day of the D-Day invasion, on Omaha Beach, two thousand Americans died."

"Yeah."

"But just listen."

The woman continued. "For six days, starting on January 12, the fighting that you see before you went on. The blockade was finally broken on January 19, 1943. On that day, our Leningrad troops hugged their Volkhov counterparts."

My mother was born on January 19. She celebrated her third birthday when the blockade was broken.

Pause. Smoke everywhere. You could barely see the planes overhead for the smoke. Fires raged along the southern shore, where the Nazis were.

"On January 20, the People's Volunteers began to build the railroad across the Neva across the very place the six hundred bodies lay." She pointed with her laser. "The first thing the civilians did was carry away the dead. The second thing they did was build a railroad from Leningrad to Volkhov."

Pause. The Finns clucked appreciatively.

"The volunteer force comprised sixty percent women."

More impressed clucking.

I saw a tarp-covered army truck with a Red Cross symbol emblazoned on its side. Beyond it a tank was treading across the ice. In front of the tank, horses lay dead.

"The women built the railroad over land and over ice on the Neva in seventeen days. On February 7, the first train carrying butter from Volkhov arrived at Finland Station in Leningrad."

Pause. The sky heaving smoke. I could barely hear the lecturer.

"The Germans bombed this railroad for the next year, and soon, in contrast with the Lake Ladoga truck route, which was known as the Road of Life, this one came to be called the Road of Death."

Pause. The Finns stopped clucking.

"But it was also called the Road of Victory. Because although it kept being bombed, the railroad did not stop working. The Germans never regained this territory."

Pause. I looked across the river at Schlisselburg — all smoke. Oreshek to the left — all smoke. I wanted to step down into the bunkers to escape the haze. I had no courage. The men in front of me were charging the river. I was next.

"The Germans remained armed in a place called Sinyavino Heights. They loved high positions, the Germans. They bombed our railroad from there. Hitler's Army Group Nord remained in Sinyavino for months after the siege was lifted because we could not get them down from the hills."

Pause.

"If you get a chance, do go up to the memorial in Sinyavino. It's fabulous."

My father whispered behind me, "Don't even think about it."

The soldier in front of me was bleeding to death on the ice, holding up the Soviet flag as high as he could. His eyes were on me. I wondered if the flag would be too heavy for me to pick up and carry. I was hypnotized by the blazing hammer and sickle. I did not answer my father.

He whispered, "Are you listening to this?"

I barely nodded, without turning around.

"Ask her a question," he said. "Ask her while I go outside for a smoke."

I thought, no need, there is plenty of smoke right here. Look at the sky. I said nothing.

"Ask her," my dad whispered, his voice breaking, "how many men died during those six days."

He left.

I raised my hand, then quickly put it down. I wasn't in school — what was I doing?

"Excuse me," I said. "Tell me, please, how many men died in this six-day battle?"

The lecturer, smiling helpfully, said, "During the six days that it took to break the blockade, nineteen thousand Germans died."

"But how many Russians?"

"One hundred and fifteen thousand."

I spun around and there was my father, standing back from me in the distance, nodding in the dark, crying.

I whirled back to my men. I needed to get inside my bunker. *115,000 boys* in six days. One of them right in front of me, holding high the hammer and sickle for Mother Russia. The truck with the Red Cross symbol couldn't get to him fast enough. The tanks and the dead horses were in the way.

America lost 300,000 men during four years of war. In this one obscure battle, 115,000 men died.

Schlisselburg was a blip on the most detailed map of the war and barely a mention in the most thorough history books. The good ones said of Schlisselburg, "And here on the shores near Schlisselburg, some of the battles for the defense of Leningrad were fought."

*

Only a moment ago I was feeling slightly resentful that we hadn't gone to Oreshek. It all fell away from me. The Battle for Leningrad flowed into me. I could reach out with my hand and touch the trenches, that's how close they were, and beyond them, I could run out myself onto that blue ice at dawn. My soldiers were exploding as German planes flew low overhead, bombarding us. We picked up one more soldier, but he died in our arms. We lay him down on the bloodied ice. Red, white, metallic blue, gray tanks, gray uniforms, red blood.

It was all in front of me, as if it had been built for me. After all my longing, I had been transported here as if by magic, by providence, for understanding. By the time I understood, I was drowned in this world. Like a drinker before her coveted bottle of wine, I opened my throat. I was no longer a spectator but a participant. I put my hand over my heart. I could barely breathe.

Then and there, between the Finnish pauses — thank God for Finland! — I felt, no, I *knew* that it was here in Schlisselburg that my Bronze Horseman came alive and jumped off his pedestal, just as he had in Pushkin's poem, and galloped away through the streets of Leningrad. I shuddered. The horseman came alive and for the rest of Eugene's days chased him through the streets of St. Petersburg, through that maddening dust, until Eugene went mad. Was my horseman also going to chase me down my days through the maddening dust?

This is what I came to see. This is what I came to Russia for.

I came for the Bronze Horseman, and I found him here, rearing up in the cold slate building in front of 115,000 dying Russian soldiers.

I felt it all inside me, twisting and warping its way into fiction, into drama.

Though not much was needed to warp it into drama.

The dead, where did they go? Were they buried in the river? I didn't ask.

THE BRAVEST OF THE BRAVE

"I know that one hundred and fifteen thousand soldiers dead seems like many — too many," the lecturer said, "but right here," — she pointed with her red dot to a tiny remote location on the south-eastern banks of the Neva — "two hundred and forty thousand men died during the course of the war, in a place called Nevsky Patch."

Nevsky Patch. That was the place Yuliy Gneze told me about as he carried a loaf of bread in the crook of his arm through a concrete museum building in Piskarev Cemetery.

I stared at the little place across from me on which her red laser dot had landed. I could barely see for the smoke. What was she pointing to? And wasn't that the German side? She must have been mistaken; the Germans must have been the ones to lose those men, because —

"Two square kilometers held by Russian soldiers in enemy territory on the southern bank," she continued. "Our men occupied this little patch in the fall of 1941. They were supplied with food, ammunition and new soldiers by boats from across the river."

I began to ask, "How long …?" but broke off. I couldn't get the words out. This was ridiculous. I was not going to get emotional in front of Viktor and the two Finns. After pausing to compose myself, I tried again. "How *long* did they hold that land?"

"For five hundred days," she replied, "they held those two square kilometers against the Germans." She paused, her own voice cracking. How many times has she given this lecture? "They were the bravest of the brave," she said.

I remembered what Yuliy Gneze had told me. *They went there to die*, he said. *No one came back from Nevsky Patch.*

I turned away from the lecturer. Behind me, my father was listening with his own stricken face. There was nowhere to hide.

I turned back to the blue diorama.

"Right after the war," the lecturer said, "the Leningrad city council attempted to plant some trees at the memorial site for Nevsky Patch. Nothing grew. They tried again — twenty years later. Nothing grew. They tried again — thirty years later, on the fiftieth anniversary of the end of war. The council attempted to plant some trees in the soldiers' honor, but one tree after another died, their roots turning up."

"Why?" I said hoarsely. I cleared my throat. "Why?"

Behind me I heard Viktor whisper, "Metal."

"Because the ground was full of metal," the lecturer replied. "Nothing could grow, even fifty years later. To this day nothing grows on that fallow ground. It's all metal: weapons of the fallen soldiers, enemy artillery, bullets, knives. And their bones."

I turned to Viktor. "Viktor, did you know about this?"

He nodded. "All the Russians know. Nevsky Patch has acquired legendary status over the years."

"Have you been there?"

"Yes."

"Was it like Piskarev?"

Viktor shrugged. "At least they are buried in Piskarev. At Nevsky Patch, they lie where they fell. The soldiers made barricades out of the dead bodies."

"Oh my God."

"I know," he said. "So not quite like Piskarev."

Shell-shocked, I bought some books at the front desk and talked to Ludmilla, the woman who sold them to me. She said she had lived in Schlisselburg since she was a little girl.

The lecturer came over and shook my hand, introducing herself. Her name was Svetlana.

"So where do you girls go shopping?" I asked, me of the NorthPark and Galleria malls in Dallas. I was trying to change the subject to something facile.

"We don't go shopping much," Svetlana admitted.

"But you have to buy things, don't you? Clothes, coats?"

"Not really," Svetlana said. "We don't need much."

Ludmilla and Svetlana had been working at the Diorama Museum since it opened in 1994. They got paid seventy rubles a month. "Theoretically," interjected Svetlana with a chuckle. "We haven't been paid in three months."

"I almost died in Schlisselburg," Ludmilla said, as if that was the reason she could not leave town.

In September 1941, Ludmilla explained, as she was crossing the Neva with her family to evacuate, their boat was torpedoed by the Germans and sank. Her parents drowned. Ludmilla grabbed her one-year-old brother and clung to him in the near-freezing water.

"We would have gone down for sure," she said, "but for an eighteen-year-old nurse who saved us."

"How old were you?" I asked.

"I was four."

Ludmilla was a year younger than my father.

My father appeared next to me and was nodding as if he were listening; he even mumbled, "That's incredible." But suddenly he said, "Girls, I cannot tell you how this place would change with a little money, a few restaurants, some vacation homes. I mean, you have a beautiful place here in Schlisselburg. World-class beautiful. If I had a million dollars, I would buy up all the land between those canals of yours, and then this would really be something. That's all that I'd need. A million dollars."

The two women smiled blankly at him.

"Papa, let's go," I said.

*

Outside, I turned to him, exasperated. "What are you doing? Those women haven't been paid in three months and you're going on about what you would do with a million dollars?"

"I'm just saying."

"Okay. Do you want to go and look at the tank?"

"Not really. We need to get going. We spent too long in there."

I didn't think we spent long enough.

I heaved myself into the car. "Papa, do you think this place we're going to, the Road of Life, will have a bathroom?"

"Are you joking?"

"Or somewhere along the way?"

"You are joking, right? I can never tell with you."

"I *really* need a bathroom." I had gotten my period, but I was hardly going to tell my father that. I needed a bathroom *that instant*.

"Go back to those women. Maybe they'll let you use theirs. They must have a latrine. It's a world-class military museum. Even the Finns have come."

I returned to the women, while my father and Viktor waited in the car.

"Svetlana," I said, "do you have a ladies' room I can use?"

She glanced at me awkwardly and then gestured toward the exit.

"Come," she said walking with me. "I'll take you. Frankly, I'm ashamed. It's in the woods, behind the museum. But someone stole the doors off it."

"Stole the doors off the toilet?"

"Yes."

"Well, why doesn't someone, maybe the city council, give you new doors?"

"They'd have to pay us first."

We walked down a path along the highway until just before the entrance to Mariinsky Bridge. The few sparse white birches did not look like a forest; they were more like an anomaly. The grass was uncut — naturally.

In the near distance I saw something I thought could *not* be an outhouse. It was a tall rectangular structure of corroded steel with a letter M on top.

It was the outhouse. M was for men, engraved helpfully above the opening where the door used to be. I could smell the toilet from thirty feet away. The stench was particularly harsh because we were in the open country. You'd think the freshness of the flowing Neva and the blooming grasses would've masked it, filtered it. But no. Nature was inadequate to battle a smell of such intensity. The men's side was first.

The outhouse was all metal. The missing door had probably been metal too. Maybe the door pilferer sold it for scrap. Maybe not *sold* it, but *bartered* it.

The toilet inside was a square hole in the ground lined in concrete, and the concrete was covered in excrement.

Pressing my lips shut, I looked at Svetlana. I was trying not to breathe. I didn't want to offend this nice woman by retching. People can be sensitive to that sort of thing. Can take it the wrong way.

"The men's side *is* awful," Svetlana said. Her face was full of acute embarrassment. "Please come around this way," she said. "To the women's side. The women's is cleaner."

We walked around the metal structure to the women's half. There were no doors on the women's side, either. Inside was a square hole in the ground lined in concrete. The concrete was covered with excrement.

I couldn't divine Svetlana's criteria for "cleaner," and I didn't dare ask. I could think of nothing to say except a limp and desperate, "Is there any toilet paper?"

"Nnn — no," Svetlana said, furrowing her brow. "There is no toilet paper." She paused. "Do you … *need* toilet paper?"

I stepped away. "You know what? I'm fine. I'll wait. But thank you anyway."

"Are you sure?"

"Absolutely."

As we walked back, she said, "Excuse us, please."

"No, no," I said. "Please don't worry." I wanted to say, it is *I* who needs to be excused by *you*, for intruding on your life. I am the last thing you need.

"We usually just go into the woods," Svetlana said.

"For everything? Even the, um, the big things?"

"Well, usually, we wait for those until we get home."

I walked carefully, trying not to rattle my bladder on the uneven ground.

"So whoever stole them, stole both doors?"

"Yes. Both doors."

I was silent.

Brightening up a little, Svetlana said, "You know, President Yeltsin came to see our diorama a couple of years ago, and we thought maybe they'd give us some new doors for the toilet then, but his people just brought a portable toilet with them. When he left, they took their toilet. And can you believe it, they didn't even let us glance at Yeltsin. They locked us in the basement."

My astonishment must have been bald on my face, because she nodded and chuckled. "I know. Not a single peek at him." She sounded more upset about not getting a glimpse of the Russian president than she did about the toilet.

"But who got to tell him the story of breaking the blockade?" I wanted to know. "You tell it so well."

Svetlana shrugged. "They have their own people for that."

When I said goodbye, I held her hand for a moment.

In the car my father asked how it went.

"I decided to wait."

He whirled around. "There was no toilet?"

"Oh, there was."

When I told him, my father didn't know whether to laugh or shake his head. He did both.

"It's easier for them to requisition a port-a-toilet from somewhere, like Poland," he said, "than to replace those metal doors. In any case, they were hardly going to send Yeltsin into the woods to pee in a hole." But that was funny to him. He laughed again.

We drove away from the diorama, from the tank with the roses, and the dying man on the ice.

On the way to the Road of Life, my father told me the story of the writer André Gide, who came to Russia in 1936 and wrote a scathing book about his visit. Gide's chief complaint was that there was no toilet paper to be found anywhere in the Soviet Union. Aleksei Tolstoy, a Russian writer and Leo's nephew, after reading Gide's book said viciously, "That's right, because of course all André ever thinks about is his ass." Gide, apparently, was a known homosexual.

We drove northward up the western coast of Lake Ladoga. Viktor called the road "The Broken Ring."

"Why do you call it that?" I asked.

"Because," he replied, "the memorial to the start of the Road of Life is a concrete ring that's broken at the top, symbolizing that the Soviets broke the blockade with this ice route years before Schlisselburg."

"Papa, what did you think of the diorama?"

"What *can* one think of it? What about that Nevsky Patch?" He shook his head. "You know your dedushka, my father?"

"Yes, I know my dedushka, your father."

"Don't be fresh. Do you remember his brother, Semyon? He was an engineer during the war; he repaired airplane engines for the Red Army. Semyon told me that *all* the pilots in his company died. They either died in the air or they died while landing, because in those days planes didn't have the stabilizing third brake. He said before the pilots went out, they drank, they smoked, went to sleep and when they woke up, they flew out to die."

"All of them?"

"That's what he said. All of them."

"Papa, do you think we'll have time to go to Nevsky Patch?"

"Are you crazy? We don't have time today to eat. Have you noticed we haven't eaten?"

"That's because there is nowhere to buy food."

"We can't go to Nevsky Patch."

"It's worth seeing," Viktor piped in.

"Everything is worth seeing, Viktor!" my father exclaimed. "But we cannot see everything."

"What about Saturday? Isn't it on the way to somebody on Saturday?"

Shaking his head, my father said, "Nevsky Patch is on the way to nowhere, I already told you."

We stopped to get some food at a small open market. "Fresh bread," a sign read.

"Will there be a toilet here?" I asked. It had now been over a half hour since the time I had to use the ladies' room *instantly*.

"Absolutely not," said my father. "Not even a possibility."

We bought some bread of dubious freshness, tomatoes, cucumbers, cherries, 200 grams of bologna, 200 grams of lamb bologna, and *kvas* — a Russian drink made from bread. For one ruble, or sixteen cents, Viktor also bought a replica Swiss Army knife.

"For a ruble?" I said. "Wow."

"Pretty good, huh?" He smiled. "Made in Taiwan."

On the way to the car, I bought a crème brûlée ice cream, which was the only thing I wanted. I sat in the back of Viktor's car and ate the ice cream with the gusto one usually reserves for reading a fantastic book: greedily, then slowing down at the end because it is too good to finish. Every few licks, I paused to gaze at the caramel-colored ice cream in its plain wafer cone.

My father kept turning around and asking, "Well, how is it? How is it?"

"It's everything I thought it would be."

These three things: the smell of Shepelevo, the smell of the metro and the taste of crème brûleé ice cream. The essence of my childhood in Russia.

The rest of it — well, I didn't want to remember.

Viktor pulled over to the shoulder.

"What are you doing?" I asked. "We're not there yet, are we?"

"This is a good place," he said, turning to me. "There is no one here."

"A good place for what?" I said, staring deep into the well of my diminishing ice cream.

"Go into the woods, do your business. You'll feel much better."

"Viktor," I said. "Please. Who are you talking to? Drive. I'm not going into the woods."

My father scowled. "Stop it, you fool. You will have to go in the woods in the end. Go now and end your misery — and ours. You haven't stopped talking about a bathroom."

"No, I will not end your misery," I said. "At Broken Ring, there's bound to be something."

"There will be nothing, I tell you!" my father said. "Nothing! Go now."

"I can't."

"Ah, hell," said my father. Viktor pulled out into the road and drove on.

He slowed down several more times before we got to Broken Ring. Each time he said, "This is not a bad spot. Secluded. Go here."

"No."

How they laughed at me. Yes, my father laughed, but underneath I could tell he wished he could just order me to go, as if I were still a child or an employee under his control.

The Broken Ring memorial, near the tiny village of Kokorevo, is on the west coast of Lake Ladoga. The Road of Life stretched twenty miles (or thirty kilometers) across the iced-over lake to Kobona, on the other shore. During the desperate winter of 1941, the Leningrad city council and the Red Army fashioned this trail across the frozen lake. Army trucks inched their way through the night to bring bread to the dying Leningraders. They built the road across one of the narrowest points of the lake, which at its widest is over seventy miles: three times as wide as Long Island; as wide as the entire state of Israel.

The trucks carried bread and sugar from Kobona to Leningrad and picked up evacuating Leningrad residents and transported them to relative safety in Kobona, while being bombarded by German air power. The Russians set up land-to-air artillery missiles to fight the Luftwaffe, and little by little, in the dead of night, with only the headlights of the trucks showing the way, they rolled across the ice to save dozens, possibly hundreds, from dying. Some trucks fell to German air strikes. Some fell through the ice.

The narrow road we were on extended pin straight into the distant horizon. There were no crossroads, no houses, just birch and pine forest. Up ahead, two kilometers away, we could see the memorial rising up out of the ground like a shorter Arch of St. Louis. From a distance, the ring didn't look broken.

The highway ended at the monument. We stopped the car. There was no place to park. Viktor pulled onto the grass. The ring still didn't look broken.

"Where is it broken?" I asked Viktor.

"Right on top. Do you see?"

The ring was a giant concrete semi-circle. Under it, tire tracks snaked through the asphalt, vanishing into the wetland cattails of the flattened lake.

Only when I came close did I see the break in the ring, at the very apex, barely six inches wide. The two spans of the arch did not quite meet. Considering the ring was forty feet tall, it was a tiny break indeed.

A wedding party was gathered beneath the ring, taking photographs. The bride was clowning around, throwing her veil above her head and dancing on the tire tracks. Why would anyone want to come here to have their wedding pictures taken?

"There must be a bathroom here," I said to my father. "A wedding party wouldn't come here if there weren't a bathroom."

"Yeah, right," he said. "Why don't you go ask the bride. Ask her where she goes to pee."

"I bet *she* doesn't go in the woods."

"I bet she does," said Viktor.

I walked up to the bride. "Congratulations," I said. "Excuse me, but is there a bathroom around here?"

She shook her veiled head. I could tell she was surprised by my question.

"There are no conveniences here," she said in the casual tone of someone who expects nothing else.

I wanted to point out that a toilet was more a necessity than a convenience, but I smiled and said, "Of course. Thank you."

After the bridal party left, my father came up to me and said with a smirk, "Did you ask the bride if she lifted up her wedding dress when she peed in the woods?"

"No, I did not."

He laughed heartily. "What did I tell you? I told you there would be nothing here. I told you to go in the woods. Who told you?"

Viktor pointed out that there were still plenty of woods around us.

"She can't go here!" my father said in an affronted tone. "It's the Road of Life memorial, for God's sake."

Besides the memorial and, nearby, an old Zenith land-to-air artillery gun, there was nothing else around, and I mean nothing. It was marshland. Long grasses grew right out of the water. After ten minutes we left. It was three o'clock. My father and Viktor were starving.

*

We decided to go down the dirt road to the beach, where we could have a swim and then a picnic.

"It's a paid beach," my father said, "so there's bound to be a toilet there."

Not bloody likely.

The potholed road was hard on my bladder.

"Viktor, gently. Please."

"Harder, Viktor, harder." My father laughed. "That's right, like that. Teach her a lesson."

At the gate to the beach, an attendant took ten rubles from us. Papa asked him about a toilet.

"Toilet? No, no," the man said, surprised by the question. "No toilet here."

"Why would there be?" I said.

"Exactly," the man replied.

"Makes you wonder what we're paying for," my father remarked as we drove on.

After Viktor parked, he retrieved from the trunk some harsh-looking unbleached toilet paper he had bought at the market for just such an occasion.

"Take this," he said. "Go down the path and into the woods."

Vanquished by the merciless demands of my treacherous body, I went into the woods. How ridiculous I must have seemed to Viktor, walking lamely down the forest path, holding my little purse in my hands as if I were at the Plaza Hotel, and was just popping into the marble bathroom to freshen up a tad.

I did what I had to. In a matter of seconds, every part of me that was exposed was stung by black ravenous mosquitoes.

As I was returning from the woods, I saw my father and Viktor changing into their swimming trunks by the car. That was the last thing I needed to see, so I turned around.

"Paullina, where are you going?" my father called after me.

"Giving you some privacy, Papa."

"Come back."

I came back.

"Papa, I read somewhere that there is no word in Russian for *privacy*. Is that true?"

He frowned. "Let me think about it," he said. "I'll tell you in a minute."

In a minute, he said, "There is a word for private property."

"No, Papa. I want a word for privacy. As in *I'll give you some privacy.*"

Clearing his throat, he said, "No, I can't think of it. I guess there isn't."

"I understand," I said. "Suddenly I understand everything."

As we walked to the beach, Viktor said, "You mustn't feel bad about the woods. The woods are often the best place to go. Clean, hygienic."

Yeah, I wanted to say, with 150 million people using the woods as one large *unprivate* public toilet, very clean and hygienic.

My father and Viktor had a swim in Lake Ladoga. The day was blazingly sunny, and almost warm, 63°F — as warm as a sunny winter's day in Texas. I touched the water gingerly with the tip of my big toe. It was cold. Standing up to his torso in the water, my father called out, "Paullina, what a shame you didn't bring your bathing suit!"

"Yes, isn't it just," I said, taking the tip of my big toe out of the water.

I went back to the car, sat on a rock and leafed through one of the books on the blockade I had bought at the diorama.

Two hundred and forty thousand dead at Nevsky Patch, a place the rest of the world has never heard of.

The memorial there reads:

You the living — Know this!
We didn't want to leave this land,
And we didn't.
We stood to the death on the banks of the dark Neva,
We died so you could live.

*

Viktor and Papa came back and dried off. At the market, Viktor had very smartly bought a plastic picnic set that came with a little plastic picnic rug, which we now laid out on the ground next to the car. Problem was, it kept blowing away. So we put the bologna and the tomatoes on it to hold it down. Then we put our shoes on it. Then there was nowhere left for us to sit.

My father stood. I sat on my rock. Viktor squeezed in between the shoes and the bologna. Getting out his replica Swiss Army knife, he attempted to cut the tomatoes. Instantly I saw why his knife had cost sixteen cents. He may as well have been cutting the tomatoes with a spoon. First the juice started pouring out. Then the seeds. Then only the tomato skin was left in his hands, intact except for the gouges.

"Viktor, the knife is no good," my father said.

"What do you expect for a ruble?"

"Here, Viktor, let me," I said, fishing around in my purse. I took out my small bought-in-America Swiss Army knife, which cost ten bucks and was actually made in Switzerland. The knife effortlessly cut a tomato into paper-thin slices and then cut some neat squares of pumpernickel bread. Those Swiss. They were busy designing a perfect utility knife while the rest of the world was making and using automatic rifles.

We ate. My father and Viktor drank the *kvas*.

"Plinka, do you want some?" my father asked.

"No thanks," I said. "I'd rather have my bread in a sandwich."

Besides, I had learned the hard way: *liquid in, liquid out.* I wasn't going to drink another sip of anything until my flight home on Sunday.

We talked in more detail and at further length about the real estate possibilities of Lake Ladoga, the largest lake in Europe and the least inhabited. So what if it was covered with a sheet of ice two solid meters deep for eight months of the year? That didn't matter. This was *the* tourist attraction of the twenty-first century, according to my father and Viktor.

I wasn't paying attention to them. I was thinking of Schlisselburg, of Nevsky Patch.

The diorama of Schlisselburg, January 1943, Operation Spark, to show the breaking of the German blockade around Leningrad.

*

On the way back, my father slept. I was silent. All I could think about was the blue Neva ice at dawn, of losing 115,000 men in six days, of two square kilometers flooding with Russian blood.

As we passed Schlisselburg, I leaned forward and whispered, "Viktor, how about if you drive on, to Nevsky Patch?"

"Oh, Paullina," said Viktor. "Your father will kill me."

"He'll never know," I said. "He'll be asleep until Grand Hotel Europe. We'll be quick. Fifteen minutes."

"But it's an hour or more out of our way."

"So?"

"Your father will wake up."

"Trust me, he won't."

"He will wake up at the hotel and wonder why it is eight o'clock instead of six."

"Tell him we were stuck in traffic."

"Oh, Paullina. What traffic?" There was no one on the road.

I imagined walking through a land of bones and bullets on which nothing grew. I leaned back. I closed my eyes.

When I opened them again, we were at Grand Hotel Europe.

SPEAK SOFTLY LOVE

My father showered in my room.

I phoned home and talked to my three-year-old Misha — finally! Poor boy. It had been five days.

He began with, "I'm so happy, Mommy." So happy he finally got me on the phone.

Afterward, while my father was getting dressed, I went for a walk around the hotel. I found the clothing boutique and looked for a black dress. I would have bought it had I been going inside the cathedral for tomorrow's funeral.

All I can say is thank God for President Yeltsin. The only wearable dress cost three hundred and seventy-five units, and it wasn't black.

*

Without our coats, because it was a sweet warm evening, we walked five minutes to Dom Knigi — House of Books — Leningrad's most celebrated bookstore, located in the shabby splendor of a green and gray Art Nouveau masterpiece of a building, glorious but desperately in need of restoration. My father was not talkative and told me he would wait for me on the street.

"Hurry up," he said, leaning against the historic gray granite and lighting a cigarette.

There are a few fundamental skills one needs to run a successful bookstore. One is a loose knowledge of alphabetization and some of its practical applications.

Dom Knigi disagreed.

Perhaps they had some other system of classification of books that I was not aware of.

"I'm looking for books about the blockade," I said to the clerk.

A young, bleached-blonde, sloppy-looking girl stared at me wanly and spoke only when she was good and ready.

"The blockade? Berlin?"

"Um, I was thinking of Leningrad."

"Oh." Silence. Then, "Did you try upstairs?"

"No."

"Try upstairs."

"Thanks," I said. "What about maps?"

"Maps of the blockade?"

"No. Just generally of this region."

She sighed. "Try upstairs."

Upstairs was run-down, unfriendly, and had no maps. There was no one at the service desk, and I had to wait five minutes before I could ask where they were hiding their history section. The man pointed me to the front window, where I found five shelves of books in no discernible order. I went back to the desk, and after waiting for him five more minutes asked where I could find books on the Leningrad blockade.

"Leningrad? What are you doing upstairs?"

"Well —"

"They're downstairs, of course, in the World War II section. Just look through there. You'll find what you need."

I left the store.

On the street my father looked cranky and hungry. He was having a little trouble walking.

"I just need to pick up my photos," I said to him. "It's not far."

"I'm going to wait for you right here," he said, settling into a stone bench beneath a lone tree on Griboyedov Canal.

"Are you okay?" I asked.

"We haven't eaten," he said. "I'm not feeling very well. I'm a little dizzy — it's just my diabetes. Go get your pictures. But hurry, I want to eat."

I ran to get my silly photos from the Kodak store, so my poor diabetic father wouldn't have to wait too long before we ate.

*

We had dinner at Sankt Peterburg, a Russian restaurant on Griboyedov Canal, next to *Spas Na Krovi*. A lifetime ago on Monday, my father had promised me we would see this church again, and here we were, casting it a passing glance as we made our way down the steps of a darkened restaurant.

I had exquisite black caviar with *blini*, excellent *pelmeni* and substandard chocolate mousse. My father had *solyanka*, a thick meat soup, and *pelmeni*.

He said he didn't want any dessert but then polished off my mousse.

Since the tap water in all of Leningrad was undrinkable, I was forced to buy a tiny bottle of Evian, which at thirty rubles was twice as expensive as my father's giant glass of beer, which he drank down to chase down his similarly low-priced double shot of vodka.

He was tired at first, but after a bit of food and drink he brightened. We talked about his retirement.

"Papa," I said, "there are two things you love: fishing and gardening. Where are you going to grow your tomatoes on Maui? How are you going to sit in your boat?" He couldn't have a boat on the ocean; too dangerous and unfamiliar, and he was too old to learn.

"What boat? What tomatoes?"

"Exactly."

My father mentioned something about fishing off a pier. I remained unconvinced. "Are you really going to stand on a pier? Are you going to stand in two feet of water?"

"If I have to."

"It's not the same as sitting in a boat."

"No," he said. "But the sun sets on the ocean; do you know what that's like?"

"No," I said sadly. I knew only the Atlantic with its sunrise-facing shores.

"Well, it's quite a sight. Besides, you are wrong. I love three things. Yes, fishing and gardening. But the third one is your mother. Maui is the perfect place for her, so I will be happy there, too. I can be happy anywhere."

I thought. "You also love the Yankees."

"What, they don't have television on Maui?"

"You won't be able to watch the games live." Hawaii was on tape delay for sports coverage because of prime time.

"I'll tape them. It'll be fine."

"You also love movies."

"Yes."

"Instead of gardening or fishing, you can watch *The Godfather* with Mama over and over."

He smiled. "What a splendid life." *The Godfather* is my father's favorite film.

We ate, we drank. I wished it weren't so smoky. My eyes were burning.

"Are you scared, retiring? You've worked your whole life. You love your job."

"I *have* worked my whole life," my father said. "And I *do* love my job. There are very few people in the world who can do what I do." Perhaps if he had done his job less well, Communism would still be flourishing in the Soviet Union and he would still be in New York, and my mother wouldn't be sick in her soul.

He shook his head, took another gulp of beer. "Paullina, it's time for me to leave work. I don't feel well. I do not live a healthy life. I don't. And also, your mother." He fell quiet.

"I'm leaving for her," he said when he spoke again. "She needs me to stop working, she needs me to be with her, to take care of her. I'm going to do that. I want us to have a good life."

"You will, Papa," I said.

"We're going to get up at seven each morning," he said, "and we're going to go to the beach. We will walk, swim, sit, talk. Then we'll come home and have breakfast."

"By the time you're done with all that, it'll be time for lunch."

"Then we'll have lunch. After lunch a nap, and maybe a little internet."

"Good plan," I said. The red dust went unmentioned.

"We'll walk back to the beach in the late afternoon. Then dinner. Then movies. It's a splendid life, isn't it?"

I agreed that it was.

"And any time we want to, we can hop on a plane and in three hours be in San Francisco. We'll rent a car, we'll drive down to see you and the kids in Texas, we'll drive to New York, visit Liza, Dedushka, Babushka. We'll travel. Mama will see Las Vegas finally. That's her dream. Paullina, I want to give her that."

"I know."

"You and the children and Kevin of course can come and visit us any time. Any time. For as long as you want. You have a place to stay. With us."

"Papa, you have a two-bedroom condo!"

"We'll fit."

"Papa, the indirect flight to Maui is thirteen hours from Dallas. What are we going to do with my kids on the plane for thirteen hours?"

He paused. "It's not thirteen straight hours. You change in San Francisco or Honolulu."

It was time for me to shake my head.

"Paullina, you don't know Hawaii. You cannot imagine. You won't want to leave." He smiled. "It's not like here."

Then why didn't I want to leave here?

"Yes, I hear it's paradise on earth," I said. I sipped my water. He drank his beer. "There, not here," I added, in case there was any confusion.

We were quiet for a while. Finally I said, changing the subject, "So, I guess I'm not calling Yulia, huh, Papa?"

"Do what you like," he said. "It's going to be very difficult for you to see her." Difficult for me or difficult for him?

He seemed so reluctant to share our time together with other people besides the minimum he was obligated to deliver. No Alla for breakfast, no Anatoly and Ellie for dinner, no walking with Anatoly through the streets of Leningrad. No Yulia. Just me and my father.

Well, he did put off his retirement to paradise to come to Leningrad with me. It was only right.

"What did you think of Schlisselburg?" he asked. "You don't need any more inspiration, do you?"

I shook my head. It was all I needed. It was everything.

He drank his beer.

"But you know," I said, "one of the things that affected me most —" I broke off. I found it hard to continue. I had started well enough, couched myself in euphemism — *the thing, affected me*, so banal, so bland — but then an image sprung up, an image of the ground on which nothing grows. *We died so you could live.* Darkest Neva rose up, and tears too. This is ridiculous, I thought, and tried again, more slowly. "You know, the thing I want to say, is this …" Trailing off, I looked into my tea.

"What?" my father said, trying to understand. "What's the matter with you?"

My head twitched as I tried to compose at least my voice.

"It's those two hundred and forty thousand men at Nevsky Patch," I said, still staring into my tea, not looking at my father. "What did they die for?"

My father shrugged. "What does anybody die for? It's war, Paullina. Young boys go to die. That's what war is."

He wasn't understanding me. *What* did they die for?

I tried again. "Yes, but we've all heard of Iwo Jima, we've heard of Omaha Beach." And yet that wasn't it. That wasn't the heart of it. "But no one has heard of Nevsky Patch. No one's heard of Schlisselburg." All true, but that still wasn't the thing that hurt. It was the enormity of the sacrifice balanced against the reality of the present life that hurt the most. They didn't balance each other out. The scales were upended.

A show began in the restaurant. Elaborately dressed traditional dancers cavorted to loud Russian muzak. I kept waiting to hear "Shine, Shine, My Star," but no such luck. It was too loud for us to talk, so we asked for the check.

The Russian waiter, although polite, could not for the life of him say "You're welcome" when we thanked him for bringing us food or drink. When we tipped him generously, he didn't say thank you, but he did ask us to come back soon.

On the way out, I stopped at the gift shop to get some *matryoshkas* — the famous wooden nesting dolls — for my children while my father went outside to smoke. He had smoked all through the meal, exhaling the fumes into my face. He didn't give it a second thought, and why should he? That had been his life and mine, too, in cramped, less well ventilated rooms. I've never said a word and never could.

I must have spent ten minutes choosing my nesting dolls. When I glanced outside to make sure he wasn't getting too antsy, there was my funny dad, leaning on a railing above Griboyedov Canal, chatting happily to a young dark-haired man. The Church on Spilt Blood framed them. The man was leaning close, energetically explaining something, and my father was listening intently.

Suddenly my father came back inside and motioned for me. In the golden glimmer of the evening I saw that the young man was drunk.

"This is my daughter," my father said, smiling proudly. As if he were introducing me to his good friend.

The man shook my hand; rather, he grabbed my hand and held it. I pulled away. My father said to him, "Come, I will buy you some water."

I glared at my dad, but he wouldn't give me the satisfaction of meeting my eyes, so we started to walk along the Griboyedov, the drunk man close behind us. He never for an instant stopped talking. He kept reciting obscure Boris Pasternak poetry:

Under willow trees with ivy ingrown
We are trying to hide from bad weather.
I am clasping your arms in my own,
In one cloak we are huddled together.

I was wrong.
Not with ivy-leaves bound,
But with hops overgrown is the willow.
Well then, let us spread out on the ground
This our cloak as a sheet and a pillow.

A few hundred feet down the canal, my father bought the drunken poet an Evian. The man promptly offered to share it with my dad, who promptly refused. We started to walk again. The man continued to zigzag beside us, quoting Pasternak all the while. It took me two more blocks to realize he was repeating the same poem over and over, about sitting down and drinking from the common cup. But when he expressed contemptuous distaste for the saxophonist playing by the canal, heckling him loudly, even my father had had enough. My father was partial to saxophonists. Earlier, he had given the same musician twenty rubles for a Russian jazz rendition of "You Ain't Nothin' but a Hound Dog."

Thankfully, it was time for us to cross the bridge over Griboyedov Canal. My father bid goodbye to his new friend. I was surprised by my dad. He was utterly unperturbed by being accosted and followed. He bought the man another Evian from a street vendor, and then walked on.

The golden onion domes of the Church on Spilt Blood filled the sky down the canal. The saxophonist continued to play. When we were quite far from him, he started to play "Speak Softly Love," from *The Godfather*. My father and I stopped, looked at each other, and returned to him. Papa smiled at me. We were back in America, at the movies, at our Kew Gardens apartment, in our Ronkonkoma house, dancing together to "Speak Softly Love" at my first wedding.

We didn't move until the man finished playing. To hear the dulcet strands of Nino Rota drift through the air while walking through the streets of Leningrad on a warm sunny night, having drunk, having eaten, having lived a full life in one day, it was a halcyon snapshot of our post-Russia existence. My father and I were suspended in the air with the minor chords of the melody.

We returned to Grand Hotel Europe for a quick bathroom break, and at 10:30 set out for Decembrists' Square and the statue of the Bronze Horseman.

As we were walking past Kazan Cathedral, my father asked me to lift my eyes. I didn't want to look too closely. The gold of the domes was black and green; the walls of the cathedral black and dingy gray. But at the top of the dome shined a gold cross, polished and luminous. This was what my dad was drawing my attention to. Before 1991 and the fall of Communism, there were no crosses on any of the cathedrals, he told me. They weren't houses of God but storage facilities or museums. After 1991, brand new crosses, beacons of a religion other than Communism, were placed atop all the Leningrad cathedrals. It was the only new thing on their otherwise faded façades.

We passed only an occasional pedestrian as we made our way through the deserted streets. I wanted to get another crème brûlée ice cream, but the street seller had run out. All she had was vanilla. I shook my head.

We walked down Nevsky Prospekt.

"Where is that sign?" I asked my father. "That famous sign from the blockade?"

"We're about to pass it," he replied. "Cross the street." Just past the alphabetically challenged Dom Knigi, a rectangular blue and white sign hung on a wall: "Comrades, during enemy attack, this side of the street is more dangerous." During the siege, the Germans aimed their missiles at Nevsky Prospekt. The bombs flew all the way from Pulkovo Heights, the site of the current airport eleven miles away, and landed on the northern side of the boulevard. The southern side was safer.

Underneath the sign was another, smaller one: "Left in memory of the besieged."

"The war is everywhere, isn't it?" my father said as we crossed Nevsky again and made our way to Decembrists' Square.

"Yes," I said. "War, poverty, beauty, white nights, Communism, our whole life."

"Heartbreaking, isn't it?"

"Yes."

THE BRONZE HORSEMAN

In Decembrists' Square stood one of Leningrad's most celebrated cathedrals, St. Isaac's.

Its paint was so faded, its magnificence so tarnished that I was too sad to take a photo.

"It's incredible," my father said. "Look at it. Why aren't you taking a picture?" I did, hoping the falling dusk would camouflage what I did not want the lens to capture.

My father told me Decembrists' Square had been renamed Senate Square in 1992.

"Who can keep up with all the name changes?"

"Nobody," he replied. "That's why everybody still calls it Decembrists' Square."

Between St. Isaac's and the Neva embankment stood the statue of the Bronze Horseman — Peter the Great atop his horse. In Aleksandr Pushkin's epic narrative poem, after the Great Flood of 1830, the luckless hero Evgeni comes to stand in front of the Bronze Horseman. The stallion rears against the setting sky, comes to life and chases Evgeni through the streets of Leningrad for eternity.

The statue stood on top of Thunder Stone, a monolithic 1500 tonne red granite pedestal, said to be the largest stone ever moved by man. It took nine months to move the stone over less than four miles of land and ten miles on a barge down the Neva. On the side of the rock was engraved simply: "To PETER I, CATHERINE II, 1782."

I took exactly three pictures. Then my film ran out. I didn't have another in my purse. I was so foolish. I had used up two rolls, on Schlisselburg, on the Road of Life, on Lake Ladoga, and reserved barely three clicks for the Bronze Horseman.

My father was already ahead, walking toward the Neva embankment, smoking. I circled the statue with acute regret, then followed him to the river. He seemed to be searching for something.

"Is there anywhere to buy film around here?" I asked.

There was a bar, where young people sat outside, drinking their beer, laughing, talking. Somewhere else on the plaza, music blared. The Beatles were singing "The Things We Said Today", one of my favorites.

My father didn't answer.

"Do you see across the river?" he pointed. "Along the embankment is Leningrad University. That's where I studied as a young man. See that resplendent building right there? Right in front of us across the river?" My father laughed. "That is not the university. That is Menshikov's mansion. Do you know who Menshikov was?"

I shook my head.

"Peter the Great's chief deputy. Peter told him to build Petersburg University, as it was then called, on the banks of the Neva. Then Peter left for the country, thinking he was the Tsar, and his orders would most certainly be followed. But Menshikov decided to take matters into his own hands and built himself a mansion instead, overlooking the river. He built the university perpendicular to the river, as you can see, so just the short sides of the buildings are exposed to the river, while his house spreads out gloriously right along the shoreline. When Peter came back and saw what had been done, he was upset, of course. He threatened banishment, and worse, but the deed was done."

The anecdote was funny, but as my father gazed across the river at the university of his youth, his Russian life was in his eyes.

We resumed our stroll down the embankment.

"Do you want to get a beer or something?" I asked.

"No. I'm getting tired. We have such a long way back. But I just can't leave. Look at this river, Plinochka."

"I'm looking, Papa, I'm looking."

We stood at the Neva and watched the northern sun ignite the sky as it set in front of us behind Leningrad University. My eyes traveled to the right, to Peter and Paul's Cathedral, where we were going to bury the Tsar tomorrow, the hazy sunrise already glimmering behind its golden spire. There it was: the sky ablaze with sunset in front of me but sunrise just upstream, all in the same lapis lazuli Leningrad sky. It was after midnight.

In 1984, when I had gone to live in England, I sent home a photo of the glum, cloudy Colchester sky with the inscription, "The sky is the same all over the world."

I was wrong. The sky was not the same all over the world.

When my dad asked, "Isn't it beautiful?" he was seeing his youth. He closed his eyes and saw himself young and handsome, in love with many girls, funny, brilliant, popular. Of course it was beautiful. It was mystifying. It was mystical.

"Yes," I said, wanting so much to see what he saw. But what I saw was what mattered to me. The war, the water, the midnight sun. I saw the streets not of my youth but of my fiction. I hadn't loved in Leningrad. I was a child in Leningrad. But now, by his side, for the first time I saw streets of passion, of adult drama, of lovers, of heartbreak. I saw the streets of my Alexander and Tatiana.

"Tonight," my father said, "is the last official night of white nights. Tomorrow the streetlights are turned back on."

"Then it's good we are here."

We sat down on a bench by the river. No sooner had we sat down than my father sprang up again, and said, "We must go."

I willed myself up. Suddenly I was old, and my papa was young.

Taking a deep drag of his cigarette, he said, "Thank you, Plinka. Thank you for making me walk the streets of my life with you."

I couldn't speak for a moment. I placed my hand on his back.

"But Papa," I finally said, "you've been to Leningrad three times since 1991. You must have already walked these streets."

"Never," he said. "I have *never* walked here since the day we left Russia in 1973."

"How can that be?" I was incredulous.

"That's how it is."

"Not even when you came here with Mama?"

"Never."

"What did you two do when you came here?"

"I don't know," he said. "Nothing. When Mama came by herself, she walked. She walked everywhere, but not with me."

No film in the camera for these irretrievable seconds of my life, walking along the Neva with my papa.

"Oh, Paullina," he said, moving more and more slowly. It was nearly one in the morning. "What are you doing to me?"

*

Back in my room, I undressed, lay on the bed and prayed for sleep.

Getting up, I opened the window to hear the sounds of Leningrad, and to air out my room, because a pungently malodorous cleaning lady had been in it. A mosquito flew in. It was three in the morning.

I found myself thinking in Russian, something I hadn't done in years. I was not only thinking in Russian, but thinking in Russian words I didn't know I knew.

I suddenly realized why I could never remember the *bon mot* in English: because my brain was Russian, and my Russian brain scrambled the signals. The neuron was Russian and I tried to send English electrical impulses across it. Every once in a while, the neurons rebelled.

I thought back to this morning. What did I do? Morning, morning, morning. Ulitsa Dybenko … sunshine … the highway … Mama's gall bladder … the scrap-steel yard at Schlisselburg … the stolen metal doors of the outhouse … the bride under the Broken Ring … crème brûlée … *kvas* … Ladoga … Maui … caviar … *in one cloak we are huddled together … speak softly love …* in memory of the besieged …

You the living — Know this! We didn't want to leave this land,
And we didn't. We stood to the death on the banks of the dark Neva.
We died so you could live.

Not them. You. We died so that you could live, Paullina.

I tossed, sleeplessly, mournfully. I wanted to cry. I'm not a Cimmerian, why can't I sleep? I thought about my Bronze Horseman and Pushkin's Bronze Horseman, and remembered a verse from his poem.

At last, his eyelids heavy-laden
Droop into slumber ... soon away
The night's tempestuous gloom is fading
And washes into pallid day.

DAY FIVE
Friday

THE IPATIEV HOUSE

When I woke up at eight in the morning I was sick.

I must have drunk the Leningrad water the day before. Somewhere in our travels, the Neva water must have run unfiltered into me.

Grimly I got ready for the Romanov funeral. I couldn't believe we were in Russia — *I* was in Russia — on the day of their funeral. What coincidence, what irony, what destiny.

I put on my taupe pant suit, my taupe shoes. I threw some makeup on my face and stumbled out to meet my father.

"Tired, Papa?" I asked. Remarkably, he looked fresh, shaved, and happy to see me. He was all dressed up in a dark blue suit, white shirt and tie. Our driver Viktor was also in a suit.

Peter and Paul's Cathedral is a slender, beautiful old yellow stucco church, set into a cobblestone courtyard, which was itself set into the middle of Peter and Paul's Fortress — a tiny island on the Neva that for many years stood as the sentinel of Leningrad and then became a prison. Most fortresses in Russia became prisons. Peter and Paul's, Oreshek. Like Alcatraz but not as well appointed.

Before the guards would let us inside the grounds of the fortress, we had to stand and wait behind the police barricades like groupies in line to glimpse the stars at the Oscars.

No one knew exactly what we were waiting for. The people with press credentials like us, and the people without, like the woman in front of me from Novgorod, were all standing in the same line. At the front were two metal detectors, but no one knew which one we were supposed to go through.

"With invitations here, without invitations there," the puzzled guard said doubtfully, as if he himself wasn't sure. The line wasn't moving. What did he mean, invitations? I broke through the crowd and made my way toward the guard.

"What invitations?" I started to ask, but he cut me off immediately. "Please go back to the sidewalk. Get off the road."

I got off the road. We waited, wondering if our press credentials were going to mean squat.

"Papa, what are we waiting for?"

"Damned if I know."

Finally, the guard spoke to the restless block of tightly packed people. "Those of you with press credentials, move over here. The rest of you will not be able to get in. Unless you have an invitation."

The woman from Novgorod in front of me, in a housecoat and unkempt hair, waved her invitation, or whatever it was, at the guard, and said, "I'm here to see the Tsar. I'm here to see the Tsar."

At long last, we passed through the metal detector and walked over a short bridge and through a portico to the interior square. The church's canary stucco had faded, giving the courtyard the look of ancient Rome or Marseilles.

Marseilles has a church, Notre Dame a La Garde, set on top of a high mountain overlooking the city. That church looks like it's from the days of Francis of Assisi. Why did the faded paint seem endearing in Marseilles yet so heart-rending in Leningrad?

My father's colleague Viktor Ryazenkov was waiting for us in the square.

"So what are we supposed to do now?" I asked.

"We wait," he said. "It'll start soon."

"Will we be able to hear the funeral from here?"

"Yes, they've set up microphones and a television set," he replied.

"Where?"

"Right there? Do you see?"

"I don't see the television."

"Do you see the screens?"

"Yes, but they're not turned on."

"Be patient. See the cameras on the crane? They'll be televising who is coming inside the church, all the church proceedings, and all the speeches."

"Where will the sound come from? There are no loudspeakers."

He pointed off into the distance. "Right there is a loudspeaker."

I saw a solitary loudspeaker hanging from a light post. "Okay," I said. "We wait. Is there anything to drink?"

"Nope."

"Is there anywhere to sit down?"

"What's the matter with you?" my father said. "We just got here. You just woke up." He tutted. "You never did like standing."

Viktor R. gave me some warm mineral water that tasted like Gatorade.

I walked around, trying to shake off my crippling stomach blues and the nagging sense that this grand occasion might not be the dignified commemoration I'd been expecting.

The political in-fighting surrounding the burial of the Romanovs was vast and petty. No one could let Nicholas II and his family rest, even eighty years later, even in death. Not the people who loved them, not the people who couldn't care less. They died a bad death, the *worst* death, yet somehow that wasn't suffering enough.

In one night, on July 17, 1918, three hundred years of the Romanov dynasty were wiped out. Eighty years ago to the day. And now, all the pretenders to the throne were fighting with one another. The priests were fighting with the politicians; the politicians were making conciliatory speeches about healing, repentance, redemption, while playing their political games.

I couldn't see anyone going inside the church. Had any of these big shots even come to the funeral?

*

The beginning of the end for poor Nicholas II began in February 1917, when he abdicated his throne. Afterward he and his family lived in voluntary exile in their summer residence south of Leningrad. When the Bolsheviks took power in October 1917, he was forced deeper into Russia, to a town called Tobolsk.

Nicholas became an insurmountable problem for the Bolsheviks, who were embroiled in a bitter civil war. They were deathly afraid their enemies would use the living Nicholas to rally opposition to

Communism. In May 1918 the Bolsheviks moved the Romanov family to Ekaterinburg, an inconspicuous city deep in the heart of Russia, where the family was placed under house arrest at a building known as Ipatiev House. Nicholas was fifty, his wife Alexandra forty-six. Their four daughters, the grand duchesses, were Olga, twenty-three, Tatiana, twenty-one, Maria, nineteen, and Anastasia, seventeen.

Their son, the heir to the throne, Tsarevich Alexei, was thirteen. His body was ruined by hemophilia, his limbs and joints permanently swollen and misshapen from a lifetime of internal bleeding. He was unable to move around by himself. His mother sat with him in the room day and night and read to him, or slept next to him.

They lived quietly for seventy-eight days until July 17, 1918.

At midnight on July 17, Nicholas and Alexandra were woken up and asked to get dressed and come downstairs into the basement. They were told the Bolsheviks were afraid for the family's safety.

Because Tsarevich was so sick, Nicholas carried him to the basement himself. Twelve people piled into a sub-basement room with one small window. The chief guard spent some time positioning them — ostensibly for a photograph to prove they were still alive. One of the girls asked for a chair to sit on; two chairs were brought in. The mother and the young son sat down.

The doctor, the maid, the nurse and the cook stood behind Nicholas. The youngest duchess, Anastasia, held the family poodle in her arms.

Eleven more guards stepped into the thirteen by eleven foot room. There were now twenty-four people in it, twelve of them with weapons. The chief guard took out a piece of paper and read aloud that by the order of Lenin himself, Nicholas and his family were to be executed. Nicholas turned to his family and said, "What? What?" The chief guard repeated himself, then took out his pistol and shot Nicholas in the head. Empress Alexandra and her daughter Tatiana started to cross themselves but there was no time. The other guards raised their rifles and opened fire on the rest of the family. The guards had been ordered to shoot for the heart rather than the head, to minimize the flow of blood. They fired more than one hundred and fifty shots. Many of the guards went partially or completely deaf.

Suddenly the guards noticed that the bullets were ricocheting off three of the girls. The frantic men were stunned to discover that the girls were still alive. Stepping closer, the guards began to shoot at point blank range, yet the girls kept moaning and trying to crawl away. The maid even grabbed one of the rifles from the guards as she edged along the wall to the door. Now hysterical, the guards turned their bayonets on her and on the duchesses. Eventually the girls stopped moving.

The massacre had taken twenty minutes.

Later in the woods after the guards undressed — and *touched* — the duchesses, they discovered over eighteen pounds of diamonds sewn into their breastplates like armor. The bullets had ricocheted off the diamonds.

Except for the jewels, all the personal belongings of the family and their servants were placed in a heap and burned. The bodies were hacked to pieces with axes, doused with sulfuric acid and gasoline, and burned in a mining shaft. The following day, the executioners came back, retrieved what was left of the bodies and buried them in another mining shaft, which was then blown up.

It took seventy years to locate the remains. All except the Duchess Tatiana and Tsarevich Alexis had been identified.

*

I wandered around the cobblestones, thinking of the Romanovs lying undiscovered for eighty years after such a death, unburied, uncommended to God. But not unmourned, I thought, as I came up behind a row of press agents, photographers, writers, all straining their necks to see the double doors. They were beautiful doors, made of solid wood — oak maybe.

"What are we looking at?" I asked a tall thin man with a camera. Really, I just wanted him to move out of my way so I could see, too.

He turned around, gave me a haughty look, and said in Russian, "For the dignitaries to arrive."

"Oh."

Finding my father again, I asked, "Papa, when are the Romanovs going to be carried through those doors?"

"No." Viktor R. stepped in. "They're already inside the church. Remember? They were carried here yesterday."

The day before, the royal remains had arrived by plane from Ekaterinburg, where they had lain on a metal slab in a laboratory since their discovery a few years earlier. Quietly they rode through the St. Petersburg streets toward their overdue burial.

Again politics and poverty ruled. There was not enough money in the city coffers to hire limousines to carry all five of the caskets; there was only enough money for one — to carry the Tsar's remains.

"How did the rest get to the cathedral?" I asked Viktor R. when he told us this story. My father had walked away, disgusted. "By bus?"

"No, by other means," was Viktor R.'s evasive answer.

I had seen horses on the Palace Square, waiting patiently for amorous couples to rent a carriage for a half-hour ride through

St. Petersburg. Why couldn't the city rent a horse and carriage to carry the coffins to Peter and Paul's? Viktor R. shrugged. It's more complicated than that, he told me. Why? Princess Diana was pulled by several horses. Why couldn't the Romanovs be pulled by just one?

That was England. This is Russia, he said.

So the Tsar was driven slowly through the city streets in a black stretch limo. Only a few hundred people turned out to watch him pass by. There was a bigger turnout for O.J. Simpson's slow-motion car chase on Interstate 5 in Los Angeles.

During the press accreditation, we had been told that the funeral service would start at 11:00 in the morning. Yeltsin had changed all that. He was supposed to arrive at 11:00 and make a speech; the funeral would start at noon.

I had been standing since 10:30, in high heels on uneven stones. My back hurt, my legs. My stomach. I was not in prime spirits.

Surprisingly, there were toilets in the yard. Port-a-Potties, four of them. They had been brought in for the dignitaries, because, although Peter and Paul's Fortress is a national treasure, a museum, a prison, a shrine, there are no permanent toilets in it.

The Russian choir, when it started to sing, had a lovely, melancholy tone. I wished I could smell the incense. Outside, we were doing nothing, saying nothing. We had no role. We just stood. My father smoked more than usual. I could tell he was frustrated. This momentous occasion, this once-in-a-lifetime moment, thousands of journalists from all over the world, piled together on the cobblestones and ignored.

When Yeltsin finally arrived — at noon, by helicopter — he addressed the gathered dignitaries inside. "This is the time for repentance," we heard over the loudspeaker.

I wished there were a question-and-answer session. I wanted to ask him about Ipatiev House. Yeltsin had ordered it razed in 1977 because there was such a push to canonize the martyred Romanovs, Ipatiev House had become a place of pilgrimage for many Russians. Yeltsin, who had once been an avid Communist, figured that if there were no Ipatiev House, there would be no pilgrimage. He was wrong.

"As a human being and as President," he continued, "I could not *not* be here."

Then the microphone went dead.

We heard nothing more for the rest of the funeral. Which was only fitting because we could see nothing, either. Although a bank of televisions had been set up — twenty-five small screens in all, five rows of five — so that we could watch what was happening inside, we could have been watching reruns of *I Love Lucy*, for all we could see in the hazy sunlight.

It was hot on the cobblestones. Everything on my body hurt, my stomach worst of all. A gray-haired Frenchman in front of me had dandruff that flaked off in the breeze in my direction. I moved away. I didn't want to see Yeltsin that badly.

The women in the crowd were dressed in too-tight clothes, even the career women. *Especially* the career women. Too-tight clothes that didn't match. And they smoked. Everybody smoked.

There was a small boathouse next to the church. I sat down on its steps. It was the hottest day yet, 80°F and humid. There was no more Russian music. No more Yeltsin. Just a bunch of suited-up people with cameras, clamoring to glimpse the closed oak doors of a church.

This was the Romanov funeral eighty years in the making.

*

Later *Newsweek* ran an article on the burial of Tsar Nicholas II, and *People* magazine had one, too. I read these articles and felt a sense of propriety about that Friday morning. I wanted to say: I was there. I was there when the Tsar was buried. I saw …

Nothing. Wait: that's not true. I saw the courtyard. What I didn't see was what the rest of Russia saw beautifully on television. Or what the rest of the world wrote about.

They saw the meaning of the Romanovs to history: the power of repentance, the virtue of forgiveness. I didn't see any of that. I saw a courtyard, and sun, and the backs of the crowd. The only excitement was when the governor of Krasnoyarsk, Aleksandr Lebed, emerged from the church and walked quickly through the courtyard. He was wearing a suit, and he looked distinguished. I saw that much. Dozens of microphones were thrust in his face.

"Quick, quick," my father urged. "Climb up here, take a picture of Lebed for Dedushka."

I climbed up. I couldn't get a picture of him. By the time I balanced myself atop a divider and focused the Pentax, all I saw was his back.

I should have realized the funeral was going to be much like the accreditation process. In literature, they call it foreshadowing.

Finally Papa said, "Paullina, have you seen enough? Do you want to go?"

"Yes," I instantly said, and thank you, God.

But it wasn't about us. It wasn't about Viktor R., or the press, or *Newsweek*'s lofty musings. It was about a family being buried.

I wish we could have seen it.

We left at 1:30 p.m., with the funeral still in full swing. Or not. Who could tell?

BETWEEN THE FUNERAL AND THE HERMITAGE

We dropped off Viktor R. at Radio Liberty. While we waited for our driver Viktor to come back downstairs, my father read to me from his newspaper: world weather and Yankees stats. Finally our driver reappeared. "Where to now?" he asked us.

"Viktor," my father said, "what do you suggest?" He actually asked someone's opinion! "It is our last day in Leningrad. Tomorrow we drive to the Karelian Isthmus. We need to make today count." He turned to me. "Do you want to go to the Defense of Leningrad Museum? It's near the Field of Mars."

"Yes," I said.

"Or do you want to go to the Hermitage?"

"Yes," I said.

"We can also take a walk along the Neva to the Summer Garden. You can't leave Leningrad and not see the Summer Garden."

"Yes," I said.

Viktor studied me briefly. "Paullina, I don't think you should go to the Defense of Leningrad Museum."

"No?"

"No. You've seen too much, you're overwhelmed."

"Yes," I said.

"You have been bombarded with too much information. I can see it's becoming hard for you to absorb it all. To process it."

"Yes."

"The museum is overkill. You will remember only five percent of what you see. What's the point? I suggest the Hermitage."

"Why not both?"

"Seeing the Hermitage in one hour," Viktor said, "is like not seeing it at all. You'll barely have time to pay and go up the marble staircase."

"Plina, here's a plan," my father said. "We go back to your hotel, you change, so you're more comfortable. Then we walk to the Hermitage, and spend a couple of hours there."

"Three," said Viktor. "At the very least three hours."

"Okay, okay, three. Then we walk along the Neva to the Summer Garden, and afterward I will show you the courthouse where I was tried and convicted. Then we will go and have our last dinner in Leningrad. What do you think? Is that a plan?"

"Yes," I said.

But what about Yulia? I wanted to ask. Was I really going to leave Leningrad without calling Yulia?

DANAË

At Grand Hotel Europe I changed from my taupe suit into a black shirt, white skirt, and sandals. I looked longingly at my bed, wishing I could fall into it and sleep until it was time to leave Russia.

We walked in the afternoon sunshine to Café Nord, where we ate smoked salmon in an open sandwich. I had cream cake and a bitter espresso. I picked at my food. I didn't like the espresso, didn't like the salmon, didn't like the bread. I was feeling glum inside and out.

"Are you feeling all right?" Papa suddenly asked, a remarkable question coming from my usually oblivious father.

"Yes, thank you," I replied. I wasn't about to ruin our last day together, just us, by whining about my stupid stomach and my stupid feelings.

In the underpass from one side of Nevsky to the other, a beggar woman sat with her infant. Another beggar woman sang Russian songs I'd never heard before. Farther along, two men and a young boy played the guitar.

Back above ground, we headed down Nevsky on the way to the Hermitage. We walked past a sign that said "THE INTER-CITY PHONE BUILDING."

"What is that?" I asked my father.

"It's the Inter-city Phone Building," he replied. "When you wanted to call another city from Leningrad, you came here."

"Oh," I said, thinking, how quaint and cute, how good to know this, how handy this information would be in my Bronze Horseman novel. How provident that we were passing this ancient relic of the past. "How long ago was that?"

"Until two years ago," replied my father. "They finally closed it in 1996."

On we walked through the Triumphal Arc of General Staff, this time in daylight. Beyond that we saw Palace Square, the Alexander Column, and the glistening green of the Winter Palace.

We stopped for a few minutes before the arc and just stood. What my father was thinking I don't know. I didn't ask. I was thinking that I had no room left inside for impressions — not of beauty, not of pain, not of nostalgia. I was full up.

But the Alexander Column was worth some feelings. Built by Nicholas I for Alexander I, who saved Russia from Napoleon, it took three years to extract the seven hundred-ton piece of granite from the Karelian Isthmus.

As we walked past it, I touched it with my hands. It was smooth and cold.

"What a square, huh, Papa?"

"Humph," he said, as though to say, *Well, of course. What did you expect?*

But it was more than that. The French feel the same way about Paris, and I know the Italians feel the same way about Rome, and the British, having fought Hitler practically single-handed from 1939 to 1941, certainly feel this way about their blitzed but still standing London.

My father and I are not French; we are not Italian; we are not British. We are Russian, and what we feel when we touch the soul of our city we don't feel for anywhere else in the world, no matter how historic, no matter how meaningful. We feel it for Leningrad, hero-city, the Calvary of Russia's war with Hitler.

*

We walked on, to the Hermitage.

The Hermitage is one of the greatest museums of the world, housed inside a palace so opulent it defies comprehension.

"Nothing on this scale could ever be built today," my father told me. The Winter Palace, the Leningrad residence of the Tsars, is an immense rectangular edifice of green stucco, built around an enormous interior courtyard. The building stretches nearly a kilometer along the Neva. It was built by Rastrelli with lavish Baroque gusto for Elizabeth I in the late eighteenth century, but the art collection dates back to the early 1700s, when Peter the Great bought two paintings by Rembrandt that still hang in the Dutch Room.

Today, the Hermitage is home to a thousand years of art and collectibles, and twenty-three more Rembrandts.

"Can we see all of it?" I asked my father.

"Yes. It will take us nine years, and we will only be able to spend thirty seconds on each exhibit, but yes."

"Huh," I said slowly. "What if we spend fifteen seconds on each? Listen, some I don't really want to see."

"Wait till you see the doors," my father said. "You won't believe the doors."

"Can we see Picasso?"

"We won't have time. It's already three. We'll try. Wait till you see the doors."

Each door — twenty feet high, handcrafted from solid walnut and then gilded — must have cost a million dollars, and there were hundreds of them.

We decided to limit ourselves to a couple of halls, a couple of throne rooms, one coffin room, a little Italian art, and one Rembrandt.

"Oh, and we must see the Fabergé room," my father said.

"I hear he makes nice eggs."

For some reason my dad didn't find me funny as we walked up the Grand Staircase.

He led me to one of the windows in the Catherine the Great Hall on the second floor. "I want to show you something. Do you know why the curtains are drawn?"

"To block out the sunlight?"

He shook his head. "I've been coming to the Hermitage for fifty years, since 1946. Today I haven't looked outside yet, but I just want to show you that I'm right about this. What do the Americans say? They say, the devil is in the details. Check out the courtyard."

He pulled aside the curtain. Down below, in the rear courtyard, were several dump trucks loaded with garbage. Old chairs, dirt, mess, weeds, rusted pipes. In the rear courtyard, the decorative lions on the windows were not gilded and restored as they were on the front walls. It looked like the backyards of Shepelevo, albeit on a larger scale.

"Fifty years and they still haven't moved those pipes," my father said. "On one side of the Great Hall, a beautiful garden. A fantastic garden built on the second floor. Imagine building a garden with earth and trees on the *second floor*. But on the other side of the hall, this. That's Russia for you. Nothing has changed."

"Why don't they clean it up?"

"Why? Why should they? They just keep the curtains drawn."

My father was quite taken by Catherine II's second-floor garden, "with lilacs!" He had mentioned lilacs a few days before, when we passed the Field of Mars, when he told me about the time he had cooked meat over the eternal flame. "It was spring," he'd said. "And the lilacs were blooming."

My father is partial to lilacs and saxophonists.

In the Italian section we found a sculpture by Michelangelo, called his "grouchy boy," two Raphaels and two da Vincis.

The Fabergé exhibit had unfortunately closed an hour early, but the Gregorian Hall was quite a sight with splendid gold columns and veined marble floors.

When we bought our tickets for the Hermitage, the sign said, if you want to take pictures, please pay now, five dollars per picture. Eight dollars for video. Well I didn't know how many pictures I was going to take. Maybe none. So I didn't pay. But when I saw the Gregorian Hall, I knew that I had to take a picture for my Natasha, to show her the famous hall where Duchess Anastasia danced with her daddy in the animated film *Anastasia*.

No, my own daddy said. You cannot take a picture. You didn't pay.

Thinking he was joking, I turned on the camera. My father took it out of my hands and turned it off.

"I said no. I told you to buy the use of the camera. You said no. Well, now you can't take the picture."

"Papa," I said, "they wanted five dollars per picture. How did I know how many pictures I wanted to take?"

"No," he corrected me. "They said, five dollars for use of camera. You didn't pay. Now you can't use it."

It seemed so absurd, standing in the middle of the immoderate Gregorian Hall, arguing.

"Fine," I said. "Wait here. I will go and buy the right to take one picture."

He relented, and I took the picture. And then two more. He was all right after that.

"Look at the doors," he said. "How do you like the doors? I told you about the doors. What do you think about them?"

"The doors are spectacular, Papa," I said. "But this whole place is something. Everything is gold and marble."

In the Napoleonic Hall we found a portrait of Shepelev, one of the Russian lieutenants who served in the war of 1812 against Napoleon. We concluded it must have been the eponymous Shepelev for whom our village was named.

We filed past Peter the Great's throne and stopped at a solid silver casket made for Alexander Nevsky, engraved with intricate sculptures of his battles.

"Wouldn't you like to be buried in a coffin like that?" my father whispered. "I would."

"I prefer not to *have* to be buried at all," I whispered back. "But Papa," I added, slowly, thoughtfully, "if Nevsky's coffin is here, um, where is Nevsky?"

He just shook his head.

"I'm just saying."

"Stop it," he said. "That's what I'm saying."

In the Dutch Art section, a whole room was given over to one painting called *Danaë*. Finally! A Rembrandt.

Back in 1986 some rotten bastard spilled acid all over *Danaë*. The museum spent six painstaking years restoring it. Now it was behind glare-free glass.

Danaë was King Acrisius's daughter. Because the Delphic Oracle prophesied that Danaë's future son was going to kill Acrisius, the king, having no sense of humor, had his daughter locked up in a tower of brass, which is how Rembrandt painted her, locked up, lying naked on a bed, waiting for Zeus. Sure enough, Zeus, being a god, was not going to be kept away by a flimsy tower of brass, so he broke in, and found Danaë naked. Nine months later, Danaë bore Zeus a son. She named him Perseus. Acrisius, afraid for his own life, set mother and son adrift at sea in a chest.

Zeus rescued them. Perseus, upon growing up, did indeed kill his grandfather, accidentally, during a friendly game of catch.

The moral of the story? As the Hindus say, do what you like, because the result will be exactly the same.

The Hermitage taught me that Russian art consisted mainly of icons, but also included some dishes. My father said, by way of commentary, "Your mother bought better dishes at Karlovy Vary" (a resort in the Czech Republic). There were Russian paintings by unknown artists, Russian swords, and some precious stones.

The Malachite room impressed me. I concluded that as a stone, the sparkling vivid green malachite is magnificent, one of the best. Could I get a kitchen counter made of it? That's right, because that's how I wanted to live, in a house made of stone and gold, with rusted pipes and trash outside my gilded windows.

It was nearly five and the Hermitage was closing. Tired, my father sat and rested while I went to get some souvenirs. I bought a book for my daughter and four large pastel prints of Leningrad for the breakfast nook of my Texas house. As I was paying for some *Danaë* postcards, I wondered why the women were always naked in the old days. No wonder they were having babies all over the place.

I wanted to buy an ornate Easter egg with Nicholas II on it, but it was ninety-five dollars. I didn't buy it.

We were on the way out of the Hermitage when Papa announced he was going to the bathroom.

"They have bathrooms here?" Really, only a quarter of a joke.

"Yes," my father said, deadpan. "I know that for a fact, because I used to drink vodka with my buddies in the bathrooms."

"Was that after you cooked the shish-ke-bob in the Field of Mars?"

He looked at me as if he had no idea what the hell I was talking about.

THE SUMMER GARDEN

We spilled out onto the granite Palace Embankment and strolled along the river, sun on the water. Through the clouds, the gilded spire of Peter and Paul's Cathedral across from us was bathed in light. The Romanovs' sacred remains can rest there now, in peace, the old Communists having repented. Water, stucco buildings, cars whizzing by, Winter Palace, Peter and Paul's, Palace Bridge, the University where my father studied when he was a young man. It was all in front of us and we were flooded with Leningrad. We didn't speak.

As we walked along the embankment, I wondered why more of these buildings had not been restored. There was one building on the Neva that was being renovated as we walked past. The façade overlooking the river had already been re-stuccoed and repainted pink and yellow. All the window frames had been replaced. The doors were new. The Baroque window molding was restored to its ornate white beauty. The front of the building looked like it belonged in Kensington Gardens. But the side of the building — well, that was another story. That belonged squarely in Russia.

My father must have read my mind, because he said, "You know, when you and Kevin and the children come back, maybe in five years, when you come back to Leningrad, the whole city will look like this. It will be a different city. They will renovate it for the tricentennial celebration in 2003."

He paused. "But it's beautiful nonetheless, isn't it? Look at the Neva, look at Leningrad around it."

"Yes, Papa," I replied quietly.

He left me and went to talk to two fishermen standing with their lines in the river.

We were at the wrought-iron gates of Letniy Sad, or the Summer Garden. I bought a vanilla ice cream (they didn't have crème brûlée) and some water and sat down on a bench to rest, while my father remained with the fishermen.

Letniy Sad, alongside the Fontanka Canal, was a breathtaking Sad, so green and alive with straight paths and majestic canopy elms, and sculptures of the Greek and Roman gods. Ice cream in one hand, I bought a photo postcard from a woman named Catherine.

"Where are you taking this photograph?" she asked me. "Back to Moscow?" No, I said; to Texas. She couldn't believe it. I was happy my Russian was good enough to be mistaken for a Muscovite.

One sculpture in particular impressed me. It was of Saturn devouring his own child. I had always liked that one. I used to have a postcard of Saturn, his half-chewed offspring in his mouth, hanging on my wall at college, a pointed reminder of the French and Russian revolutions. It hung next to a photo of my baby sister jumping off the diving board in the backyard pool of our American home.

My father came to the bench where I was sitting and took a drink of my water. We saw a woman in a wedding dress at the gated entrance to the gardens.

"Papa, look, another bride. They're everywhere."

"Yes," my father said. "The divorced ones are all in bars." He got up. "It's custom. Don't you know? Every Russian bride and groom must go to a national monument on their wedding day. It's tradition."

"Where did you and Mama go?"

"To the beer bar."

We walked along Fontanka Canal to City Court or Gorsud, where my father was tried and convicted in three days back in 1969.

"For what, Papa?" It must have been the first time I had asked him that question directly. "What were the charges against you?" My mother once told me he was arrested for writing letters. My father confirmed he was arrested for writing a letter to the newspaper *Pravda*, advocating rule of law. Another time he told me, "For good cause, Paullina, for good cause." Another time he told me, "I was lucky I didn't go away for longer, and wasn't found out sooner."

Today he said proudly, "For anti-Soviet agitation and propaganda with the aim of undermining Soviet power and workers' rights." Then he laughed.

I photographed him outside the wrong building at first. He momentarily forgot where it was. "Paullina, I didn't go into Gorsud by the front door, if you know what I mean. They brought me in handcuffs the back way. How do I know what the building looks like from the front?"

We cut across to the red Mikhailovsky Palace, built on the locus of Fontanka and Moika canals. I was so busy walking with my father, thinking about Gorsud tummy Romanovs hunger Leningrad Ladoga Lomonosov Shepelevo Schlisselburg, that I strolled past Mikhailovsky Palace without a glance at its impregnable red stucco walls, behind which, in 1801, Paul I was assassinated by his own men, so that his son could ascend to the throne.

"Take a picture of that palace," my father said. "It's worth it." I trudged back, took a picture.

A rusted tram rattled past, a sign on its side cheerfully proclaiming, "Leningrad Trams! 90 Years Old!"

These ninety-year-old trams schlepped through Leningrad on rails not embedded in concrete but suspended above ground: the low-quality concrete around the rails had disintegrated, leaving clefts in the road. You had to be careful when crossing because your foot — hell, your whole body — could easily get stuck in the gaping hole. You'd disappear and not be found again until more of the concrete broke off.

It was amazing — the whole city nearly untouched in eighty years. Like a holy relic. What had the Soviet government been doing for nearly a century? Vacationing in the Crimea?

I say untouched, but the Soviets did build. They built the KGB building next to my father's prison. They built the housing blocks Anatoly and his family lived in, prime residences in the workers' paradise. They built hotels: obscene industrial concrete boxes. The hotels were the shape — and size, it seemed — of the state of Kansas. Hotel Leningrad and Hotel Moskva were perfect examples of the Stalinist–Khruschevian aesthetic: Doric Ugly. Perhaps if they'd built one less hotel, they could have fixed all the potholes in the city with the concrete they saved.

We were walking so slowly now, we had nearly stopped by the time we entered Alexander's Park at the back of *Spas Na Kvovi*. Inside the park, we collided with a large gathering, discussing the Romanovs. I couldn't tell if the vocal priest was for or against. There were many Russian words strung loosely together. I felt like I was listening with my legs. My father didn't want to listen. He had had quite enough. Either that or he was hungry. It was after 7:30 in the evening and we had only eaten that little half-sandwich at Café Nord. He was tired of the whole thing.

We walked with agonizing slowness back to my hotel, where he had a shower and I went out to explore our dining possibilities.

LAST DINNER IN LENINGRAD

When I returned to the room, my father was standing in the hallway, dressed, washed, and smoking.

"You know," he said to me, "a shower is the key to civilization."

Nodding, I said, "It's not the shower, Papa. It's running water."

"Well, what is a shower then?"

"A perfect example of running water."

Though we liked the menu at the European Restaurant, we settled on the Caviar Bar after we realized that the elegant European had the same menu as the Caviar Bar but was thirty percent more expensive.

In the Caviar Bar we had Russian *zakuski*, borscht with no meat or potatoes, beef Stroganoff (with potatoes but no noodles). Papa had *kamchatka* — lobster with sauce. It was delicious. He said it was the most delicious lobster he'd ever eaten.

Thinking of Leningrad and how much I longed for it to be restored, I said, "Someday, the city will have money. Things will improve. Roads will be renovated. Buildings repainted."

My father shook his head. "It won't matter. No matter how much money there is, it won't matter. Look at Stalingrad. Never was a city more destroyed by war than Stalingrad. There was a heavy-machinery factory there, demolished. It was rebuilt after the war from scratch. So what did the Soviets do? They rebuilt it exactly the same. The same obsolete technology, the same dated architecture. That's just how they operate. It's a fallacy to think things will be different. They won't be any different."

As we were finishing up, I said, returning to the subject of Maui, "Papa, you know, it's the beginning of the rest of your life. It's an exciting time for you. You'll go to Maui, you'll get your health back, settle in, see how you like it. But Papa, if you don't like it, that's okay, too. You can always sell your condo and move back to the continent and find yourself another place to live."

He shook his head vigorously. "I am never leaving Maui."

"Don't say never. What if you don't like it?"

"What's not to like? Why won't I like it?" He squinted at me with suspicion.

"No reason. What if you get lonely?"

"I won't. I'll have Mama. I'm not leaving."

*

My stomach pretended to be all right so long as I wasn't eating, but as soon as we had dinner, I felt awful again. We had had a long day and all I wanted to do was get back to my room, instantly.

But my father asked if I wanted to walk with him to the monument to Catherine the Great, just down Nevsky near the Bolshoi Theater. I could not say no to my dad, even though I was nearly falling down.

As we strolled around the statue, several times I thought I was actually going to faint.

"What do you think?" he asked.

"It's wonderful," I said. "Can we go back?"

"Tired, Paullina?"

"Tired, Papa."

Crossing Nevsky, I lagged behind. I had no legs left. I saw his hand reach back, just as it did when I was little. I extended my own hand and took his. I think he'd forgotten himself, how old he was, how old I was, where we were. As soon as I took his hand, he let go.

"Don't forget," he said, "tomorrow, we're going to pick you up early because we're going to the Karelian Isthmus. We have a big day."

"Oh, I see, not like the days we've been having."

"Don't be fresh. Just be ready."

Back in my room, I felt better.

Running water was great as long as it didn't enter my mouth.

I took off my makeup.

Soon it was two in the morning again.

MY COPPER PENNY

Kevin called. In the movie *Somewhere in Time,* Christopher Reeve travels through time from 1979 back to 1912 to be with his beloved. When he accidentally pulls out a penny from 1979, he is instantly transported back to the future, parted forever from the love of his life. So it was with me a little bit. I had been awash in Leningrad and then Kevin called and instantly reminded me I had another life far away.

"Are you thinking of what movie you want to watch when you come back?" Kevin asked.

I was so distant, a life away from where he was, in beautiful sunny Texas, swimming with the kids, having pizza, watching TV. Thinking about movies. "I'm sorry, not at all." How far my other life was from me. There was no Texas for me here, no yellow stucco house, no heat. There was a yellow stucco church. Cobblestones. Endless daylight. A river. My father.

"I'll get back in the swing of things soon, I'm sure," I said without feeling. When I hung up the phone, I thought, will I? I didn't know if I would get back in the swing of things. What if I didn't?

Outside, the streetlights had been turned on. No more white nights.

I lay in bed and regretted not buying the Nicholas II Easter egg for ninety-five dollars. I would never find one like it again.

A fly buzzed around. Where would it be three days from now? Flies die in three days. In two days the fly would still be alive, but I would no longer be in Russia.

Would I still be alive?

How big was the wall around our breakfast nook? Would the wall in Texas hold my four watercolors of Leningrad?

Sleep, please, merciful sleep.

White nights, July 1998.

At Radik's dacha. From left: Alla, Alla's husband Viktor, Radik holding court, my dad, Ellie, a miserable-looking Anatoly, Luba and Anatoly's brother Viktor.

DAY SIX
Saturday

FIVE RUSSIANS IN A CLOWN CAR

In the morning it was raining and cold. Of course I had overslept.

When the phone rang, I had just jumped out of the shower.

"We're downstairs," my father said.

"Um, not quite ready yet."

"But Paullina," he said, in his unhappy-with-me voice. "I thought I told you to be ready."

"I know you *told* me," I said. "But I overslept."

"Ellie wants to see your room," he said brusquely. "I'll send her up."

"Papa, wait, what do you mean, Ellie? I'm completely naked."

"Well, put something on," he said and hung up.

Two minutes later there was a knock on the door. Ellie looked at me with my wet hair and no makeup and said I looked like the little Paullina from the home movie of our trip to the Caucasus Mountains.

She clucked appreciatively as she walked around the room. "Alla would've liked to see this."

"Have you had breakfast?" I asked her.

"Yes. You?"

"No, I just got up."

"You must be hungry, poor thing."

"I'm all right." No time even to eat *blini* and caviar anymore. No time to write, to call home, to sleep; no time, no time. My last day in Leningrad. No time for anything.

As I put on my makeup, I asked Ellie if my father seemed tired last night.

"I don't know about that," she said.

"When he left me, he was ready to fall down."

"I don't know about that. We stayed up until three in the morning, talking."

I did a double take. "You're joking. Anatoly, too?"

"No, Anatoly was at our *dacha*. He came back this morning. Did you see the Romanov funeral yesterday?"

"Well, we were there," I replied cryptically, scrunching mousse into my hair.

"Yes, of course I know. Do you have my dress? We saw the whole thing on television. All five hours of it. It was beautiful to watch. The service was incredible. Well, I don't have to tell *you*. You were there."

We were going to see my grandfather's and father's friends. Ellie said that on the way, she wanted to stop at her *dacha*. It was in the village of Lisiy Nos, twenty kilometers north of Leningrad.

After the Germans attacked Russia in 1941, the Finns came down the Karelian Isthmus, to reclaim what once had been theirs.

They stopped at Lisiy Nos on the outer city limits and waited for Hitler to take Leningrad.

"Don't worry, there are no Finns there now," Ellie assured me.

"That's good," I said. "I still don't know what Papa is going to say about us stopping at your *dacha*." Actually, I knew very well what he was going to say.

Slyly smiling, Ellie said, "I made you your favorite. *Blinchiki*." *Blinchiki* are rolled-up meat crèpes fried in butter. I do love them.

"Mmmm," I said. My stomach was feeling better. I was hungry.

"If we stop at Lisiy Nos, I will fry them for you and your papa. We could eat them with some tea."

"Let's talk to Papa, okay?" I said. "What's in the bag you're holding?"

"Oh, these are presents for you," she said. "I brought a few little things for you to take back to your family."

She took out three GIANT bags of Russian candy — one for each of my three children, some chocolate for Kevin, and two china cups with saucers for me.

"Ellie, thank you. But you shouldn't have. I mean it. You really shouldn't have." Where was I going to put it all?

She smiled. "It's custom. To take back something of us with you. So you don't forget us."

"Little chance of that." I hugged her.

Thirty minutes later, when we got outside and I saw my father's sour expression, I was glad I wasn't a child anymore. If I had been, I certainly wouldn't be getting any ice cream today.

Viktor drove. My father sat in the passenger seat. I sat in the back, squeezed in between Ellie and Anatoly.

Ellie mentioned to my father about our stopping in Lisiy Nos.

My father glared at Ellie as if she were mad.

"Go to Lisiy Nos? For God's sake. Why, woman?"

Even Anatoly seemed to think it was a crazy idea, and he usually never sided with my father. Ellie was visibly upset.

"But my *blinchiki*," she said. "I don't understand, I spent all day yesterday making them. I made them for you because you all said you loved them. Paullina told me they were her favorite."

"Paullina's favorite is mushroom barley soup," my father said. "Did you make that, too? You want to warm that up too at Lisiy Nos?"

"Ellie, you never make *blinchiki* for me," Anatoly said.

"Oh, stop it," she said. "I make you food every day."

It went back and forth about *blinchiki* for a half hour.

I was amused. I wanted Ellie's *blinchiki*.

With five adults in the car, two of them smoking, my father and Anatoly argued loudly about Soviet hypocrisy regarding the Finns and discussed Ellie's impossible request to stop at Lisiy Nos — until we reached a small supermarket in the middle of a wet nowhere that smelled strongly of fish. Fresh fish and smoked fish and salted fish and fish that was none of the above.

We bought some pastries and some bread, and some beer. But no fish.

In the car, Ellie had in her lap a large bag of ginger cookies and some soft meringues.

"Want a cookie?" For some reason she looked sheepish as she offered it. I took a cookie, which turned out to be awesome. I took three more. After a few minutes, Ellie softly confessed to the occupants of the car that it was a good thing we hadn't stopped at Lisiy Nos, because she had forgotten her *blinchiki* back at Ulitsa Dybenko.

Amid laughter and general mocking, we imagined how the scene would have unfolded had we acquiesced to Ellie's wishes and gone to Lisiy Nos. For many miles we laughed about what would have been said when we discovered there were no *blinchiki*.

Anatoly repeated, "She never makes me *blinchiki*."

To change the subject, I asked my father how it had been for him, staying in their apartment without hot water. He told me that every morning he boiled a kettle and diluted the scalding water with cold water in a pan.

"First I shave, and then I wash myself piece by piece."

"Really?" I said. "And how did that work out?"

My father was cheerful. "I discovered you can wash a whole person on one kettle of boiling water."

"Depending on which parts you wash," said Ellie.

"Stop it!" Papa barked, whirling to her. "What's gotten into you?"

As we drove north up the Karelian Isthmus, I stared out onto the gloomy misty distance and imagined that somewhere, on the other side of the Gulf of Finland, was my Shepelevo.

Now that I had seen it with adult eyes, would it ever mean the same to me again?

I closed my eyes.

KILOMETER 67

"How long is this trip?" I asked my father after what felt like four hours in the cramped car.

"Forty-five minutes," he replied. "Right, Viktor?"

"Right," said Viktor.

"Right," I said.

After what seemed to be another few hours, I inquired again.

Apparently we could not find the town of Orekhovo, where my grandfather's friends, the Ivanchenkos, lived.

We might as well have been looking for a Corelware factory in the middle of Tunisia, or asking a blind South African for directions to Disney World. The streets were unmarked, the houses un-numbered, the roads barely paved. It was raining, and the locals were stuporously unfriendly.

After a week-long observation, I finally concluded that, for all his other very fine qualities, our faithful driver Viktor *loved* to stop and ask for directions. It was like a hobby, a pastime for him, like photography or baseball. Every several hundred feet he would stop and ask. When he was directed to go straight for two kilometers, he would go straight for two hundred and fifty meters and then stop and ask someone to reaffirm the directions.

He would do this *every* two hundred and fifty meters.

Sentimentally, I reminisced about getting lost with Kevin, twelve years ago, before he was my husband. I was driving; we were headed to an amusement park in New Jersey. Our map had been inadequate, and we drove around lost for a half hour, missing the exit to the highway. Occasionally Kevin would mutter, "We could stop and ask for directions."

"No!"

Finally Kevin gave up and started reading a paperback.

He was a third of the way done with his dumb book before I gave in, stopped and asked for directions.

He married me anyway.

*

We drove down a wrong road, drove and drove, stopping and asking for directions every two hundred and fifty meters. Then we turned and came back to the highway, and asked someone else at an intersection. The man told us we hadn't gone far enough down the wrong road. So we turned around and drove back, and drove farther than before, without really knowing what we were looking for.

My father and Viktor finally told me they were looking for Kilometer 67.

"What does that mean?"

"Kilometer 67. Just that," said my father. "The Ivanchenkos live on the sixty-seventh kilometer from Leningrad."

"Oh," I said. "*That's* the directional marker we're going for? Kilometer 67?"

"We don't have another one."

"I see."

A man and a boy told Viktor we were going the wrong way, and had to go back to the highway, through an outdoor market, and down over the railroad tracks. Why we had to stop at the market, I don't know.

But we did stop at the market, into which Anatoly up and disappeared — ostensibly to ask for directions. We sat in the car for a few minutes, wondering what to do.

Where was he? Where did he go? And why? "Don't worry about him," Ellie said. "He always does this."

"So why did you let him out of the car if he always does this?" I wanted to know. "And what exactly is *this*?"

"This. This." My father pointed to the market. "He goes off and disappears."

Ellie shook her head. I reached for the door handle. "So let's go find him."

"Sit right there," my father said. "He'll be back."

"When?"

"Don't know."

Ellie shook her head again.

"What's he buying?"

"How should I know?" Ellie shrugged. "He doesn't have much money, though."

We sat — not all of us quietly. Viktor periodically left the car himself and approached passersby to ask directions. But how could strangers help us when nothing was marked? Russians can barely tell you how to get to their own house. The directions my father received from the Ivanchenkos went something like this: "Go to the railroad, then turn left. No, wait, right. There will be a sign — no, wait, the sign's been missing since after the war — just make a left, there will be two roads, I think it's the one closest to the railroad tracks. Make that left, then drive. We're on a street to the right. You can't miss it. It's a green house."

Feebly, my father had asked them, "Will it be the only street to the right?"

"No, there are many rights, but our street has tall trees and purple lilacs in the spring. You'll know it when you see it."

"But it's not spring. What's the name of the street?"

"It doesn't have one. I think it used to be called Sireneva Street." *Siren* is the Russian word for *lilac tree*.

"What's the number of the house?"

"Seventy-four. Or forty-seven. Can't remember. Wait, it's three.

Yes, three. But you won't know that. The number fell off a long time ago."

"Let me guess. After the war?"

Idly we sat waiting for Anatoly to return.

"Papa," I asked, "how does mail get to these people?"

"It doesn't," he snapped, puffing on another cigarette. "There is no mail here."

Viktor saw another passerby and jumped out of the car.

At last Anatoly returned — without any purchases. Everyone in the car yelled at him. He said he'd found a local street map and now knew *exactly* where to go. Apparently we needed to go over the railroad tracks, straight ahead, and Sireneva Street would be right there.

We drove to the railroad station, half a kilometer away. Viktor stopped and asked for directions three times. No one knew where Sireneva Street was. This did not inspire us with confidence. Finally, near the station, we stopped in the middle of the street. Blocking the road and foot traffic, we sat with the engine running and the rain hammering outside.

Russians filed past us, fresh from the train. Anatoly and Viktor kept getting out of the car and asking people where Sireneva Street was. No one knew. But we got plenty of dirty looks from people who had to go around our car in the rain.

Finally a man told Viktor to turn around and go back. This was *precisely* what Viktor wanted to hear, so we turned around and went back — to the outdoor market. My father kept smoking and shaking his head. Ellie was trying not to laugh. I had to use a bathroom — naturally.

I was a little concerned with the way Viktor kept tailgating, keeping barely six feet between himself and the car in front of him in the slick rain, going thirty miles an hour. Leaning forward, I said to him, "Viktor, I don't know if you've ever had a chance to brush up on the immutable laws of physics, but the laws clearly state that two objects cannot occupy the same space at the same time."

Papa laughed. Viktor, sensing the joke was at his expense, slowed down ever so slightly. The outdoor market loomed ahead.

"Can we really risk Anatoly disappearing into the market again?" I asked.

After a glare in my general direction, my father said, "I see that I have to take matters into my own hands. This time I'm going with him."

So my father, Anatoly, and Viktor — who could not keep still — set out to look for another street map. Five minutes later, when they came back, my father was yelling at Anatoly and shaking his head.

"The man doesn't know how to read a map! Did you read it upside down? It was clear as daylight where the street was. We went completely the wrong way. One hundred and eighty degrees from where we were supposed to go. Mother of God, what am I going to do with these people?"

Anatoly looked sheepish and said simply, "I got us here, and now everyone is yelling at me."

We drove away from the market and the railroad. Viktor stopped four times to ask directions. The last time he stopped to ask where Sireneva Street was, the man stared at Viktor, then pointed directly to the left of us and said, "Right here."

We made a left and finally found a green house.

"I can't believe we're here," I said. "What the hell time is it?" It felt as if we had been in the car for weeks.

"Two o'clock," said Ellie.

The forty-five minute trip had taken three hours.

"Ladies and gentlemen," my father said. "A fair word of warning. We can't stay long. I told Radik we would be at his house by two. We're running late." He glared at me again. "If only you'd gotten ready on time like I told you."

"Of course," I said. "It must be my fault it's so late."

They were waiting for us, my grandparents' old friends, Nikolai and Valya Ivanchenko.

The Ivanchenkos lived in a small *dacha* with a large wet yard full of tall wet pines and birches. They had a vegetable garden, and a little hammock. The hammock reminded me of the one I used to play on with Yulia in Shepelevo when we were children. Remembering Yulia prickled my heart. I was leaving tomorrow. There was nothing to be done now.

Valya and her husband Nikolai were very happy we had come. I knew immediately it was the right thing to do. Apparently, however, there had been some confusion. My father originally told them we were coming four days ago, on July 14, so Nikolai had gone back to the city and spent all day by the phone, waiting for my father's call. When my father didn't call, Nikolai thought we weren't coming. When my father did call — on July 15 — there was confusion again. Nikolai thought we were going to arrive *yesterday*, on July 17. I wanted to tell him that we might have — had it taken us less time to find him.

So to me it sounded for a moment as if they hadn't known we were coming.

Yet, when we stepped inside their house, I saw that the table on the veranda was set for ten people.

"Oh, no. Please," my father said, looking at the spread, "we can only stay for a little while."

"Well, then, let's hurry and eat," Valya said.

Their two-story *dacha* was very small. I don't know where Valya and Nikolai slept, but they shared the house with their daughter, her husband and her two children, a three-year-old boy and a shy sixteen-year-old girl.

"But there's an upstairs?" I asked.

"Yes, but we only have the downstairs," said Valya. "Somebody else lives upstairs. Are you looking for something in particular?"

I had learned my lesson well and that morning had drunk no water, no coffee, no liquid of any kind. But feminine demands being what they are, I still desperately needed to use the facilities.

What kind of modern woman plans a trip to Russia during the most inconvenient time of the month? The kind who says I will have mastery over my body. I will not be ruled by the minutiae of discomfort and subservience, I will act as a man, undaunted and free. Well, here I was. Free. Undaunted.

"Toilet?" I inquired meekly.

Valya Ivanchenko's face struck the same expression as Svetlana's had in Schlisselburg at the Diorama Museum. As if she wished I hadn't asked.

She pointed to a green wooden structure in the backyard. In the rain, I walked across the soggy ground.

I had to hold my breath and hoped I could do what I had to do before I needed to breathe out again.

The toilet in the outhouse was a wooden platform at thigh level with a hole in the middle. In Shepelevo we had one just like it, except ours was *inside* the house.

What disturbed me was not the hole in the ground, which I had expected, but the brevity of time between liquid leaving my body and making a dense, thudding sound below me. It sounded uncomfortably close; I couldn't help but look.

Usually the hole in an outhouse is dug three meters deep in the ground. Here, two feet below me stood a cannister filled with human waste.

Yet inside the house there was running water. *Cold* running water, granted, but I was able to wash my hands. I understood nothing.

As Valya got lunch ready, I *quietly* asked Ellie why there would be nothing but a bucket in the outhouse.

Ellie *loudly* explained to me that in many villages, when the canister got filled up, they took it out and used the contents for fertilizer.

"Oh," I said, wondering — *silently* — if feminine sanitary dressings made good fertilizer.

The Ivanchenkos' half of the house included the veranda, where we were eating, a small kitchen-slash-hallway, and one bedroom. Maybe there was another bedroom somewhere? It was all so small.

What did I mean when I said small? Small compared with what?

With my house in Texas?

With our *dacha* in Shepelevo?

With any other *dacha* I'd ever seen?

With the Winter Palace?

What was I comparing it with? I was ashamed. It wasn't small. It was their life, and they were happy in it.

Valya was bubbly and despite being seventy-eight, looked like a young, energetic girl. Nikolai was eighty-two ("a baby," my ninety-one-year-old grandfather had called him), and reminded me of my grandfather. He sat with quiet dignity and watched everyone. Much like his three-year-old grandson, Eugene.

I gave Eugene a T-shirt I had brought for him from Texas. He immediately took it, mumbled a thank you, and disappeared into his bedroom. When he emerged seconds later, the T-shirt was no longer in his hands.

Where did the boy play? I wondered. Where were his toys? Outside, yes a hammock, but today was cold and raining. There was nowhere to go. He sat silently on his father's lap.

Sunny and animated, Valya moved quickly, carrying large pots of food. Nikolai sat and watched, above the fray. I saw why my grandfather liked him.

We had black caviar on bread with butter, beef Stroganoff, cucumbers and tomatoes. We also had hot potatoes with dill, sardines, some ham, and then coffee with unchewable stale waffle cake.

"I didn't know you liked sardines, Paullina," Ellie said when she saw me ladling sardines onto my plate.

"Love 'em."

"I would have opened two cans for you. We have so many. Too bad you're leaving tomorrow."

"It *is* too bad, isn't it, Ellie?"

"Next time you come you have to stay for longer. You can stay at our *dacha*. Bring your whole family and stay for as long as you want."

"Thank you."

Nikolai said to me, "I am glad and proud you are sitting next to me. I should be so lucky as to have a writer, a real-life novelist, sit to my left. But Paullina, your books, I've never seen one in Russian. Are there any in Russian?"

My father promised he would send Nikolai *Tully* in Russian as soon as he returned to Prague.

Then he raised a glass of vodka to Nikolai. "I just want to say how glad I am we came to see you today. I remember you so well from when I was a child, and it means so much to me ..." He couldn't finish the toast. He just downed his vodka.

Nikolai turned to his wife and said, "Is there anything for me to drink, *kotik*?"

Kotik is a Russian endearment literally meaning *kitty cat*, but the connotation is one of great tenderness, like *my sweetest beloved darling*. You would not say *kotik* to someone you did not completely and unconditionally adore. It was inspiring to hear a husband call his wife *kotik* after sixty years of marriage.

The Russian way was to finish everything on your plate, because of the war, but I didn't know what to do with my stale waffle cake. When Ellie wasn't looking, I slipped it onto her plate. Now it was her problem.

Viktor finished the film in my camera, taking pictures of us by Nikolai's house, outside in the cold rain. Just as I was thinking that my grandfather would love all these pictures, I opened my camera to load a fresh roll of film, thinking — erroneously — that Viktor would have rewound the finished one. He hadn't. I had inadvertently exposed it. How much of it would be lost? And what would I tell my father and grandfather when he asked for photos of the Ivanchenkos in front of their green *dacha*?

We said our goodbyes and drove to Radik's house, also on the Karelian Isthmus but closer to the Gulf of Finland, not inland. I was afraid to ask how far it was. Finally I mustered up some courage. "Papa," I said, "about how long is it to Radik's house from here?"

"Like I know," he said.

"Forty-five minutes," Viktor told me.

"Paullina, you'll be happy," said Ellie. "Radik's house has a toilet *inside* the house. You'll see."

"Paullina," Anatoly said, "I promise you that when you come back to see us in Russia, my *dacha* in Lisiy Nos will have a toilet that flushes. I'm working on that right now. You will have it when you come."

My father promptly interjected that the key to civilization was a shower.

"But Yura," said Ellie, who never forgot anything, "you said you could wash your whole self with a kettle."

My father grunted and fell asleep.

RADIK

As we drove, Ellie told me about Radik. The gist of it was: "Radik when he was young was the most handsome man you ever saw. Now he is older, you know he is nearly sixty — or maybe he is sixty. He has gained weight, but still. Yes, still, but not like *before*."

"Before what?" I ventured.

"*Before*, he was just — you could not stop looking at him. Well, you'll tell me what you think." She stopped. "How can you not remember him?"

"I was very young," I said. "I was nine. What did I know of handsome? I had my own father. I remember Radik's son, though, Korney." Korney was born in August 1963 to my November. My mother and his mother, Lida, Radik's wife, were pregnant girlfriends together. We grew up knowing each other. Each of us was our parents' only child. But in 1973, we left Russia, and they stayed behind.

And that made all the difference.

In 1984 Korney died of acute alcoholism. When he died, Radik and Lida were left childless. Rather than tear them apart, Korney's death brought Lida and Radik closer together; at least that's what Ellie told me.

Ellie said that no one could understand what Radik saw in Lida, because while he was extraordinary, she was plain and had always been on the heavy side.

"I don't know if he's ever been unfaithful to her, but I think so," Ellie said, "because women have thrown themselves at Radik all his life."

"They have, have they? *All* women?"

"Without exception," Ellie said firmly.

We sat. I looked out the window.

"You do know the famous story about Radik, don't you?" Ellie asked.

"No," I said. "I know no story."

"When Marilyn Monroe was in Russia with her husband Arthur Miller, shooting a film —"

"What film?"

"I don't know what film. Her latest film. Radik was working on the set. When Marilyn Monroe saw him, she said, 'Oh yes! I want to act with him in my next movie.'"

"Oh?"

I wanted to correct her, tell her that Marilyn Monroe had never gone to Russia with Arthur Miller. It was Arthur Miller's third wife, Inge Morath, who had gone to Russia with him in the mid-sixties, and Inge was no actress, but a photographer; and Marilyn Monroe had been dead several years by that point. But I said nothing, except, "Oh?"

"Paullina," Ellie said, as if I hadn't understood, "he was handsomer than *Alain Delon*."

"Not Alain Delon," I said, smiling. Ellie with her little round face and youthful freckles was contagiously enthusiastic. As if the French heart-throb of the 1960s was the universal benchmark of manly good looks.

She could not stop talking about Radik. Even I, overwhelmed as I was by exhaustion, affection and heartache, discovered that I had room for one more emotion: curiosity.

All this in the crowded backseat of a Volkswagen, traveling on a country road, the Gulf of Finland a gray blur through the sodden birch trees and the pines. We passed a beautiful old-style Russian church in Zelenogorsk: tall-spired, round-domed. A little farther north, in Ushkovo, we made a left onto an unpaved road. We didn't ask anyone how to get to Radik's. We simply found him.

*

He was standing in his front yard in the rain, waiting for us, and on his face was the biggest smile I ever saw.

He was extremely happy to see my father. They embraced like lifelong friends. Then he came to me with open arms and said, "Plinochka, let me look at you!" After giving me a bear hug, he pulled away to look at me again, and as he scrutinized me, the smile never left his face.

I didn't remember Radik; I didn't recognize him from old photos. But even now, at fifty-nine, he was striking. He was tall and tanned and broad-shouldered, with brown, happy eyes and a shocking amount of longish salt and pepper hair. He didn't look like a hobbled man whose only son had tragically died. Aside from his physical presence, he had a confident manner that had obviously charmed many over the years. A well-used, smiling, casual manner that said, "I know what I am. I don't even have to try. I'm just going to smile." He was so happy to see me. It lifted my heart to know that despite all the things I had wanted to do on my sixth and last day, we had done the right thing by coming to visit him.

We were still outside getting soaked by the heavy rain when Radik's wife Lida came down the porch steps, a huge smile on her face, too. She hurried over to me, hugged me tight, pulled away, and then both she and Radik stood close with their arms around me.

Lida said to Radik, "Look at her, Papulya. Isn't she something?"

She said it as if they had talked about me many times before, as if they had seen me before, as if they knew me well. But how could they? When they told my father they would never forgive him if we didn't spend one-sixth of our trip at their rented *dacha*, what were they looking forward to? What were they expecting?

As they pulled away again to look at me, Lida tenderly touched my hair.

I was confounded.

Confusion reigned inside the house as well.

For one, it was chock full of people.

Ellie's daughter Alla and her husband Viktor were already there, without their kids. Anatoly's brother Viktor and his wife Luba were there. I was so taken aback by the welcome I'd received, I barely managed to grunt in their direction.

And second, the men started making plans to go to the public baths.

"The what?" I said.

"The public baths," replied Radik, as if that was explanation enough.

"Papa, are you crazy?"

"Why? Why do you say this?" he demanded.

"Has anyone noticed it's raining and cold?"

"So? In the baths it's warm and hot."

"And wet. How far are these baths?"

"I don't know. Radik? How far?"

"Not far. Maybe half a kilometer. I go all the time in the rain. Paullina, it's refreshing." He smiled. "It makes me feel young."

"Hey, girls," I said. "Maybe we should go swimming in the Gulf of Finland."

"Paullina, you're welcome to do it!" Radik exclaimed. "Have you brought your bathing suit? What a pleasure it is to swim in the Gulf. Am I right, Lida?"

"Yes, Papulya. But we're not going swimming," she said, frowning. "It *is* raining."

But the men, Anatoly, Viktor, Viktor, Viktor, and Radik, all left. They walked half a kilometer in the cold rain, got naked, went into the steam room and beat each other with bundles of birch twigs.

Meanwhile, we girls sat in the warm glow of a little ceramic wood-burning stove, and chatted. Lida took me into her bedroom and showed me a picture of Korney at age twenty with their family dog.

"Both are dead now," she said. And sighing, she showed me another picture of Korney as a child.

"He is a very good-looking boy," I said.

"Yes," she said sadly. "He was." And then she clicked her tongue and looked upward as if to say, "Ah, life."

Lida's features were broad and her skin was coarse, but she had an air that was funny and natural and I liked her enormously. She was a true woman: beaten by life but not defeated, and apparently still in love with her husband.

"Lida," I said, "I hate to ask, but do you have a bathroom?"

"Do we have a bathroom? What do you think, we live in the woods?" She laughed heartily at her own joke as she took me to a room behind the kitchen. They did in fact live in the woods.

Maybe once upon a time their toilet was flushable. But to flush a toilet, you needed running water. And Radik and Lida didn't have any. Lida showed me the toilet, and the large bucket of water next to it. There was a small metal saucepan in the bucket.

"You do your business, and when you're done, you take the saucepan and use it as a ladle, all right? Fill it with water from the bucket and pour the water into the toilet."

"All right," I said.

So that's what Ellie had meant by flushable.

The toilet paper could not be thrown into the toilet but had to go into a receptacle provided, which had a helpful note attached: "For paper."

To wash my hands, I pressed hard on a short metal nozzle attached to a refillable tank above the sink. Cold water poured over my fingers.

To give credit where credit was due, there was toilet paper! — and it was *soft*. Also, the bathroom *tried* to smell clean. There were cleaning supplies in the bathtub, the first I'd seen all week.

I went out onto the covered veranda and looked at the sumptuous dinner table that was set for us.

"Hungry, Plinochka?" Lida asked, carrying the wine and cognac to the table.

"Starving. I am so happy you have marinated mushrooms. They're my favorite."

"I wish I had known!" exclaimed Lida. "I would have opened another jar. But I'm going to put them in front of you, and I want you to eat all of them."

I walked into Lida's kitchen, saw the dog on the twin bed on the floor, and just as I was about to go to the dog, and to inquire about the twin bed standing next to a wall in the kitchen, my nose got a whiff of something so wretched that I needed to get out of there instantly.

Before I could move, Ellie cornered me near the twin bed and the abominable odor. I held my breath, but I didn't want her to think I didn't want to smell *her*, so I exhaled. Bending me to her four-foot ten-inch frame, she whispered, "Plina, don't laugh, but I brought my *blinchiki* after all."

I laughed.

"Don't laugh, I said. They'll laugh me out of the house when they come back and find out."

"I don't understand," I said. "How did you miss them in the trunk the last time you looked?"

"I don't know," Ellie said. "They must have fallen behind the ginger cookies."

"What are we going to do with these *blinchiki* now?"

Ellie asked Lida if she could fry the *blinchiki* after dinner for me to take back to my hotel.

"Of course," said Lida.

The men came back, wet and flushed. Everyone was wearing their coats; everyone but Radik, who strolled in wearing just his shorts and no shirt, exposing his wet tanned body as he stood in the doorway, laughing. A blurred picture could not do justice to the life Radik breathed into that small kitchen when he walked in.

Lida gazed at him with a delighted expression and laughed with him, saying he was simply crazy for being half-naked in this cold. "I always come back from the baths like this," Radik said to me. "It's so rejuvenating."

It was time for dinner. Radik at the head of the table demanded that I sit on his left side. That's how Radik wanted it, so that's how it was.

I wanted to be next to my father, who instead sat several people away at the rectangular table. I suddenly became acutely aware that after this dinner, I was going to get into the car and Viktor was going to drive me back to Leningrad, and my trip with my father would be over.

We ate canned herring and tongue with horseradish.

Radik spooned the horseradish onto my plate himself. He made sure I had some tongue and some herring and all the cucumbers I wanted. Lida must have told him about my affection for marinated mushrooms, because every ten minutes, he would ladle some more onto my plate with the words, "Eat, eat."

He poured me the cognac, glass after glass, as he made the toasts and we all drank with him.

Alla sat to the left of me, and Lida next to Alla. Alla's husband Viktor was next, then my father, and on the opposite side of the table was Ellie, who watched us jealously, Anatoly next to her, then Viktor and Luba. Somehow, I don't know how, Viktor the driver finagled a seat on Radik's immediate right.

Alla tried to talk to me. She would start, "Plinochka, my daughter Marina wrote your Natasha a letter in English." And Radik would tap on my shoulder and say, "Plinochka, a toast, I would like to make a toast." After his toast, we would down a glass of vodka, and then Alla would try again. "Plinochka," she'd say, "I hope Marina wrote the letter correctly. She is learning English and she wanted to make a good impression on Natasha. I asked her if there were any mistakes, and she said no. It's hard for me to tell."

Radik would tap me on the shoulder and say, "Plinochka, I have a story for you, listen to this story." Toast after toast after toast, anecdote after anecdote, he talked and we listened and laughed and commented. My father talked, too, but less than usual. Radik ruled that table.

We ate cucumbers, tomatoes, warm boiled potatoes with dill and garlic, and marinated mushrooms. I ate plenty of those. I must have eaten the entire jar.

Viktor the driver hung on to Radik's every word and laughed loudly at every small joke Radik made. Viktor didn't just hang on to Radik's words; he could not take his eyes off Radik. Finding this amusing, I glanced at Luba, then at Ellie, then at Lida, and at Alla: every one of them was transfixed by Radik.

Occasionally he and his wife exchanged a small remark about food. "Lidochka, your borscht is very good. Very good. Let me drink a toast to this borscht," he would say. Or Lida would ask, "Papulya, do you think it's time for the stuffed peppers?" Papulya, a diminutive of Papa, must have been what Korney had once called his father. It was a vestige of the old days. Fourteen years after Korney's untimely death, Lida couldn't go back to just Radik, as if calling him something other than Papulya would remind them both of something they wished to God to forget.

Alla mentioned how handsome Radik had been. I studied his face as she paid him this compliment. He shrugged casually and said, "Ah, youth."

I turned to Lida and she said, leaving to get her stuffed peppers, "You're asking the wrong person. I'm biased." But Viktor could not stop staring at him. When Radik cracked a joke, Viktor was nearly always the first to laugh. Sometimes Ellie beat him to it. She never glanced at anyone else, certainly not at her husband, who sat glumly next to her. Finally Anatoly went out for a long smoke.

I went out at the same time to use the bathroom. As I was coming back to the dinner table, he cornered me on the veranda. "I've been thinking that I want to show you something," he said.

"Oh, yeah?" I said, staring longingly at the door.

"Yes. I want you to read my novella. What do you think?"

"I'd be happy to, Anatoly."

"Your father is in it."

"That's fine."

"As a young man."

"I'll be glad to read about my father as a young man."

"And as a grown man, too."

"That'll be fine."

"Yes, but ..." he stumbled on his words and stopped.

"What is it?"

"It's just that ... I hope it doesn't make you uncomfortable ..."

"What kind of stuff is in there?" I smiled. "Something saucy?"

"Well, I don't know if you know this, but before Ellie and I got together, your father had quite a crush on her."

"Really?" I didn't know that.

"Yes. How do you feel about that?"

"It's all right," I said, wondering how he wanted me to feel about it. He was obviously bothered by something.

"When I found out he liked her, it almost ruined our friendship. We didn't talk for two years. He didn't want to talk to me either." He spoke about it as if it happened last week. The discomfort was all over his face.

"Anatoly," I said, patting him on the arm. "It's in the past now. Ellie married *you*."

"Yes," he said, "but I wonder how your father feels about it."

I didn't know how to respond to that. He married my mother. "I'm sure," I said, "that it's in the past for him, too. Has he read it?"

Shrugging, Anatoly said, "He did, or not. I don't know. Maybe he read some of it, maybe most of it. I don't think he read the whole thing. He didn't seem to like it. I think it's because of the Ellie stuff. He thought it was too personal."

"Well, the more personal the better. Personal makes for very good drama," I said. "I'll be glad to read it. Now let's go back to the table."

Pensively looking out onto the wet yard and stepping away from me, Anatoly said, "I'll stay here for a minute."

Radik quickly poured me another drink, made a toast to my father's and mother's good health, and we drank.

The subject of the Russian Revolution came up. My father said, "Yes, my wife was due to give birth to Paullina on November seventh, the anniversary of the Bolshevik uprising. I told her if she gave birth on that day, I would have no choice but to leave her." He laughed heartily. "I was only half-joking," he added. "But my wife took me very seriously in those days, and gave birth the day before."

"The day before what?" Radik asked, filling my cognac glass, and smiling at me.

"The day before November seventh," replied my father.

"Oh my God," Radik said to me, "What day were you born?"

"November sixth."

"No," he said. "It can't be. So was I."

I had not met anyone who was born on the sixth of November. I studied him for a moment.

"Well, well," I said. He raised his glass and we drank to our birthdays.

"Plinka," Radik said, smiling, "I will always think of you now on my birthday. We will have this bond because we were born on the same day."

Sometime before the stuffed peppers were brought to the table, Radik leaned over to me and said in a quiet voice but not a whisper, "Plinka, but you are very beautiful."

What could I say? I smiled politely. My father sat across the table; Radik's wife was just one wife away.

"Thank you."

"You are. You are," he said. "Do I embarrass you by talking like that?"

There was nothing I could say. "Of course not."

Lida served the stuffed peppers.

Radik drank a toast to the stuffed peppers.

Radik and Papa drank a toast to fishing together tomorrow on Birch Island.

Lida served us all, getting up, going around the table, hardly sitting down. She was lovely.

She did everything while Radik sat and drank and ate and presided. No one could fault him for that. As if anyone had ever faulted him for anything. He acted like a man whom no one ever faulted.

He poured me another glass. "Radik, please," I said. "I can't drink any more. How many have we had?"

How many *had* we had? We drank to me, to my father, to my mother, to my father and me, to borscht, to the stuffed peppers, to our birthdays, to fishing. And to my parents' good health. Perhaps I was leaving some toasts out.

"Please," Radik said. "You have to drink to this one. Yura, please, you too, where is your glass?"

My father carefully poured himself half a glass.

Radik stood up. "I want to drink to my beloved friends, my old friends." He teared up and had to sit down. The way my father had teared up at Nikolai Ivanchenko's house, and for the same reason: for the passing of time, for the loss of those he loved, for nostalgia, youth gone by, heartache. For Russia.

Some of us needed to leave Russia to have a life, he said when he could speak again, but the rest of us stayed and took our hits and went to our rented *dachas*. We continued to fish and pick berries, and our wives cooked our food, and we worked without getting paid, and we cried for our old friends who had flown to all the corners of the globe.

My father raised his glass to Radik. "*Moi dorogoi*," he said. "My dear. We are all getting old. We have known each other forty years. Who knows when we will be together again. Who knows if we will ever be together again. This could be the last night we are together. Tonight I drink to my lifelong friends, Radik, Anatoly. Let's promise to bury each other when we die."

There was not a dry eye at the table.

"Yurochka," said Radik. "Do you remember New Year's Eve, 1971?"

My father rolled his eyes. "Do I remember New Year's Eve, 1971? I never forget anything."

My ears immediately pricked up. "What happened New Year's Eve, 1971?" In the chronology of my life, it was my penultimate New Year's Eve in the Soviet Union.

Radik said, "Plinochka, listen to this story. It's a good story, and it's about your father. New Year's Eve, 1971, I took my son Korney to a pioneer camp for New Year's school holiday week. The camp was in Tolmachevo, one hundred and one kilometers south of Leningrad."

"So you would say that Tolmachevo was on the one hundred and first kilometer?" I asked.

Radik laughed. "That's exactly what it's called: the one hundred and first kilometer. Now listen."

I smiled at the droll way Russians measured distance.

Radik continued. "It was about twenty degrees below zero Celsius, and I was wearing a long wool coat with an Astrakhan fur collar. As I was slowly walking back to the train station, I ran into a man in a torn dark ratty coat with god-awful black and injured hands. On his head he wore a shabby black hat." Radik looked at me. "It was your papa."

"Yes, yes," my father said. "My hands really were terrible looking. I hurt them bad."

Radik went on. "'Yura!' I said. 'What a coincidence! What are you doing here?'" Your papa told me he was in exile on the one hundred and first kilometer, working and living in a factory that made concrete and steel telephone posts. We hugged. He showed

341

me his injured hands, all blue from the cold. I asked how he hurt them. He said he worked as a cutter of reinforced steel fittings for the telephone posts and cut himself.

"We went to a local cafeteria, where they were serving three selections for dinner and some wine. After we had plenty to drink, your papa asked if I could take him with me to Leningrad, so he could spend New Year's Eve with you and your mother. 'Let's try,' I replied, and together we went to speak to his parole officer, the captain of the local militia.

"But we couldn't go empty-handed, so first we went to a store and bought bottles of cheap wine that we put in a mesh carry bag, so that the captain could see right away what we had brought him."

Lida interjected. "And you should have seen Radik then, Plinochka, oh, my. The militia man took one look at him and stood up. Radik was so tall, and his coat was so beautiful. He looked like a captain in the army."

I glanced at Radik to gauge his reaction. He was utterly unmoved. Yes, that was me, his expression read. What of it? Can we get on with the story? I know what I am.

He continued. "Your papa's parole officer sat behind a desk in a dark, dirty, extremely well heated little room, in the middle of which stood a cylindrical cast-iron wood-burning stove. The room was poorly lit, which cast the officer's expression in a pale, mournful tone. It was the thirty-first of December and he was on duty behind an empty desk, probably all night. He was not a happy man."

"But when Radik walked in," Lida said, "looking so handsome and tall in his coat, the man stood up."

"Lida, wait," said Radik. "Can *I*?"

Lida smiled and waved him on. I could see most people in the room had heard the story before, knew it by heart. Radik was telling it for me.

"So I said, 'Hello to you,' to the parole officer, standing before him and holding out my hand to him. In my other hand I held the bag of the cheap but delicious wine, *Rubin*.

"Because it was *I* who extended my hand to him and not vice versa, he was impressed and assumed I must be someone important. I was counting on that, and that's what happened. I shook his hand and said to him, 'Sit down, sit down.' He sat down."

Everyone laughed.

"I handed him the bag with the wine and said, 'This is my present to you for New Year's.' Then I pointed to your papa. 'You know this man?' The officer said, 'Of course I know him. It's Gendler.'

"I said, 'Well, this man is my brother, and I have come here to take him home with me. He would like to spend the holidays with his family. Say five days or so. I hope you will let him go. If you want, I can leave you my passport as a guarantee of his return.'

"The parole officer opened my passport and read my last name. '*Tikhomirov*,' he read. 'Why is *Gendler* your brother?'

"'Our mothers were flesh and blood sisters.'

"The captain immediately hid the bottles of wine under his desk and returned my passport to me. 'Take him,' he said. 'But make sure he is back at work by January 2!'

"As soon as we left the man's office, your father and I bought some more wine for ourselves and went to wait for the steam train, on which we cheerfully rode to Leningrad, drinking and talking in English so that your father could get some practice. He already knew he wanted to go to America. So — happy end."

Thus my father spent New Year's Eve, 1971 with us. I remembered it well. My mother had been happy beyond belief to see him. Her happiness was a faint memory. What I vividly remembered was Papa walking inside our rooms on Fifth Soviet and her crying out to me, "Look how our poor Papochka hurt his hands."

My father raised another glass of vodka and with a stricken face said, "To my old friends, still in Russia."

"Forever in Russia," said Radik resignedly.

*

Lida told a joke over tea and cognac.

"A man's wife has left him for his best friend," she said. "Both his children have died and he lost his job. Finally he feels he has had enough, and decides to kill himself. He goes to a hotel room, planning to hang himself in the bathroom. When he stands on the edge of the bathtub to tie the rope to a hook in the ceiling, he sees on top of the cabinet a hidden bottle of vodka. There is a little left at the very bottom. He takes off the cap and drinks what was left. 'Better,' he says. 'Okay, now I'm ready.' He jumps back up onto the edge of the bath, ties one end of the rope to his neck. As he is about to tie the other end to the ceiling hook and jump to hang himself, he sees on the floor near the bath a cigarette butt. Getting down, he picks it up, finds a match in his pocket, and lights the butt. Sitting down on the edge of the bath, with the noose still around his neck, he inhales the smoke from the cigarette into his throat, and says, 'Yesss ... life is slowly returning to normal.'"

And then Lida took a swig of cognac and laughed uproariously. We all laughed with her.

*

"Yura, why aren't you drinking?" Radik asked my father indignantly before we were served dessert. "Why are you drinking like a woman?"

My father, refusing more drink, said, "Forget it. I don't want to get drunk in front of my daughter. Wait until she leaves. Wait until tomorrow."

Radik threw back his head in laughter. And then he sang the beginning of a well-known Russian ballad. "If only there was enough vodka for one, how great it would be, but sometimes there's vodka for two and sometimes there's vodka enough for three, unlike a wife who's only for one, and for one she is the cradle and the grave." He had a good voice. But of course he did.

My father told me that song was one of his all-time favorites.

For dessert Lida had made blueberry cobbler and raspberry meringue pie. Radik asked his wife to pass him the platters. I thought, how nice, the man enjoys his wife's sweets. But he spooned it all onto *my* plate and poured himself some cognac instead.

When I lifted the jug with the blueberry compote to pour myself a glass, Radik practically ripped it out of my hands to pour it for me.

As he was a little too enthusiastically spooning the blueberries onto my plate, some of them fell and stained my cream-colored capris. I was to be traveling back to the States in these pants the next day, so I wished he hadn't done that.

Minutes later, Radik stood, motioning me to come with him.

The two of us got up and left the table. The rest of the guests stayed where they were, chatting. No one said anything, as if no one had noticed.

Radik took me into one of the bedrooms, the one with his son's photo in it, and told me to sit down on the bed. Before I could ask him why, he took something from his closet. It was a laundry stick. "This will get the blueberry out. This is the best thing for stains. It's from the *West*," he said. "You'll see. I'll get the stain out for you."

He knelt down in front of me and rubbed at the blueberry on my thigh with this stain stick. After five minutes of this, he got up, left, came back with a wet rag, kneeled back down and rubbed my thigh with it. Of course he didn't get the blueberry out but now I had a Frisbee-sized wet purple stain on my pants.

We talked about the stain stick, and about how it was supposed to remove *all* the blueberry, if we scrubbed hard enough. "It's from the West," Radik kept repeating. "You'll see. It'll work."

I could hear that outside the bedroom, the others had started to carry the dirty dishes to the kitchen.

Giving up, Radik shrugged, got up off the floor, threw the stain stick emphatically into the garbage and went to get more cognac.

Lida came to me, holding a large glass jar of marinated mushrooms. "This is for you," she said.

"Lida, I can't take this."

"You can and you will."

"Where am I going to put it?"

"In your suitcase."

"What if the jar breaks?"

"Then carry it onto the plane."

That opened everyone else up. Suddenly Alla out of nowhere procured gifts for me and for my family. There was the letter for my daughter from her daughter, and there were coloring books for my young boys, and there was a huge box of chocolate-covered prunes.

"If you get hungry, you can eat them on the plane," she said. Yes, I thought, because you know, there's nothing better than having prunes on a nine-hour flight.

Then Viktor and Luba gave me *rocks* to take home with me, not exaggerating, actually rocks, and a book of poems. Anatoly stuffed a manuscript of his novella into my coat pocket.

"This is for you," he whispered.

I wanted to cry.

Did I want to cry because they had nothing and I must have seemed to them as someone who had everything, and yet here they were giving *me* things while *I* hadn't even brought enough T-shirts for all of them? Or did I want to cry because I couldn't tell them that I'd only brought a garment bag, which couldn't even properly fit my seven pathetic little skirts, much less chocolate-covered prunes and rocks from the Gulf of Finland?

Anatoly hadn't been paid in four months. They got vouchers to pay for the apartment they couldn't afford, and lived on Ellie's pension, three hundred and sixty rubles a month.

As Ellie fried the *blinchiki* on Lida's stove for me to take home to America, she told me that she felt happy each month until the money was all gone, and then she was miserable until the next check came. I understood that, living check to mouth when the check did not last a month. Ellie told me that Alla and Viktor were in better shape financially. They were considered middle class in Russia, whereas Ellie and Anatoly were considered poor.

And here she was, giving *me* gifts.

Radik gave me his business card and told me that if I needed anything in terms of research for my Russian book, he would be more than happy to help. That was his gift — his business card.

Radik, I decided, was more used to others giving *him* gifts. That was all right with me.

It was time to go, but my friend Alla wouldn't let me. She kept talking about coming to visit me and my family in Texas, how we would go about it, what kind of visa they would need, who could come, what they would have to do.

Anatoly pulled on my sleeve and said, "Read it, read my novel when you can, but soon, and tell me what you think, write or call and tell me what you think, whatever it is, but tell me the truth."

I promised I would.

Ellie continued to fry the *blinchiki.*

Anatoly's brother Viktor read aloud to me one of his own poems from a self-published poetry book he had given me.

Lida cleaned up.

Lida's dog lay on the twin bed in the kitchen, growling and baring his teeth at anyone who got within a foot of him. Since the kitchen was only seven feet wide and there were ten of us, that was pretty much everybody. Finally the mongrel bit one of the three Viktors. Lida came up to the dog and in the tenderest of tones said, "Darlinkin, Vasia, what's the matter, bunny rabbit? Too many people for you?"

Viktor rubbed his finger and stayed away from the twin bed.

It was 9:00 in the evening.

It was time to go. Time to say goodbye to all of them, and to my father. My driver Viktor was taking me back to Grand Hotel Europe. My father was staying with Radik for a week. They were going fishing. Ellie and Anatoly were driving back to their *dacha.* I was the first one to be leaving. I didn't want to go.

Eventually we walked outside and took some pictures. A whole roll of pictures. Some with Radik, standing next to me, beaming. Some with Radik and Lida. Some with my father.

The goodbyes proceeded slowly: too many people to say goodbye to. When you haven't seen your friends in twenty-five years, you are saying goodbye promising to write, to call, to visit soon, but you can't help thinking that it may well be another twenty-five years before you come back. And what if you never come back?

Radik walked around, filming us with his video camera.

Everyone else was leaving, too, except for my father. Lida said, "No one leaves before Plinka. She leaves first." The guest of honor always left first, she said.

Viktor and Luba wanted me to get in touch with their son who lived in Princeton. I knew that in the Russian mind, Princeton was just *over there* from Dallas. A car ride away.

Several times Viktor and Alla reminded me not to forget to give my daughter their daughter's letter.

I looked over Alla's shoulder. "What's that?" I pointed.

She turned around. "It's a well."

"A what?"

"A well. Have you never seen a well?"

"In movies," I said. "In my kids' *Hansel and Gretel* book."

"There was a well in Shepelevo," Alla said.

"Really? I don't remember."

"Where do you think you got your water from?"

"I don't know," I confessed. "I never thought about it. Is this a working well?"

"Of course. Didn't you notice there was no running water in the house?"

I'd never thought about it.

I asked them to take a picture of me by the well. Unfortunately I had used up the last of the film. And I had to give my father his camera back, anyway.

Anatoly gazed at me with moist eyes as he hugged me. He said he loved me.

As Ellie said goodbye to me, I could tell she wanted to ask me something.

I thanked Lida for her great hospitality, for the dinner and the mushrooms, which I was carrying along with the other gifts in a heavy plastic bag. "Are you kidding me?" she said. "You're like family. We feed you for life."

There were only my father and Radik left to say goodbye to. Radik put down his video camera, waved everyone else away and opened his arms. He hugged me and kissed me, and shaking his head without letting me go, said, "Plinka, I can't believe it. Not only are you beautiful but you smell great, too."

I said nothing. He still wasn't letting go of me. How far that charm must have gotten him in life.

Stepping away, I patted him gently on the chest. When I glanced at our audience, they were completely unfazed. They all knew him.

I saw Ellie's sparkling eyes. I felt stabs of pain for Anatoly. Could he help that he was wracked with misery? Why wasn't Radik? Anatoly still had his only child. Why hadn't the death of Radik's only son hunched his shoulders and made him weak? Why did he still entertain on a grand scale in his rented *dacha* without running water as if he really was Marilyn Monroe's leading man?

Finally I embraced my father. He actually hugged me back. Maybe he was moved, too. I couldn't tell.

I was about to get into Viktor's car when Ellie pulled me aside.

"So what do you think?" she whispered.

I played dumb. "What do I think of what?"

She lowered her whisper a notch. "Of *Radik!*"

I nodded. "What can I say? You're right. He is handsome."

"I told you," Ellie said. I thought she might start to giggle. "He is really something, isn't he?"

"He certainly is."

Viktor and I got into his car. "Are you okay to drive, Viktor?" I said. Had he been keeping up with the toasts?

"A little late to ask me this, don't you think?" he said, adding, "I'm fine." He looked and sounded fine. "I stopped drinking three hours ago." Slowly he drove away, honking. I rolled down my window and waved. It suddenly felt gloomy and cold. I saw them waving back, receding in the distance.

In the half-kilometer drive to the paved highway, Viktor stopped twice to ask for directions. It was a straight line to the highway, but he wanted to be sure. The second time was merely to confirm the first set of directions.

I was about to offer him Ellie's *blinchiki*, but then had a better idea.

"Hey," I said, "let's eat them tomorrow morning together." My flight was early and we wouldn't have time for breakfast.

He agreed.

We drove quietly through the rain.

I was unspeakably sad. I turned to my window, hoping to glimpse the miraculous Gulf of Finland, but all I saw was white. The Gulf was white. The sky was white. White gray. I couldn't see the horizon. The sky and the sea were one: the sky, the water, they were all gray, like me.

Viktor expressed regret for not taking me to the Inform Bureau, a radio station that reported during the war, using a generator from a sunken ship. He said it would have been invaluable for me to see. "Oh, well," he said. "Maybe next time?"

"Viktor, do we have time to go to Nevsky Patch?" I asked. "It's on the way, isn't it?"

He almost laughed. "It couldn't be farther away from us. It's on the southeastern shore of the Neva . We're up northwest."

"We have time," I said. "Papa's not here."

"Have you packed?"

It was 10 p.m. "Not really," I said. Not at all, actually. "Hey, maybe next time?"

We talked about the importance of radio during the war. The radio station would get reports from the front and broadcast them daily; that's how everyone knew what battles were being fought. "With a spin on them, of course," said Viktor, "and a spin on who was winning."

"Were there lists of the dead?"

"Of course," Viktor said.

"Wounded? Missing in action?"

"Of course."

I fell quiet.

"But so many dead," Viktor said, "and it took so long to identify them that sometimes the news didn't get to the families for many months. Sometimes years. They were always running behind with news of the dead. Eventually you knew."

"I'm sure."

Viktor had treated me so well. I was grateful to him. When we got back to the hotel, I gave him one of the *blinchiki* to eat on the way home.

I was back in my room around 11:00. It took me two and a half hours to pack one garment bag. Don't ask.

The mushrooms were in my purse, right underneath my journal and my Siege of Leningrad book.

LAST NIGHT IN LENINGRAD

The sponge of my heart had filled up sometime during the evening. Now it began to drip.

I couldn't remember anything I saw or read. I was going back to Texas tomorrow. I remembered that.

Kevin called. "Are you looking forward to getting back to our routine?" he asked. "To Cici's Pizza?"

I was so far away from my other life.

"I feel a little bit bad," he said, "because you're having this incredible experience, and I'm not part of it."

"I wouldn't describe it as incredible," I said.

"How would you describe it?"

"It's hard for me to tell you over the phone."

"You'll show me the pictures," he said. "It'll be great."

"Yes, great," I whispered, lying down, looking at my garment bag.

When we hung up, it was nearly 2:00 in the morning. I was supposed to be getting up at 7:00 to leave Russia.

Truth was, I didn't want to leave Russia. I didn't want to *stay* in Russia; I was just afraid I was going to leave *me* in Russia.

*

353

"Sit on my lap," says my grandmother, crying. "Sit, Plinochka."

I am nine years old, nearly ten. I am staying with them on my last night in Leningrad. The next day we will fly to the new world, to our new life in America.

"Babushka," I say, "you told me I was too big to sit on your lap. You told me that two whole years ago."

"Please sit, darling," she says, pulling me onto her knee. "The last weight is never heavy."

I sit on her lap through the whole movie, a black and white film about the war. As usual, everybody dies. Tearfully she keeps patting my back. I do not get down.

*

Jumping up, I put on my coat and went out. I hoped it wasn't raining.

It wasn't. It was cold and wet and dark, and the streetlights were on.

I walked down Nevsky Prospekt to the Neva. There was no one on the street. Occasionally a car would pass. I remembered my father's admonition about not going out by myself late at night but I didn't care. I wanted to see the Neva one last time.

On the embankment in front of the Winter Palace, I found a damp bench and sat down. I was cold, but it was nothing compared to how I felt inside. Tightly I wrapped my arms around my chest and rocked back and forth. The Neva was dark. The Palace Embankment was poorly lit.

The beginning of my trip seemed so long ago. A lifetime ago. Six days ago I was a harried, multi-tasking American with a dim memory of my Russian childhood. I had come to Russia with an academic interest. I had come to do "research" for my Russian book, looking for facts, or inspiration. When I left Dallas, my mind was filled with brass knobs and carpeting and handscraped floors.

It took one flight on Aeroflot to forget all that. And then I, like Dorothy in *The Wizard of Oz* books, went back through the wet dark tunnels, by boat and by foot, standing waist deep in cold underground water, until I found my way to underneath the Land of Oz. Except my fairytale was cramped into one room on Fifth Soviet and into one *dacha* in Shepelevo, into a dozen smells, and into the streets of Leningrad. I was embedded in the wet sidewalk, on the street I used to walk with my sullen mother, on the concrete steps of the Concert Hall, where I played as a child.

I became a child again now — first broken and then patched together from the pieces into a fractured whole.

But broken I would be returning home. I didn't have a deeper understanding. I understood less than when I had set out. I didn't have a greater appreciation. I had a greater shame.

What did I want?

I wanted Alla to have a future. I didn't want Anatoly to be hunched over by his life. I didn't want Ellie to keep an empty bottle of Trésor on her nightstand.

I couldn't fix this. I couldn't fix any of it.

How could so many Russias be flying inside me all at once? There was the Russia of my childhood, the nearly forgotten, small-child Russia: mute mother, absent father. Shepelevo, Fifth Soviet.

There was the Russia of my grandparents: the impoverished, bombed-out, war-torn Russia, full of death, Stalin, purges, soldiers, evacuation, starvation.

There was the Russia of my parents, Dzhubga in the Caucasus Mountains where they first met, my mother and father falling in love by the Black Sea. *Me and your mother, we had a great love,* my father once told me when he was trying to talk me out of marrying my first husband. I never forgot that. He was telling me not to compare myself with him and Mama, because they were different, they had something different that bound them together all these years. A great love.

There was the Russia of Anatoly, of the tenement halls and the flowers wrapped in newsprint, and the wallpaper from Europe, and the absence of hot water for three weeks in the summer.

There was the Russia of Shepelevo, of the village life, without chocolate, without clothes, without laundry machines or running water. Still. Ever.

There was the Russia I saw now, by turns exquisite and stupefying, the glory of the northern river emptying out into the cold Gulf waters, the colorful stucco buildings lining these banks for centuries, since the days of Peter the Great, dignified, bent, bowed, broken, their crumbling exposed brick a testament to the ages.

There were the white nights, an astonishing act of God.

And then there was me, starting out in Russia and ending up in Texas, on the prairie. How did that happen? Why was that my life? Why wasn't it Anatoly and Ellie's life? Why wasn't it Alla and Viktor's? Radik and Lida's?

That's what my sadness was. I had been given something I did not deserve. I had been given something I took so woefully for granted.

What was I going to do with it, now that I knew I had it?

I didn't want to go to sleep. I didn't want this to be my last night. I didn't want to go home. I wanted to understand, and after I understood, to feel better.

In the last *Wizard of Oz* book, before she goes back to Kansas, Dorothy asks the Good Witch if she will ever come back to the Land of Oz. The Good Witch replies, No, child. You will never come back. Dorothy starts to cry. The Good Witch says, Don't worry. Soon the pain of it will fade, and your memories, too. Eventually it will become distant, and one day it won't even seem like yours anymore. You won't remember you were the one who had lived through it. It will be just like a fairytale.

It was so cold. I was shivering.

By the time I stumbled back to the hotel and fell asleep fully dressed, it was after 3:00 in the morning — outside, inside.

Friday, July 18, 1998.

PART III

AFTER RUSSIA

Attempting a serious face, 1968.

COMING TO AMERICA

LEAVING LENINGRAD

I hadn't eaten breakfast — my *blini* and caviar — in three days. Who had time for breakfast when I didn't even have time to see Yulia? I didn't have time for Ellie's *blinchiki*, either. They lay in the hotel room refrigerator until I grabbed them at the last minute to give to Viktor. I carried my ridiculous and overstuffed garment bag downstairs. Conveniently, I had been already dressed, my day-old make-up a suit of armor on my face. My stomach felt better after Friday's debacle, while the rest of me felt worse. But there was no time to feel anything, because I was running late: it was 7:30 and I hadn't checked out yet.

Viktor was waiting outside in the rain.

"Take this," I said, handing him the *blinchiki*. He chivalrously took my garment bag first; then he took the *blinchiki*.

"You want to share them?" he asked.

"No, I want you to have them."

We passed by the Moscow Gates on Moscow Prospekt, by Moscow Square with its statue of Lenin and its Communist-era government buildings. It all looked different to me now. Like home.

"We should stop here," Viktor said, as we were passing the Monument to the Heroes of the Defense of Leningrad. "So you can see. It's a very nice monument."

I could see that from the car. It was raining. Each dreary drop fell into my heart. I said, "Okay, we'll stop for just a sec. But we really must hurry, Viktor. It's eight o'clock."

We got out of the car. In the rain we walked up the steps to the eternal flame in front of the sculpted victors: soldiers, workers, women. After a few silent minutes, we went back to the car.

Before we took off, Viktor said, "I have a small gift for you. I know you were looking for some Russian music. I got you this." He pulled out a CD. "It's Russian marches. I think you'll like it. Listen to it on my portable CD player while we drive. Here are the earphones."

I was afraid I'd cry. "Thank you, Viktor."

"It's nothing," he said. "Just a small gesture."

Yesterday, on our way to Radik's, my father told me I should give Viktor a T-shirt for his young son's birthday. But when we got to Radik's and my father distributed the too-few T-shirts to the too-many guests, he forgot and gave away the T-shirt to somebody else.

I asked Viktor if my father had given him a shirt, and Viktor shook his head. Shaking my own head, I said, "Viktor, after you drop me off, please call my dad and casually ask, 'Yuri Lvovich, remember you promised my son a T-shirt?'"

Laughing, Viktor said, "No, I cannot do that, it will torture your poor father his whole remaining life."

"That's the point," I said. "That's the point! What did my father say to you at Lake Ladoga when I desperately needed a bathroom and you were driving over potholes the size of dinosaur footprints? He told you to drive faster. Drive faster. *He* doesn't mind torturing *me*. In fact, he revels in it."

Viktor laughed.

Closing my eyes, I put on the earphones. "Tell him, Viktor. Call him."

The rest of the ride to the airport, I listened to Russian military marches. I would open my eyes, see Russia, and then close them again, retreating into cymbals of Soviet war.

Pulkovo's tiny parking lot was full. We pulled into a taxi rank.

"Write down your address for me, Viktor, will you? I want to send your kids some T-shirts from Texas."

"Oh, no," he said. "You absolutely don't have to do that."

"I know I don't have to. I want to. Please."

He wrote down his address for me but forgot his zip code. "Viktor, you don't know your own zip code?"

Smiling sheepishly, he said, "You know, my wife handles all that stuff. She knows everything."

"Well, where is she when you need her?"

"Call me from Texas. Can you do that? Call me at home or at the office, and I'll give it to you. Better yet, don't send anything."

I promised I would call.

I opened the car door and got out. He went to get my bag out of the trunk. When he saw my face in the rain, he said, "Paullina, you don't want to leave, do you?"

I was filling up, so I said nothing. Just shook my head and stared at the ground.

"You should've come for longer," he said. As if that would have solved anything. "Maybe next time?"

"Maybe next time." I smiled. "Let's go. We're so late."

Inside, the airport buzzed like Dallas–Fort Worth on a Sunday afternoon. It was swarming, amass with people. Everyone behaved as if they wanted only one thing: to get on my flight. Moreover, they behaved as if they wanted to get on my flight *ahead* of me. There were long lines everywhere and a lot of pushing and shoving. It was 8:20 in the morning. My flight was scheduled for 9:50.

Patiently Viktor and I stood and waited, I wasn't sure for what. To find out what to do next?

"Viktor, what are we waiting for?" I finally said.

"I don't know," he said calmly. "They'll tell us."

"Who's they? And when? And tell us what?"

"I don't know."

Thirty minutes we stood. Finally I figured it out: we were waiting so my bag could pass through a metal detector while an indifferent man indifferently studied my customs declaration, and waved me on. "You're checking that bag, right?" he said. "Because you can't bring it on the plane."

"Yes, I know, I know." I grumbled under my breath. "I can't bring carry-on luggage on the plane. I got it."

Hurriedly Viktor and I said goodbye.

"I'll send you the T-shirts," I called out to him, but he didn't hear me.

To the metal detector man, I said, "Can I get on the plane now?"

I was only joking, but he glared at me as if I had just insulted his mother.

"You and your bag go stand over there," he snapped. "In the check-in line."

I joined the check-in line.

On the digital display board in front of me, the deadline for checking in flashed as 9:10 a.m. I glanced at my watch. It was 8:50.

Do I even need to say that 9:10 came and went and the line did not move? I stood and watched two enterprising men wrap suitcases in plastic wrap for twenty dollars a bag. They asked me three times if I wanted to protect my bag from unnecessary nicks and cuts. Three times I told them no, each time wanting to ask what kind of a sharp and pointed instrument would I need to use to cut through the plastic wrap, and what would that sharp and pointed instrument do to my bag.

I looked up at the LCD display, which now boldly proclaimed that the check-in deadline was extended to 9:40 a.m. It dawned on me that the end of check-in was simply thirty minutes ahead of whatever time it was now. How convenient.

The woman standing behind me was beginning to get on my nerves. She wore black platform shoes with tight black pants and a tight black shirt, and she had drooping, absurdly giant breasts. But no, that's not what got on my nerves. What got on my nerves was that she and her boobs kept bobbing and weaving and undulating their way to get in front of me. When that didn't work, she tried to use her ridiculous chest to influence the man behind the counter to let her check her luggage *right now*.

Despite the enormity of her foundering bosom, he was not swayed.

It was 9:40 a.m. I looked up at the LCD display. The end of check-in time for my flight had disappeared completely. The display now carried the check-in time for a flight to Portugal.

Finally — my turn. I had a choice: aisle in non-smoking or window in smoking. Idiotically I asked, "Could you put me at the very beginning of the smoking section?"

"Yes," the check-in woman said in Russian. "You *are* at the beginning."

I don't know what I was thinking. That all the smokers would be behind me, far away? She handed me my boarding pass. It had no gate number on it.

"What gate?"

"Gate?"

"Gate, yes. The plane, where is it departing from?"

"Oh." She waved me over to the central terminal. "Ask passport control. They'll tell you."

My brain cloudy, I waited in the passport control line so they could stamp my passport and take my visa.

I waited fifteen minutes. It was 9:55 a.m.

"It's five minutes past my scheduled flight time," I said to the passport lady when I reached the front of the line.

"It is?"

"Yes."

"Oh." She looked at a piece of paper on her desk. "Yeah," she said slowly. "I hope they're holding the flight. I'd hurry."

"Great," I said. "What gate, please?"

"Gate?"

"Yes, gate."

"Didn't they tell you at check-in?"

"No, they said you would know."

"I don't know why they would say that. I have no idea. Go and check the departure and arrival board. It should be up there. You have a few minutes. Don't worry."

"So they'll hold the flight, right?"

She shrugged. "I hope so. Sometimes they do."

I had to go through yet another metal detector, this time for my carry-on bags, all the white plastic bags filled with gifts from my Russian friends.

Deciding that the flight would hold, I ran to the duty-free shop because my father had told me to. He'd said, "Take the remainder of your rubles, how many do you have?"

"Six hundred."

"Take them and buy yourself black caviar in the duty-free shop at the airport."

"But, Papa," I said, "doesn't caviar need to be refrigerated?"

"Yeah? So?"

Russians were not big on refrigeration.

"Eat it as soon as you get home," he said. "You'll be fine."

Eat six hundred rubles worth of Beluga when I got home? Through the glass door of the refrigerator I stared at the caviar, squinting to read how much I could buy for six hundred rubles. In the six days I'd been in Russia, the ruble had suffered a catastrophic collapse, and on this Sunday, six hundred rubles amounted to only sixteen dollars.

However, those six hundred rubles would buy me six ounces of Beluga! Long live the worthless ruble. I opened the refrigerator, but I couldn't stop thinking of Ellie, with the empty bottle of Trésor on her nightstand. Knowing my mother, I bet she hadn't even bought the Trésor for Ellie: I bet she had given her one of her gently used own, since she had a dozen more at home, fuller and newer.

I closed the refrigerator, empty-handed. I didn't buy the near-half-pound of Beluga for sixteen dollars.

Instead I bought four T-shirts, one each for Kevin and the kids. Time was ticking. It was after 10:00. I couldn't be sure how long the flight would be "held." Neither could anyone else, I suspected. After paying for the T-shirts, I still had over three hundred rubles left.

I decided to buy a bottle of Trésor for Ellie.

After paying for the perfume, I would still have two hundred rubles left. Geez, I couldn't give this money away.

I asked the duty-free clerk if she knew what time my flight was leaving. She looked at her schedule. "9:50." She eyed me with alarm. "You better hurry."

It was 10:03 a.m.

I ran out of the duty-free to the flight information board.

There was nothing on it about my flight.

I rushed to the nearest metal detector and asked the man sitting behind it. He spoke no English and refused to help. Don't ask me why I didn't ask him in Russian — I don't know.

I tried another man.

He said in Russian, "No English."

I gave up and asked him in Russian.

He replied, in his most apathetic Russian, "Dunno."

"Does anyone know?" I asked feverishly.

"Dunno," he said, lazily pointing me back to the flight information board.

My state now was three notches above frantic. I flew up an escalator. There was no information anywhere, either what time the flight was, or what gate it was at. I ran down the escalator, past the metal detector and again asked a woman at passport control.

"Oh, you're on the New York flight!" she exclaimed.

I didn't like the panic in her voice.

She talked quickly into her walkie-talkie. "Sergei! We have another one!" Then to me, "Hurry, hurry, upstairs to the left."

I airlifted myself up the escalator and sprinted through some double doors. At last, a hundred yards down the long hall, I saw a small sign above an actual gate: "New York."

There was no one at the desk. There was, however, a soldier on the gangplank. He checked my passport. Then the woman who had checked me in at 9:50 a.m. took my boarding pass, ripped it in two and impatiently pointed me toward the plane, where the stern stewardess demanded to know where the other half of my boarding pass was.

My seat was 35K, five rows from the very back of the plane. Didn't the check-in woman tell me I'd be sitting at the front of the smoking section?

I felt in Russian, I did everything else in English. At that moment, I was feeling *tense* — in any language. I couldn't find the words for tense in Russian. Hyperventilating, breathless, shaking, nerve-wracked: none of them were coming to mind.

I squeezed into my window seat, and the power went out. When the electricity goes out on an airplane about to fly 4500 miles, I don't see it as a good omen. Don't they need power for the black box? Outside my oval window was incessant, driving rain.

The young man in the seat next to me was dark, extremely hirsute, and busy drawing in a notebook. He was so hairy, he had thick black hair growing out of his sketching knuckles. Then he was busy snoring, with his hairy elbow all over my armrest. I longed for my own armrest. At least I had a window.

Finally the plane took off. The young man woke up and started chain-smoking. When I had asked to be put at the beginning of the smoking section, it hadn't occurred to me that the man sitting *next* to me might smoke. *Duh*, I thought, coughing his exhaled nicotine into my sleeve.

I excused myself. When he stood up to let me out, his cigarettes fell to the floor and his charcoal pencil smudged his coat. His lighter dropped under the seat. I smiled sweetly as I inched past him and went to wait by the OCCUPIED lavatory.

BETWEEN TWO WORLDS

When I got back to my seat, I read Anatoly's novella.

Anatoly thought his wife was beautiful. He is right. She was. She still is.

I was really only interested in my mother and father, but there was disappointingly little of them in his book. The story, if you could call it that, had only one main character, and that was Anatoly's heartbroken nostalgia for a youth long gone. Everything else was subordinated to this prevailing and poignant sense of loss for the past.

Although Anatoly told me that he and my father had both been in love with Ellie, I would not have gleaned it from his book. It was too impenetrable for something as straightforward as a love triangle. Ellie had chosen Anatoly over my father, and this created a rift between the three of them during which, for two years, they did not speak. Eventually things got back on track. Again, I knew this only from what Anatoly had told me; these details were invisible in the murky pages I read. What was clear, however — absolutely conspicuous — was Anatoly's jealousy about the episode to this day, forty years later.

I put the manuscript down and closed my eyes. Maybe youthful hurt never mends. Could you really feel pain about a forty-year-old incident? I knew you could. I had my own youthful hurts. They didn't feel raw anymore, but you never forget your first heartbreak. I still carried it with me.

As I carry Leningrad with me. I carry Leningrad with me in a little box next to my heart. The smell of Shepelevo, the memory of me reading in my bed, my mother and me having dinner mute and alone, my father taking me to the movies on Saturdays, as if I were a child of divorce. I carry all of it inside me.

Shepelevo is with me whenever I walk outside and smell the air. I always search for the familiar smell that will take me back home. What I want to smell is smoking fish and fresh water and burning firewood and nettles. But in Texas I smell hardly anything but heat. That has its own, somewhat limited, appeal. Besides, Texas carries no personal history for me.

When I was growing up in Russia, I didn't constantly want something I didn't have, something else, something new. As Sinead O'Connor wisely wrote many years later, I did not want what I didn't have. What no one had. I never even knew that another world besides the one I was living in existed. We were all fish swimming in the same water. I didn't know I had gills. I just lived. I was a kid with really only one dream. I dreamed that I might one day write books that would transport other people to other worlds, as I myself had been transported, by Dumas, by Dickens, by Verne. I wanted to make other people feel like D'Artagnan had made me feel.

And now I wanted that simple child back. I wanted to be happy with the sunrise and fishing on the Gulf. I wanted to be happy, not ashamed, or anxious, or worried about money or work. I wanted to ride my rusted wobbly bike and smell the fish and the pines and the clover and believe I was lucky.

I had too much time to think on this flight — last thing I needed. I opened my eyes and reluctantly turned to my smoking seat buddy. The scruffy artist pumped my hand, announcing he was Andrew. He didn't even ask for my name. He was an unkempt twenty-four-year-old *artistpaintersculptor* with fingers permanently blackened by charcoal pencil, or by tar from the cigarettes.

He offered me a cigarette.

"No, thank you," I said, poorly suppressing a judgmental cough. He smiled. "Your bad luck to be sitting next to a chain smoker, huh?"

"No, no, it's fine." Perhaps not so lucky?

Andrew was a Catholic and an art dealer, though he told me the two things were not "conjoined" (his word not mine). He was the middle son of an Atlanta businessman, engaged to a Russian woman named Olga who, he said, spoke perfect English. Andrew told me he didn't care about money and was eventually moving to live in St. Petersburg with Olga because he didn't like government, any government, but *especially* the U.S. government. His three-month visa had just expired and he was unwillingly returning to his art gallery in the hated United States.

"Russia is so pure," Andrew said. "There is no pretense."

"Well, they can't afford it."

"Yes, but that's the beauty of it. The Russian people have to make up their own reality."

I laughed, perhaps too loudly.

He looked at me seriously, then half-chuckled. "I am totally serious."

"Of course you are."

I wanted to ask him if he didn't think the Russian people had had just about enough of their own reality without having to make any up, but didn't want to get into it with him. I'd met his type before. Everything about the most pungent poverty everywhere else in the world is noble and glorious, and America sucks.

Andrew loved Michelangelo ("He's a god") and Florence. He hated working at an art gallery. "I'm not meant to work there, I know. Soon I'll be fired, and then I'll *have* to go back to Russia. I'll be fired because I can't stand all that bullshit. People come in and they want to buy paintings to go with their furniture. It drives me crazy. Once a lady came in and said, 'Do you have anything blue? I've got a blue couch I'm trying to match. I want that blue painting.' I said to her, 'Lady, get out. Don't buy something blue from me. What's going to happen when you get tired of your blue couch? The painting is still going to be on your wall.' I got into a lot of trouble with my boss, but most people just don't understand art. They don't understand that real art doesn't *go* with anything. It has to be something that you walk by every day and see. Every day. Every time you walk by. If you forget to look at it as you pass by, it's not art. Forget the fucking couch." He laughed. "I almost got fired."

"Really?" I said. "For a painting? How much was it?"

"A hundred and seventy-five thousand dollars."

After an hour and a half, I was done listening to him so I read my Defense of Leningrad book in Russian, then slept, really slept, waking with a hurting neck. I dreamed about giving my cleaning lady a raise. I woke up groggy at 10:20 p.m., Leningrad time.

Time to come home to Grand Hotel Europe.

They fed us twice on the flight. First, a choice of beef or salmon;

the second time, oily fish plus ham, salad, and pound cake with chocolate fondant. Coffee. Ginger ale for my funny tummy.

Actually, they forgot to feed Andrew and me. Clearly we weren't art because they walked right past us. They were coming around with the coffee carafe by the time we looked around and realized everyone else had finished eating. There was a grudging non-apology and some food.

When we landed, Andrew got up, walked off and didn't even say see ya. He was too busy smoking.

I went to the bathroom at Kennedy Airport. I marveled at how clean the toilets were, how they flushed! How soft the toilet paper was! I was excited about toilets at an airport, can that just sink in a little bit?

I made beautiful time getting to LaGuardia, and then sat on my hands for three hours waiting for my connecting flight to Dallas.

At the airport everyone spoke English. I spent ten dollars on Chinese food of dubious quality. I was back home.

I wished I had time to go see my grandparents on Long Island. I couldn't call home: before I left Russia, Kevin told me that a lightning strike had knocked out the power in our subdivision. The phones weren't working.

In Leningrad during the war, in December 1941, the authorities had to turn off the electricity to conserve it. Russian winters are brutal, dark and long. Without electricity, they must have been unbearable. Without electricity or food. The only thing that took people's minds off the darkness was impending death by starvation.

Every rat, every mouse, every dog and cat in the city had long been eaten. People sat in the dark and starved. That's how it was. But every apartment had a little wood-burning ceramic stove, by which they could heat their small rooms, not quite seven meters for every man, woman and child.

The men were at war, the women and children were dying. If there had been soup, they could have heated it up on their ceramic stoves. But there was no soup, and there was no firewood either. The Leningraders burned their furniture and their clothes. They ripped apart abandoned homes to make firewood. Then they started cutting down trees in the parks. The city council by emergency decree protected the Summer Garden, declaring it a felony punishable by death to steal the trees out of it, but everything else in the city was cut down and burned.

I ate my mediocre Chinese food and was grateful.

I stared out the airport window, noticing that in the flat of green between one runway and the next the grass had been cut. Someone had paid for a mower and a person to cut the grass. Not a lot of money. But what I'm saying is, after paying for air-traffic control, electricity and payroll, there was money *left over* to get the grass cut.

My eyes hurt from being up, from reading, from being alive.

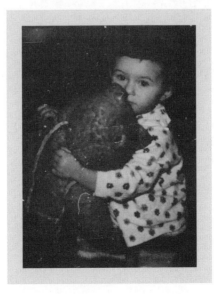

February 1965.
Fifteen months
old.

THE BLUE SILENCE

COMING HOME

An uneventful American Airlines flight back to Dallas, a flight marked only by my ravenous hunger. I inhaled the entire platter of Southwestern chicken plus two cookies. It was a struggle to keep myself from asking the woman next to me if she was going to finish her chicken.

She didn't.

My flight landed at 6:00 p.m. Kevin was supposed to pick me up by the gate with the kids. I was looking forward to the sight of my daughter holding a homemade sign that said "MOM."

Not only was there no sign, there was no family either. I tottered over to the baggage claim, where I stood dejectedly for fifteen minutes until the luggage started coming out, and then my family appeared. Apparently there was confusion over arrival time. I was so tired and happy to see them, it didn't matter. I just wanted to be done with my day.

We went to the Rainforest Café for dinner.

Misha, my three year old, said, "Mom, do you know what we had for breakfast? Ice cream! And do you know what we had for lunch? Cookies! We had popcorn for dinner and we watched TV all day!" He laughed joyously.

Playing along, I furrowed my brow and turned to Kevin.

Smiling, Kevin shrugged his shoulders. "I don't know where he gets this stuff."

I didn't know how I kept myself upright.

"So tell me about Russia," Kevin said in the car on the way home.

The thought of relating my trip to Kevin in the car in between traffic lights filled me with exhausted dread. We were driving past McDonald's, a Mobil station, a Boston Market. Gamely I tried.

The children interrupted us like a stutter as I spoke. My words came out in staccato half-sentences. "Shepelevo, border patrol, Misha stop yelling at your brother, give him the toy, Natasha stop complaining, smell, poverty, wait I can't hear myself talk, you kids are screaming so loud, okay, Fifth Soviet, the toilets, Radik, Misha stop scratching the window with your rake, sit down, don't take your seatbelt off, okay if you kids don't stop it, we're turning right around, and there will be no *Magic School Bus* tomorrow. Kevin did you get that? Did you get what my Russia meant to me?"

We didn't get home until 10:00 in the evening, which was 7:00 in the morning Leningrad time, which meant I had been up for twenty-four hours.

I don't think I fell asleep so much as fell unconscious around midnight.

FIRST DAY BACK

The next morning my husband walked into our bathroom and found me gazing at our toilet.

"Um, what are you doing?" he asked cautiously.

"Nothing. Look how nice it is."

"What? The toilet?"

"I mean ... well, yeah. Clean. And white. I'm so happy we didn't get a black toilet."

I felt Kevin staring at me. Turning around I said, "It's just so clean, don't you think?"

"Yeah ... sure," he said. "Do you want to go look at the other five toilets?"

"Let's go get the kids ready," I said.

We got the boys dressed and ready for the day. The babysitter came and Kevin went to work.

I trudged upstairs to my office. Phil the foreman called me on the cell phone, because the regular phones still weren't working — which reminded me I had to call the phone company. The alarm guy came to the house supposedly to fix the alarm, but really just to tell me that if lightning struck my house and ruptured the alarm signal, he would have to charge me three hundred dollars to fix it. Did I still want the work done? Our homeowner's insurance was being cancelled. The landlord from our old rental house hadn't sent us our security deposit back. Kevin hadn't listened to the answering machine the whole week I was gone. There was a panicked message from my mother. She was about to go in for her gall bladder surgery and needed to speak to someone — could Kevin please call her as soon as possible? Not only had *he* not called her, but my father hadn't called her either. We'd been too busy dissecting the dire real estate situation in Schlisselburg to call my mother, who was having gall bladder surgery.

I was too scared to call her, so I called my grandparents in New York instead in preparation and then called my mother at the hospital. She was groggy and recovering but clearly not happy not to have heard from any of us.

That took the whole morning. In the afternoon I made Russian beef soup and *blinchiki*. It took me three and a half hours to make dinner. As I cooked, I became uncomfortably aware that my house was too beautiful. Granite island, white cabinets, brass hardware, handscraped floors, crown mouldings, tall ceilings. Lots of large rooms with solid-core doors. Not in-laid with gold doors. But still. Two staircases. A three-car garage. A swimming pool. A spa. My head bent low, I tried not to look at any of it.

Kevin came home and we ate dinner, went swimming, put the kids to bed, watched some TV …

The next day we got up and did it all again.

And the next day.

And the next.

Life continued as if I hadn't been to Russia, hadn't been to Shepelevo, hadn't been to Leningrad.

Except … I couldn't lift my head, my eyes, my heart to my house.

I said I would tell Kevin about Russia after I got my photographs developed. Once I had the photos, I said I'd tell him when I had organized them. After I had put the photos in order, I said I didn't want to tell him without putting them in context.

This book is that context.

It took me eight months to write it. I wrote it when I should have been writing *The Bronze Horseman*, the book three editors in three different countries were desperately waiting for, the book that was egregiously late, like years late.

In my photos, Leningrad doesn't look quite so drab. The lens softens the peeled paint, flattens the dimensionally broken stucco. Rust looks like a ray of light, you can hardly see the dirt on the street. The Neva is gorgeous, and so is the sky.

And there is no smell in photographs.

No smell of Communist toilets, or the subway or Shepelevo or crème brûlée or wet trees.

WET DOGS

I had a very difficult time talking about it to Kevin. It became a thing between us, a wedge, a widening unhappy gap. I couldn't find the words to explain, was afraid he'd never understand, and he resented my silence. How to reduce Russia to a pithy sound bite over the dinner table, or over the joyful chattering of our children on the way to Baskin Robbins?

My six days in Leningrad didn't fit into my life. I'd known that even as I was flying home. I knew there would be no time to stop and talk about Russia, and I was right. The longer it went on, the *not* talking about it became both a solace and a disgrace.

Talking would require a break in our daily ritual. Who needed that? Not Kevin, he just wanted things to be good, like they had been, like they still were to him. Talking would need us to enter into a different reality than our Texas reality, which by the way seemed less and less real by the hour because I spent all my waking seconds hidden so deep inside my head.

In the evening we would clean up, maybe unpack some books, go to bed, read for a few minutes, kiss and fall asleep. In the morning we would once again stumble out of bed. Kevin went to work, and I was left home with the contents of my heart.

*

I came home one afternoon to find a message on the answering machine. A female Russian voice I didn't recognize was saying, "Misha, is this you? Pick up the phone, Misha, I want to talk to your mama." All of this was in Russian, like Misha could understand a word of it.

I went up to my office and the phone rang. A woman's voice in Russian said, "Plinka? Plinka is this you?"

I didn't know quite what to say.

Was it me?

I said yes.

"Plinka, do you know who this is? It's Yulia! Yulia. Oh, Paullina, how *could* you have? How could you have come to Russia and not called me, and not seen me? How could you have done it?"

Thank God I was sitting down.

Yulia wept.

"I'm sorry, Yulia," I said. "I'm really sorry. We had no time. We only had six days. Six lousy days, Yulia, I'm sorry."

But she didn't understand. She talked and talked, railing at the injustice, at my callousness. Her voice, high-strung and emotional, carried with it such regret, such sorrow. "I would have come to the airport to see you off," she said. "I found out only on Friday and I called Anatoly the whole day Saturday but no one picked up.

You were leaving Sunday, and I would've come to the airport to see you; I was so desperate to see you, I must have called Anatoly seven hundred times, that's all I did Friday and Saturday, I dialed his number over and over, but no one picked up. But in the end I couldn't have come to the airport — do you know why? Because I was going into labor! Labor, Plinka. I had another child, can you believe it? The day after you left, I had my little girl. So now I have two children, can you believe it, two, a boy and a girl. I named the girl Maria. For our Babushka. She liked it. I just talked to her. She was very happy."

I was mute.

"How could you not have come to see me, Plinka?" she repeated mournfully.

"Yulia, I didn't even know where you lived."

"I live in the same place, Plinka! Where else am I going to live? The same apartment I shared with my mama. I still live there on Prospekt of Veterans! But who cares where I live, I would have come anywhere to see you, anywhere, you tell me where and I would have come, you have no idea how I think of you every day of my life, how I think of you, I've never had anyone who was a sister to me. You were my only sister. I love you so much, how could you have not come and seen me?"

She was sobbing.

We are swinging in the hammock all afternoon. We have our bare legs in the stream and our hands are trying to catch the little fish that swim by. We are staring in wonder at Dedushka's bleeding heel. Yulia is running to our grandmother, yelling, "Babushka, Babushka, Plinka split her knee open, Babushka come!"

Here we are, here we are.

"How are you, Yulia?" I said, my voice breaking. "How have you been?" I squeezed shut my eyes so I wouldn't see the sparkling swimming pool and the soaking wet golden retrievers leaping into it from the diving board. What did she see while she spoke to me? Did she see the Prospekt of Veterans outside her window? Did she see the Khrushchev concrete tenements through her tears?

"I know nothing about your life," Yulia said. "Nothing. What are you doing now? I don't even know how many children you have. How many do you have?"

"Three," I said. "We'll come to Russia again, Yulia. We will come again, all of us, my husband, too."

"Well, next time you come don't you even think of staying in a hotel. You stay with me. I have room. I have room. All of you stay with me. You don't have to worry about anything, about food or anything. You just come, and I'll feed you and take care of you. I'll do everything. Just come and see me next time, Plinka."

"Okay, Yulia." I wiped my face.

"Oh, dear one," she said. "If only you knew how much I love you."

We talked for a half hour. She told me the new baby was from her current husband, who wasn't living with her. Then she told me he wasn't really her husband.

"But I really like the baby," she said. "Haven't had one in nearly eleven years."

I promised to write and send pictures of my family.

*

I couldn't look at my house the same way anymore, or my pool or my hardwood floor, or my dogs, or the view. I didn't feel the same about them anymore.

I didn't feel the same about my life, the life it took me so long to build.

Maybe if I burned wood and smoked some fish and grew nettles in my backyard and got a tub full of warm water that would slowly evaporate and draw some mosquitoes, maybe I could sit in an old wicker chair by the tub and breath in the air and recreate Shepelevo right in Texas.

What could I do? I still had a life, and I had to continue living it because it was the only life I had.

I thought about Anatoly. What if he looked at his own life and found it wanting? What could he do about it?

Here's the thing. In America, we *could* do something. We could move, get a new job, divorce the skunk, have another baby, or we could just shake our heads and call in the Prozac prescription before our psychotherapy session on Friday.

In Russia, Anatoly could find his life to be unsatisfactory on every level, yet he could not get another job. He could not moonlight, could not declare bankruptcy. There was no room for another baby, which is why most Soviet couples only have just the one. The abortion clinic is open every Thursday evening in Leningrad, and there is a long line of women snaking out into the street. And even if Anatoly wanted to get divorced, he and Ellie would have to continue to live in the same apartment, because there was nowhere else to move.

There was nothing else for him but the life he had. After a while, after a whole lifetime of having nothing else, most of us would probably look like Anatoly, the lines in our faces etched out by the grim determination to face our days unexamined. It would be the only way we could face them.

That life would have been mine, too, and I would have lived it and shrugged my shoulders just like they did, and put out my good china and crystal when guests came, and every shrug of my shoulders would have meant another gray hair, another line in my face.

That's how I felt. On the outside, I was in my glorious home, a home in which there were six working, gleaming white toilets, and five bedrooms, one for Radik and Lida, one for Yulia and her baby, one for Anatoly and Ellie, one for Alla and Viktor, and one for me and my family. I couldn't believe I was thinking like that. I guess you can take the girl out of the Soviet Union but you can't take the Soviet Union out of the girl.

But inside, I hunched my shoulders and held my breath as I walked into the bathroom on Fifth Soviet that had not been cleaned in years and never would be, and as I squatted down, I knew I was squatting down in my old life. Outside in America, inside in Russia. Who said memory is kind? Memory is merciless. My father was right. *All the things you want to remember, Paullina, I want to forget.*

Faulkner was right. The past is never dead, he said. It's not even the past.

When would the Good Witch Glinda be right? When would my old life fade? It was a race. Either my old life would fade, or my new life. The two could not live together side by side.

When we had been in Russia, I would see my father smoking and sometimes I would want to smoke, too. I wanted to start smoking now to relieve the aching, to soothe my soul, to see my papa again as I remembered him when I was small and he was taken away from me.

But because of the Gulag, we moved to America. He made that happen for us. I had to keep remembering that. He learned English in the Gulag to get us out of the Soviet Union. Wasn't that worth something? At least as much as the soldiers consecrating the earth on which Russians walk. They died so we could have the Fifth Soviet life, the Ulitsa Dybenko life. Their bones and ashes and the metal from the bullets that killed them all in the same ground while above it, nothing grows.

When I thought like this, I thought I might not make it out in one piece.

And I thought like this all the time.

I was a mom. I had kids to take care of. I had a house to run and dinner to make every night for five starving creatures.

So I did what we all do to give ourselves relief, to keep ourselves from going insane. I took my anguish and opened a drawer in my desk and I put it inside and I closed the drawer, and I left the room.

It was the best thing, really: I squeezed the elephant that was Russia into a tiny drawer in my desk and said I would open it when I didn't have too much to do.

Thank God I had too much to do.

February 1965.

August 1998.

NEW YORK IN AUGUST

Two weeks after I returned from Leningrad, we flew to New York to visit our families. My grandmother was turning eighty-seven. My father had retired from Radio Liberty and came to New York to spend a few days with his parents before flying off to Maui to begin a new life with my mother. Despite her ill health and the recent surgery, my mother also came to New York for the week.

"So how was your trip?" asked my twenty-year-old sister, Liza, before I had even made it through the front door. We were gathering in our family home on Long Island to celebrate Babushka's birthday. There wasn't enough room for me, Kev and the kids in my parents' four-bedroom house, so we were esconced in a hotel nearby.

"Fine," I said. "What can I say, Liz … It was …"

"Why won't you tell me about it?" she said impatiently. "Papa did."

"Oh yeah? What did he say?"

"He said it was the best trip of his life."

"He said that?"

"Well, was it?"

"He said that?"

"Yes. Was it?"

"What can I say …" I said.

"Oh, for God's sake," said my sister.

As I walked in, I saw my mother slowly making her way down the stairs to greet us. I put on my best smile. "Hey, Mama! How are you feeling?"

"As if you care," she said as she walked past me to hug my kids.

A little later, before dinner, I tried again. "So, Mama, how are you feeling? You look good."

"How I look is no indication of how I'm feeling. I feel terrible. Absolutely awful. I was dying all alone in the hospital while you and your dearest papochka were gallivanting all over Leningrad."

*

I was very eager to show my grandparents my six hundred photos. After all, at ninety-one and eighty-seven, they would not return to Leningrad again. "I can't wait to see the picture of Lebed!" my grandfather said. "I'm really interested in him."

Not understanding for a moment, I said, "Who? Oh. Deda, I don't have a picture of Lebed."

His face showed such disappointment.

"You mean at the Romanov funeral? No, I couldn't get him. He was hidden by other people."

"Oh." My grandfather looked dejected.

"But I have other pictures!" I said brightly.

"Oh?" he said, but nothing else interested him. He looked through them but was not enthusiastic.

I sat with my grandparents at our kitchen table while we leafed through my two albums. "Deda, Baba, look — our lake in Shepelevo. It's called Gora-Valdaisko."

"How were the Likhobabins?" asked my grandfather, after a shrug at the lake's name. "Vasily Ilyich, how was he? Did you ask Yulia why she doesn't go to the *dacha* anymore?"

"No, I didn't ask her."

Before I could say another word, my grandmother busted in with, "We talked to Yulia, you know." She stared at me with stern disapproval. "Why didn't you go visit her? You had time for Schlisselburg. But no time for Yulia?"

"Babushka, please," I said weakly. "Let's just look at the pictures."

When I showed them the pictures of my grandfather's cucumber supports in the garden in Shepelevo, my grandmother said, "No, they're not his. Yulia must have built them."

"Yulia built them? What are you talking about? She didn't build them. She doesn't go there. They're Dedushka's."

"That can't be," she said, shaking her head. "It was twenty years ago." She looked at the pictures. "They can't still be his."

"Babushka!"

My father walked by, and glancing at the picture said, "Of course they're his. As if Yulia would build something."

It was impossible for us to believe that these lives, houses, mailboxes, blueberries, brown doors, hinges, concert halls, buses, buildings, cucumber supports could all be the same. Our lives had changed so much: how could Russia be at standstill? How could it be so frozen in time, as if on permanent pause?

Looking at me dourly, my grandmother said, "Why did you take those things you took from our *dacha*? I think you were wrong to take them. Like you stole them. Yulia might need them, and you took them without even asking her."

"Babushka!" I exclaimed. "What are you talking about? Yulia abandoned that house."

"Well, maybe she will need Dedushka's notebooks about when and how to plant vegetables."

"His notebooks on weather patterns in 1978?"

"Maybe," she said gruffly.

I had no response, except to shake my head in amazement. I could see she was upset with me. I was upset with myself. I said nothing.

"Listen, Plinka," my grandfather said. "This relates directly to your trip to Shepelevo. When I was in the army during the war, I went to visit my brother Semyon, who was serving on the Volkhov front as an aviation engineer."

"Where were you?"

"On the Western Front," he said. "When I came to his airstrip, I had a little trouble getting in to see him because the border patrol kept me for a long time near the checkpoint, making sure my passport and credentials were valid."

"How long?"

"How long what?"

"How long did they detain you?"

"I don't know. It seemed like two days. It was probably two hours. Apparently an airplane had been recently stolen from the airport hangar by an army man who wanted to eat. If you were a pilot with a plane, the army gave you more food than if you were just a soldier. So the guy stole a plane to barter for some food, and because of his hunger, I was held up at the checkpoint.

"The ironic, idiotic Soviet thing," Dedushka continued, "and this is the part that relates directly to your Shepelevo experience, was that through this airport ran an unpaved road by which all the locals walked on foot to the fields and forests to pick berries. Paullina, the road ran directly *through* the airport, and they walked on this road by the dozens and no one stopped them. But at the entrance to the airport, I was stopped for several hours."

"Deda, how far away from the checkpoint was the road the people walked on?"

"Oh, I don't know," he said. "Five meters."

I laughed.

"That's Russia for you," said my grandfather, the former chief engineer for the Soviet shipbuilding industry, a mathematician, a genius, a soldier, a blockade survivor.

*

During Babushka's birthday dinner it quickly became obvious that my father had already told all the stories about our trip; there wasn't much for me to do, except pass my photographs around and clean up. Everyone asked me what I thought of Russia. Did I think St. Petersburg was beautiful? Yes, I said.

My father had told them about the Romanovs, the Diorama Museum, the metal doors of the toilet, the caviar I ate every morning.

It was a mixed relief for me not to have to recount to my grandparents, to my sister, to my mother, who blessedly didn't want to hear anything at all, things I couldn't put in perspective for anyone — most of all me.

And my family didn't want my perspective. What they wanted was for things to go back to the way they were before I left: peaceful, untroubled, unexamined, *nice, nice, nice*. While all I felt was shame. Profound shame and regret and fear. Put that into perspective.

*

"Did we have a good trip, eh, Paullina? Did we?" my father asked.

What could I say?

"Yes, Papa," I said. "We did."

He wasn't writing a book. But he told the stories. That's what life's twists represented to my father. Another good story to be told over vodka and herring and potatoes and cigarettes, with a raptly listening and appreciatively laughing audience. He could barely get through an experience before he would start forming the story in his head. Sometimes in the *middle* of the experience he was already thinking how he was going to tell it so that it would be the funniest, the cleverest, the most touching story he could create.

Feelings, those were extra. Actual pain, sentimentality, nostalgia, that was all extra. And it wasn't what he was interested in. He was not interested in his own feelings. He was interested in ours. He wanted us to feel something when he told his story to us. Privately, he may have been tremendously affected. I know he was. But publicly, he simply made every facet of his life a story and waited for his enraptured audience to react.

My father affected everyone who knew him. All his friends, all his colleagues adored him, said he was the brightest, the funniest storyteller they knew. His skills as a storyteller were legendary.

Because he was also a romantic, during the birthday dinner

he told the story of our walk through Leningrad and hearing the street musician play "Speak Softly Love" from *The Godfather* on his saxophone.

I waited for him to finish. "That's so interesting, Papa, because what I also remember from that evening is some homeless drunk striking up a friendship with you and then following us down the lovely Griboyedov Canal, reciting the same Pasternak poem over and over."

My father shook his head. "You would remember that, wouldn't you?" We laughed.

Sometime during dinner, I stood up, raising my vodka glass and was interrupted by my Russian family seven times before my mother said, "What do you want to say, Plinka?"

And my father, knowing already, said, "That she likes me. That she likes me very much."

"I want to drink to my father," I began.

My mother said, "What about me? What about me?"

"Alla, could you wait?" my father said.

"What about drinking to me?" she repeated. "Who gave birth to you? Who taught you how to read?"

"Who got us out of Russia?" I quietly asked.

My mother sneered bitterly. I raised my shot glass higher and said, sighing, "But *first*, of course, let us drink to my mother. Had she not given birth to me, I would not be standing here tonight."

"That's right," she said, nodding. "That's exactly right. You don't even know how right you are." With abortion being the primary form of contraception in Communist Russia, the average Soviet woman had anywhere from four to eight abortions in her lifetime.

"I know, Mama," I said. "I know how right I am."

We drank. I poured myself another vodka. "*Now* I'd like to drink to my father." My mother managed to keep quiet. "When we were in Leningrad, sometimes I looked at Papa," I began, "and wondered how in the world did he ever get us out of Russia? Yet, he did. He learned English in prison because he knew with absolute certainty that without English we would have no hope. He wanted to go to America; he had known that for a long time. If we came here, we might fail, but without his English, we would fail for sure. We'd be part-time hot dog vendors on the streets of Brighton Beach, or driving cabs, complaining about the government not taking better care of us.

"Furthermore," I continued, my voice cracking, "I raise this glass to him, because if not for him, we would still be in Russia, living the dead-end life of Alla and Viktor, of Anatoly and Ellie, of Radik and Lida. Papa gave Liza and me a future. With his English, he pulled us out of Russia," I said. "Tonight, I drink to him for giving life to my sister and me."

We choked up, even Papa. My mother stood up and stormed outside.

When she came back she said to my sister, "Paullina doesn't love me."

"What are you talking about, Mama?" exclaimed Liza. "She is your daughter. What are you talking about? You're crazy." That's my twenty-year-old sister.

*

When I was still in Texas, my grandparents kept saying on the phone how they couldn't wait to talk to me about Russia. But when I got to New York, they didn't talk to me about Russia at all.

I thought it was a product of too many people, too much food, too much to do. So one night, at Kevin's suggestion, I left my family at the hotel and came at 10:30 in the evening to talk to my grandparents by myself. My parents had gone to the movies.

When I arrived, my grandmother was busy watching a Mexican soap opera translated into Russian. My grandfather — an engineer, a shipbuilder, a war hero, a chess player, a genius — was too embarrassed to watch it in front of me, so he made tea and we chatted idly about nothing, biding time until my grandmother was finished. For two hours she didn't get up from her armchair. It was well after midnight when she shuffled into the kitchen, and we looked over my photos from Leningrad again and bickered about which ones they could have copies of and why I couldn't give them any of my negatives. I left at one. We had not spoken about Russia.

*

My father's old friend Mark came to have dinner with us one night and while he ate he asked me what I thought of Russia. I shrugged. I said by way of reply, "Have *you* gone back?" He had been in America with his family since 1977. My father got him and his family out. They lived with us for months when they first arrived in New York. Shaking his head, with his mouth full of my father's garlic shrimp, Mark said, "I don't want to go back. I'm not interested in seeing it. It hasn't changed. I left because I didn't want to live that life. Why should I go back and see it's all the same?" He looked at me. "And I can see by your face, it *is* all the same, isn't it, Paullina?"

My mother, 1958. She is eighteen.

RADIK REVISITED

One evening, not long before we returned to Texas, my mother was leafing listlessly through my photos and stumbled upon pictures of Radik and Lida. Holding a picture in her hand, she jumped up to run to my father, then sat back down and said, "Is this Lida? Paullina, do you know? Is this Lida?"

"Of course I know," I said. "It *is* Lida."

"Oh my God," my mother said. "She got so old. She got so old. Oh my God."

Having finished his smoke, my father came back inside, and my mother shoved the picture of Lida into his face.

"This is Lida, Yura?"

"Yes," he said, taken aback by my mother's fervor.

"Yura, do I look this old? Oh my God, do I look like this?"

He moved the picture farther away from him, and stepped away from my mother. "No. Stop it, Alla, what are you talking about?"

My mother slumped down, defeated by the photograph. "Lida was never very beautiful," she said. "But this just shocks me. Shocks me."

"Not beautiful like Radik?" I teased her.

"Oh," she said. "No one was beautiful like Radik."

I smiled. "Of course not."

She stared at a photo of him. "He got old. He's lost some of his shine. Still, he's not bad, right?"

"Right."

My mother told me that when Papa and she first met, he told her about Radik.

"During or after Dzhubga?"

My mother scrutinized me. "After," she said slowly. "But before we were married. And what do you know about Dzhubga, anyway?"

"I saw you," I said. "Saw you being painted. You were so beautiful."

"I was, wasn't I?" She looked so sad when she said it. "Beautiful and young."

"Tell me what Papa said about Radik, Mama."

Sighing, she continued, "Your Papa, well, he was not your Papa yet, said, 'I'll introduce you to all my friends, but one of them, you will stop loving me, leave me and go with him, because he is just incredible.'" My mother had assured my father that that would never happen, but when she saw Radik for the first time, she told me that her breath did stop.

My grandfather chimed in. "Radik," my grandfather said, "was the most handsome man you ever saw. Men and women both thought so. You could not stop looking at him. You couldn't even if you wanted to."

"Well, he is old now," my grandmother said.

"He may be old, but Babushka, you didn't see what I saw during dinner at his house, the way the whole table could not take their eyes off him," I said.

Always a cynic, my grandmother snorted dismissively.

My father, embarrassed by such a personal discussion of his friend, mumbled, "Ladies and gentlemen …", and went outside to smoke.

I was amused by how unforgiving older people could be of the aging process in other older people.

Particularly of the aging process in Radik.

As if, in their secret souls, they were all happy that even a star like Radik's had dulled, that old age had not spared him either. We were all beautiful when we were young, they seemed to say, but we got old, and he got old, too. *Thank God.*

I ventured, "Well, I didn't know Radik when he was young —"

"Oh, you wouldn't have been able to resist him," interjected my grandfather.

I repeated, "I didn't know him then, but I think that for a sixty-year-old man, he still looked pretty good."

My mother studied his picture for a long time.

"Not bad," she finally said. "But not like *before.*"

Oh, the pitiless old age.

February 1965.

SIX HUNDRED PHOTOS

I had shot sixteen rolls of film. Six hundred photos. To reflect on the events of six days, that's a hundred pictures per day. Surely that was enough to show what I had seen, to show a small measure of what I had felt. But I found that the pictures subtracted from rather than enhanced my memories.

Each photo, taken at an average speed of one-sixtieth of a second. During the whole trip, the shutter was open for a total of ten seconds. Ten seconds out of six days. They conveyed nothing: not the pain of Shepelevo, not the sadness of Fifth Soviet, not the crumbling stucco, not the marble halls of the Hermitage. And what about all those seconds, those minutes, those hours I didn't take pictures of? What happened to them? I regretted not taking a photo of Ellie's floors. I regretted not taking pictures of any of the toilets I had visited or avoided. Why didn't I take a photo of the outside of the Diorama Museum or of Mariinsky Bridge? Where was the mezzanine of the Grand Hotel Europe? Where were my *blini* and caviar? Where was the smell of Shepelevo? The smell of the metro? Where did the six days go?

They sat in my chest. They filled me from morning to night, and when we came back to Texas I was so glad I had my wood blinds and my Irish Cream walls and my satellite television service, so I didn't have to close my eyes and see Shepelevo, my old apartment, of the other life that was mine. No, let me swim in my pool instead, to get my heart away from Leningrad.

I still couldn't look at my house.

There was no place for me there, but there was no place for me here, either.

Blink and you'll miss it. Forget. Regret. Sitting on a plastic picnic blanket by Lake Ladoga, pouring salt onto fresh tomatoes from a folded napkin, eating bologna and Russian bread. Where was my picture of that?

And the smell of fresh water from the canals of Leningrad. All right, fresh may not be the best word for it — but the scent flowed through the city and rose up to meet me wherever I went, attaching itself permanently to my insides.

Russia was like a hard dream from which I could not wake up. When I was young I used to have a recurring nightmare in which I was being chased by a cow down the railroad tracks. Every time I turned around, the cow was behind me. I'd speed up, but I ran with a dreamer's ineptitude, tripping, falling, slowing down. Then I'd turn around, and there was the cow, just a few railroad ties behind me.

*

"Kevin, what am I?" I asked him one evening after the kids had gone to sleep. "When you have to describe me to people or think of me in your own head, how do you describe me?"

404

"Well, first and foremost, you're my wife."

"Okay, and then?"

"Then you're … well, you're …"

"That's what I thought," I said. "I can't describe myself either. What am I? Am I an American? Am I Russian?"

"Yes!" he said triumphantly. "I got it. You're a Russian-born American author who also happens to be my wife and the mother of my children."

"Okay, good," I said.

I decided I had lived in too many places. When we first came to America, we lived in Woodside, Queens, then in Kew Gardens, Queens, then in Ronkonkoma, Long Island. I lived at Stony Brook University, in one dorm, then another dorm, and another dorm, then in a house in Port Jefferson, then at a university in England. I lived in an apartment in Lawrence, Kansas, back in another dorm in England, and another dorm in England. A house in Ilford, a house in Birmingham, a house in Dagenham. Back in the States, I lived in one apartment in Forest Hills, another apartment in Forest Hills, a third apartment in Forest Hills, then a house in Lake Ronkonkoma, a rented house in Texas, and finally here, in my yellow stucco home from our own original design. That's nineteen different places since we left Russia. About one a year.

Before I was ten, I lived in only one place, and that was our apartment on Fifth Soviet. I spent my summers in only one place, and that was Shepelevo. When my spirit can't find any solace, that's where I return, because it's the only place I can call home.

I wasn't carrying Russia with me. It was carrying me.

*

I struggled to settle back into my life. How lucky I was that I had one and didn't have to make one up from scratch. In this life there was no time for feelings of raw displacement. The brass weather stripping outside my balcony door had been ruined by paint thinner, and the blower above my cooktop made a racket when it was turned on. One of the bathroom door handles broke, the garage door would not close, the Texas prairie wind blew through the gaps in my warped front door and made the cavernous formal living areas cold. I made time for these details. I didn't make time to cook *blinchiki* or send Yulia her photographs, or figure out who I was. Who I was didn't matter because the black Texas clay dirt was getting in the dog kennel when it rained and something simply had to be done about that.

*

I kept the leftover rubles from Russia in a cubby hole in the mud room. Finally I couldn't stand looking at them anymore, so I sent them to Ellie and Anatoly, along with the bottle of Trésor.

It was tough for Ellie before, but now that the ruble had been devalued by half and half again, how much was going to be left for her tomatoes and her borscht and her *blinchiki*?

I sent Viktor's sons their Dallas T-shirts. To get his zip code, I miscalculated the time difference backward instead of forward. I thought I was calling him at 9:00 in the morning but it turned out to be 2:00 in the morning. Big difference. Viktor's wife must have been *thrilled* that some woman from America was calling her husband at that hour of the night. "Oh, but honey, she is going to send our boys T-shirts."

One night, the television news carried a picture of a well-dressed man from Leningrad. He was in his fifties, and he was wearing a suit and tie. He lived in Leningrad, but on this particular evening, he left his job at 5:00, a job for which he had not been paid in six months, and he took a tram to the outskirts of the city. At the last stop, he got off and rode the *elektrichka* to a town near Leningrad called Kolpino, where he went to a local cafeteria and stood in line. Back in Leningrad he had heard that in this cafeteria in Kolpino they were serving soup. So he stood in line that evening to get some soup to bring home to his family. The picture on the news was of him standing in this line. It could have been 1941. It was agonizing to see his face.

The war was not in the past. It was everywhere you looked, just as Communism was everywhere you looked. War was the baggage we all carried with us: every heartbreak, every longing, every job, every neglect, every happiness. We all went forward into the future with the wounds of Communism on one shoulder and the wounds of war on the other. We went to our outhouse and we hoped that our cucumbers wouldn't have bitter skins this year, that our one and only chicken wouldn't get worms and die, because then we wouldn't have eggs.

We hoped for perch, and we hoped that the men who came to clean the outhouse would not ask for more than a liter of vodka because a liter of vodka was all we had to pay them with. And when, upon leaving, all they asked for was what we had, we thought we were lucky.

And then with our heads bent, we went to get a loaf of bread from the lady near the metro and coming back we said, let me just walk one more time among the graves of my soldiers, my brothers. Let me bow my head and let the tears in my eyes not spill over because I don't have a free hand to wipe them with. Maybe Yuliy Gneze and

I had more in common than I realized. Maybe he walked through Piskarev every day because he too couldn't believe he had lived, had been spared. Like me.

You'd think that Russians would be more in need than Americans of artificially induced stupor, and vodka certainly did take care of the edges. In between shots, or even during, they read books and tried to write them; they baked blueberry pies, they had children, they grew their vegetables, they caught fish, they fixed what they could and left what they couldn't. Every once in a while someone went overseas and brought back perfume or makeup or perhaps a leather jacket. They continued to live the best they could, even if it meant going to Kolpino for some soup in your best suit.

It was only right that nothing could grow on the small square of land at Nevsky Patch. The soldiers were still crying, is this what we died for, what we stood on the dark Neva for? Is this it?

In Texas, I walk out onto my balcony. Alla goes back to the Prospekt of Five-Year-Plans. Svetlana haltingly sings "Shine, Shine, My Star" as she stands in the kitchen, crying into the bowl of ground beef for stuffed cabbage, thinking about St. Petersburg, Florida, about singing arias through the palm trees.

Ina continues to rejoice that she got two large rooms for her family. She's in those two rooms till the end of her life, and she thanks God.

The Likhobabins go to Babushka's grave, pulling out the weeds, putting some fresh flowers on it, and then stroll arm in arm to the Gulf of Finland, to their boat.

Yulia pulls the curtain closed over the Prospekt of Veterans, where she has lived since 1968, and goes to take care of her infant daughter, hoping that she can get the baby's father to move in with her one day.

If he does, she hopes that he'll stick around long enough to help her bring the dacha in Shepelevo back to fighting form.

Anatoly stands on his balcony over Ulitsa Dybenko, stubs out his cigarette, and goes back inside, slowly closing the door. He sits on the couch and says, "Any more of that blueberry pie, Ellie?"

*

I walked out onto my balcony, thinking about the Likhobabins and their thirty-five-year-old couch. They had a thirty-five-year-old couch, but they got to smell Shepelevo every day. Did they even know what they had? What I would give to walk out on my balcony and smell Shepelevo.

Heat kills all in Texas. I breathed in the air. There was no smell.

But I am ashamed to say I like the sunshine.

I walked back inside, reminded of the words of the Russian writer Alexander Kushner: "Only those who have not paid a high price for the gentle joy of living and breathing can allow themselves feelings of melancholy, denial and lofty disdain of life."

I had been given more than I deserved. I hoped the angels didn't recognize that fact. Any minute now I would blink and be in Kolpino, standing in line for soup.

The doorbell chimed. It was the landscaper, wanting to know which tree I wanted him to plant in the front yard, a red oak or a live oak. I walked outside with him. It was 110°F. The prairie stretched in every direction.

"The red oak," I said. "I like my trees deciduous. A live oak with those permanent rubber leaves just doesn't cut it. It looks too fake. Don't you agree?"

"Well, yeah, in the beginning," he said. "But give it a little time and when it grows tall, a live oak looks very beautiful. Rich and green and colorful. Not at all rubbery."

"Oh, yeah?" I said, thinking about Shepelevo's oaks standing over the neat simple grave of my great-grandmother, who gave my grandfather the last potatoes she had dug up from the fields during the blockade so he could live. "How much time do I give it?"

"Twenty-five years," he replied.

I looked at him. I was thinking about seeing the sun set and rise on the Neva. I was thinking about 240,000 dead and their bones and their bullets on the banks of a dark river, dying for me, dying for Anatoly. *We died so that you could live.*

"I can't think that far ahead," I said. "I'll take the red oak. The leaves will turn beautiful in the fall, right?"

"Right," he said. "Now, what about your winter flowers? We'll plant some pansies? They're very hearty, will withstand any kind of weather. Even with severe frost, they'll die down a bit, and then as soon as it thaws, they'll come back more vibrant than ever. How would yellow pansies be?"

I am thinking about my father, who learned English in the Gulag to get us out, to get us to America, so that I could stand in front of my stucco house in Texas, smile and say, "Yes. Yellow pansies would be very nice in the winter."

My father by his favorite river, July 1998.

AFTERWORD

It has been seventeen years since I wrote the book you've just read. At the time, I had been a published author for four years. I had written only three books. I was supposed to be writing a fourth, but instead — there was *Six Days in Leningrad*.

I had chided myself for taking the time — to write, to record, to set it down. Then I spent writing time I didn't have after the trip to make it into a real book.

I wrote it, but I didn't have a publisher who wanted to publish it. Quite the opposite. I had a deadline for a novel I had barely started, a novel I kept delaying by my endless procrastinations. I needed to do more research, I needed to read more books. I needed prescription glasses, I needed to take notes, to interview more people, to go to New York again, to talk to my grandparents. I needed to go to Russia. I needed to get over my fear of the material and what it represented to me, my life, and my fledgling career as an author. And afterward, if all that weren't enough, I needed nearly a full year to write a book about going to Russia that no one cared about and no one had asked for. The book I had been delaying by all these various means was *The Bronze Horseman*.

I had hoped that *The Bronze Horseman* would convey my eternal struggle with loving my mother country and coming to terms with my Russian self, and yet loving my adopted country and coming to terms with my American self. I had hoped that a story of fiction could convey my sorrow at leaving behind the people I loved, the people who have never known what it is like to live in the land of plenty, the land of five thousand square foot homes and built-in heated swimming pools and restaurants and stadium seating movie theaters and malls and valet parking and beautiful cars and expensive shoes.

I justified writing this book by pretending that writing it would help me get into the soul of Leningrad during a war I had not lived through. I pretended it would help me to become part of the story I had not been part of. But it was a ruse. *Six Days in Leningrad* was its own means and its own end. As I lived it, and as I spent a year writing it, all I hoped and wished and prayed for was that I would be able to find the words to express the profound things I had felt during July 1998, to reflect on my subsequently transformed life.

It takes a Herculean effort to leave behind the life you know and hurl your family who speak no English to another country to begin anew. It takes something extraordinary to make that happen. In the case of my father, that extraordinary thing was an unshakeable faith in America. In the case of Alexander in *The Bronze Horseman*, that extraordinary thing was love.

In 1999 when I finished *The Bronze Horseman*, I told my agent that it was the last book I would ever write. I had left every word I knew and every feeling I felt on the page. Nervously she tittered. She said she didn't believe me. "The last book I will *ever* write," I repeated. "That's the truth."

But it wasn't the truth. I wrote *Six Days in Leningrad* in 1998–99, *The Bronze Horseman* in 1999, *The Bridge to Holy Cross* (the alternate universe version) in 2000 and the screenplay for *The Bronze Horseman* also in 2000. I wrote *The Bridge to Holy Cross* (published version) in 2001 and *The Queen of Lake Ilmen* in 2002. *The Girl in Times Square*, much of it to do with my mother and father's time on Maui, came in 2003. I wrote *The Summer Garden* in 2004–05, the cookbook *Tatiana's Table* in 2008, *Children of Liberty* in 2011–12, *Bellagrand* in 2013, and *Lone Star* in 2014. Altogether that is over a million and a half words that flowed out of the six days I spent with my father. As in Pushkin's eponymous poem, indeed that horseman had come to life in Leningrad and has never stopped chasing me since.

In 2001 I had a child whom I named Tatiana. As she says to her friends when they ooh and ahh, aww, Tania, your mom named a character in her book after you, isn't that special, "Oh no," my Tania says. "You have it wrong. She named me after a character in her book."

We left our halcyon life in Texas and now live more modestly in a seaside town in New York. The children — four of them now, not three — twenty-eight, twenty-one, nineteen and fourteen are growing, growing, grown ...

But not gone, she adds with a smile.

St. Petersburg underwent a major renovation to prepare for the tricentennial celebration of the city's birth in 2003. The old rusted tram tracks were pulled up, roads were repaved, buildings painted, new windows installed, the domes as well as the crosses re-gilded. There are new Western stops on Nevsky Prospekt, there's a Zara and a Starbucks. There are many more cars on the road. Yet, despite these improvements, my building on Fifth Soviet away from the center of town is still falling apart, seventeen years later, the concrete foundation still crumbling, the façade unpainted, the windows rotting. However, the road on Fifth Soviet has been repaved.

These six days is the only time in the last forty-two years I've been back to the place of my birth.

My grandfather died in 2007 at ninety-nine, three months before his centennial birthday. My grandmother died two years later in 2009. She was ninety-seven.

Radik Tikhomirov died of pancreatic cancer in August 2005. He was sixty-seven.

Lida lives. Ellie lives. Anatoly lives. Yulia lives — in the same apartment with her two now-grown children.

After my father retired, he joined my mother in Hawaii. Their spell on Maui was depressingly brief. They never did hop on a plane and fly three hours to San Francisco and travel the United States. They never did visit me in Texas. They came back stateside less than a year later in 1999, and settled in the southernmost corner of western North Carolina, where they lived alone and unhappily until my mother died in 2010.

A month after we buried her, my father was diagnosed with pancreatic cancer. He had been sick for a long while, sick but undiagnosed. He had lost all his weight and stopped eating, and couldn't fetch and carry like he used to, or cook for my mother anymore, or fish in the lake. The lake lost its water, and the fish died. In January 2011, he died.

There is not a day that goes by when I don't think of him. There is not a single thing in my life that has been made better because he is gone, not a single thing I can point to and say, well, at least there is this. Many things are significantly worse. I am worse. Yet on the pages of the book you've just read, my remarkable dad lives, funny, quirky, loquacious, thoughtful, sentimental, growing older, yes, but still full of energy and memory. I am so grateful that I have this chronicle of the few precious days we had spent together.

It took seventeen years to bring it into your hands. You have Shona Martyn and James Kellow at HarperCollins Australia to thank for that. Write them a note. Thank them. It should give you hope that some unlikely things are worth doing, worth waiting for, worth battling for. May 29, 2016 will have been my father's eightieth birthday. This book arrives just in time, as a small tribute to him, and a priceless gift for me.

The four pastel prints of Leningrad I bought at the Hermitage to this day hang in gilded frames on my bedroom wall. They are the last thing I see when I go to sleep and the first thing I see when I wake up.

I am Russian. I am American. I was lucky.

I'm still lucky.

Paullina

New York

2015

My dad on Maui, June 1999.

The Bronze Horseman series

The epic story of Tatiana and Alexander ...

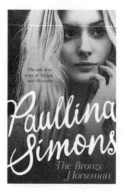 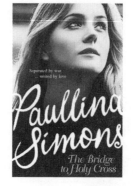 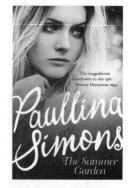

... and how it all began.

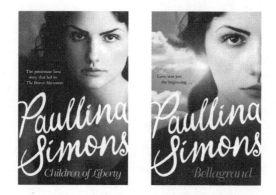